What She Go Do

Women in Afro-Trinidadian Music

Hope Munro

University Press of Mississippi / Jackson

www.upress.state.ms.us

The University Press of Mississippi is a member
of the Association of American University Presses.

Copyright © 2016 by University Press of Mississippi
All rights reserved

First printing 2016

∞

Library of Congress Cataloging-in-Publication Data

Names: Munro, Hope.
Title: What she go do : women in Afro-Trinidadian music / Hope Munro.
Description: Jackson : University Press of Mississippi, [2016] | Series:
 Caribbean studies | Includes bibliographical references and index.
Identifiers: LCCN 2015042761 (print) | LCCN 2015043754 (ebook) | ISBN
 9781496807533 (cloth : alk. paper) | ISBN 9781496807540 (epub single) |
 ISBN 9781496807557 (epub institutional) | ISBN 9781496807564 (pdf single)
 | ISBN 9781496807571 (pdf institutional)
Subjects: LCSH: Popular music—Trinidad and Tobago—History and criticism. |
 Women musicians—Trinidad and Tobago.
Classification: LCC ML3486.T7 M86 2016 (print) | LCC ML3486.T7 (ebook) | DDC
 780.82/0972983—dc23
LC record available at http://lccn.loc.gov/2015042761

British Library Cataloging-in-Publication Data available

Contents

Acknowledgments vii

Introduction.. 3

1 Woman Is Boss: Music and Gender in Trinidad's Cultural History 23

2 Woman Rising: Women Find Their Place in Calypso Music 61

3 From Calypso Queen to Calypso Monarch................................. 93

4 Carnival Is Woman: Party Music and the Soca Diva 123

5 Pan Rising: Women and the Steelband Movement 149

Conclusions 177

Notes... 183

Glossary.. 197

Bibliography.. 203

Index... 217

Acknowledgments

I would like to thank the scholars who helped me accomplish my work at the University of Texas at Austin and my research in Trinidad and Tobago. I am most grateful to the late Gerard H. Béhague. I would also like to thank Stephen Slawek, Deborah Kapchan, Dana Cloud, and Joel Sherzer for their support and encouragement. My fieldwork in Trinidad benefited greatly from the support of two wonderful scholars at the University of the West Indies, St. Augustine: Anne Marion Osborne and the late Mervyn Williams. Their guidance and encouragement helped me in every phase of my fieldwork, including the more difficult and discouraging times. Further guidance and support were provided by Jillian Ballantine, Rawle Gibbons, and Gordon Rohlehr, for which I am truly grateful. For the gender studies aspect of this work, I am particularly indebted to Rhoda Reddock, Patricia Mohammed, Eudine Barriteau, and the many other scholars and activists associated with the Caribbean Association for Feminist Research and Action (CAFRA) and Women Working for Social Progress (Working Women). I would also like to give thanks to Aileen Clarke, Gillian Goddard, and Christopher Gray at the Ministry of Culture and Gender Affairs.

While in Trinidad I also received guidance from other North American scholars working in the region, including Shannon Dudley, Peter Manuel, Ray Funk, Phil Scher, Jocelyne Guilbault, Robin Balliger, Susan Racine Passmore, and Christine Scofield, and I thank them profusely for their assistance. My classmates at UWI were also kind and supportive, and I would like to extend special thanks to Winston Garcia, Gail McIntosh, Judy Noel, Kelly Ramlal, and Nubia Williams for extending their friendship.

A large portion of my research rested on conversations with informants and attendance at rehearsals and performances, and this book could not have been written without the participation of many remarkable individuals involved with calypso, soca, steelband, and Carnival arts. Abbi Blackman and her singing partner Shanaqua Popoola were particularly supportive, welcoming me into their homes and encouraging me to accompany them to rehearsals and performances. Ms. Blackman coached me in the art of calypso singing, and I consider my lessons with her to be among the most valuable aspects of my fieldwork. I extend warm thanks also to many other musicians, especially McCartha Lewis (Calypso Rose), Denyse Plummer, Sandra de Vignes (Singing Sandra), the late Garfield Blackman (Ras Shorty I), the late Beulah Bob (Lady B), Nikki Crosby, Karen Eccles, Karla Gonzales, Cristophe Grant, Shirlane Hendrickson, Melanie Hudson, Seadly Joseph (Penguin), Karissa Lewes, Marcia Miranda, and Ann Marie Parks (Twiggy). Warm thanks go out to Alvin Daniel for his introductions to many of these musicians and a number of other resources within the music community. I would also like to thank journalists Lisa Allen-Agostini, Gillian Moor, Roslyn Carrington, and Shivonne Du Barry for their knowledge and insights on Trinidadian culture. Lorraine O'Connor and Roses Hezekiah of Rituals Music/Trinidad Tunes deserve special thanks for getting me in contact with Calypso Rose, and for their support of my work.

There were numerous individuals who helped me with my work on the steelband movement and encouraged my participation as a pannist. Special thanks go out to Sat Sharma, Michelle Huggins-Watts, Natasha Joseph, Merle Albino de Coteau, Ursula Tudor, Elizabeth Bartholomew, Richard Forteau, Seon Gomez, Jack Pram, and all the pannists of Courts Laventille Sound Specialists.

A number of people I have met "virtually" have been very helpful in sharing their knowledge about Trinidadian music and culture. I would especially like to thank Roger James, who generously shared with me a wealth of information about calypso and pan that he has collected over the years, and Ray Funk, who kept me supplied with vintage recordings. Other virtual friends I would like to thank are Alison McLetchie, Alicia Sealey, Dianne Marshall-Holdip, Liz Mannette, Harry Best, Roy Edwards, Clevil James, Cal Taylor, Ryland Burhans, Trevor West, Gene Wilkes, and Edward Pinheiro.

At the risk of making omissions, I would like to thank all the friends that I made in Trinidad, especially Christine Cardinez and her family, who hosted me in their house during my most recent visits to Trinidad. Warm thanks also go out to Elspeth Duncan, Denise Darlington, and Paula Obe Thomas—I will never forget our "limes" together.

My fieldwork was made possible by the financial support of the Organization of American States, and I thank Dr. Clement Campbell and Marina Piper in the Trinidad office for assisting and advising me.

At the risk again of making omissions, I would like to thank Sherri Canon, Laura Cervantes, Karen Blizzard, Peter Garcia, Aaron Lack, Javier Léon, Robin Moore, Rebecca Sager, Maria Alice Volpe, John Wolfe, and Ketty Wong. Other special individuals in Austin who supported me in my career and advised me on the Caribbean and Trinidad include Carrie Derkowski, Darren Dyke, C. J. Menge, Vicky Paschisch, and her husband Darius Williams. I would also like to thank Jason Gardner for the wonderful photos of Calypso Rose, Denyse Plummer, and Singing Sandra.

I would like to thank my editor at University Press of Mississippi, Craig Gill, as well as his editorial assistant, Katie Keene, for all their support and guidance in bringing this book to publication.

Last but not least, I would like to thank my family for their love, attention, understanding, and patience throughout my fieldwork and preparation of this book for publication, including my patient and loving husband, Michael Smith, who endured my long absences during my fieldwork. My parents, David and Sally Munro, inspired me to achieve and excel in my academic career, as have my sisters Heather Munro Prescott and Sara Munro. Heather was especially helpful in directing me toward sources in women's studies for various aspects of this project. I am forever grateful for my family's ongoing encouragement and support.

What She Go Do

Introduction

During Carnival 1999 two events occurred that had not happened for over two decades: female performers won the two most coveted song competitions of the festival. During the Dimanche Gras show, Singing Sandra won the Calypso Monarch crown; the last woman to achieve that feat was Calypso Rose in 1978. Over the course of Carnival Monday and Tuesday, as the various mas makers passed the judging points for the Parade of Bands, the song most frequently played was "De River," sung by Sanelle Dempster, one of the front line singers of the band Blue Ventures. This earned Dempster the Road March title for 1999, which again had been preceded only by Calypso Rose in 1977 and 1978. "De River" acted as an anthem for the thousands of female masqueraders who were reveling that season. It also described the rivers of color that flowed through the streets, and the sheer physical space these mas bands took up in the streets of Port of Spain:

> When de river, when de river
> When de river come rushing by
> If you want to be in de river
> Raise your hand up put it in de sky[1]

These events were particularly serendipitous for me. I had been in Trinidad since December 1997, collecting data on the impact women were having on contemporary Trinidadian music and related expressive forms.[2] I was drawn to doing my research in Trinidad and Tobago because of the vibrancy of Caribbean music and expressive culture, which I had loved since I was a teenager. While a graduate student in Austin, I had met a number of Trinidadians who were living in Texas, and had experienced their version of Trinidadian Carnival several times in an annual celebration in Galveston, Texas. From my previous research, I knew that Caribbean music in general was often very politically oriented, and that calypso music in particular was a unique form of social commentary allowing singers to address various social problems including gender-based oppression. From attending Carnival fetes in Galveston, I knew that there was great diversity in how various lyrical and musical ideas could be expressed. Soca music, a modern development on the musical ideas in calypso, was an accompaniment to the sense of fun and freedom that women experienced at these fetes, and appeared to be a way that they could cut loose regardless of what other obligations they might be facing in daily life.

At the same time, I had become increasingly interested in how gender is constituted and/or challenged through musical performance. I had discovered that there was a strong feminist movement in Trinidad, making it possible for women to make enormous gains in equal access to education, employment, and equal pay during the second half of the twentieth century. Women were also becoming increasingly visible as performers in the context of various types of Trinidadian musical expressions, particularly calypso, soca, and the steelband movement.

In the nineties, the face of expressive culture in the Caribbean was becoming more feminine, as evidenced by the masses of mas makers described above. Doing fieldwork in Trinidad seemed ideal to meet all of my interests. Since my initial fieldwork I have returned to Trinidad several times, most recently in January 2011. By the time I was completing this book in 2015, Denyse Plummer and Karene Asche had earned the Calypso Monarch crown, and Fay Ann Lyons-Alvarez had won the Road March several times as well as becoming the first woman to win the Soca Monarch title. Michelle Huggins-Watts had become the first female arranger to win a Panorama title. Clearly, women had become significant contributors to the performance of calypso and soca, as well as the musical development of the steel pan art form. The popular music of the Caribbean contained elaborate forms of social commentary that allowed singers to address various sociopolitical problems, including those that directly affected the lives of women. There were also various performance spaces that, while not directly related to social commentary, made it possible for women to participate in meaningful ways. In general, the cultural environment of Trinidad and Tobago was making women more visible and audible than at any previous time in its history, and this book examines how this came to be and what it means for the future development of music in that region.

My study centers on several research questions that pertain to the intersection of music and gender. My first area of research is historical: What role have women played in the creation and maintenance of various genres of music and performance contexts? Have women been involved with music throughout Trinidad's history, or is this a recent development? Are women mere maintainers of tradition, or are they key musical innovators in Trinidad's popular music landscape? I see my work as more than compensatory history, however. The first chapter of this work places Afro-Trinidadian women within the complex ethno-history of the nation, illustrating their roles as cultural agents over time. I also illustrate how stylistic changes in music facilitated women's participation and contribution to culture at large.

My second set of questions is: What role has popular culture, especially musical performance, played in sustaining Caribbean feminism and related struggles to overcome gender-based oppression? What are the dimensions and limitations of women's political agency through musical performance in Trinidad? Related to this is how popular music can be used to express political concerns. Song lyrics are the most obvious way such commentaries are expressed. Most studies on calypso, in fact, have focused on song lyrics to the exclusion of other aspects of the genre as musical expression. However, most popular music involves expressive strategies used by singers in interpreting these lyrics. Musicians create particular song arrangements and stage elaborate presentations that are integral parts of their musical expressions. Musicians choose particular musical genres to associate themselves with certain social groups and their position within the social hierarchy. Popular musicians bring together personal opinion, public persona, and various aspects of musical performance practice to create commentaries on the contemporary moment (instrumental political agency). They also create emotional bonds with their intended audiences and show that an alternate way of organizing gender representations and intergender relations is possible (constitutive political agency). Various contexts for musical performance in Trinidad offer a space to renegotiate gender identity, and I discuss these contexts in detail.

My last two questions are mirror images of each other: Have musical genres and contexts changed as a result of the improved status of women in Trinidadian society over the course of the twentieth century? Asking this from the other direction, does increased access and agency through expressive forms such as popular music improve other domains of life for women? Has musical performance significantly assisted in formulating permanent change in the representation of gender and improved intergender relations in Trinidad? I had learned from my earlier research that women became increasingly prominent in the Trinidad music industry from the seventies forward. It seemed that women's advancement in the music industry reflects as well as supports the social advancement of women as professionals, government officials, and more generally as individuals with inalienable rights. As female musicians win space for themselves in the music industry and performance contexts associated with Trinidad, they also discuss women's issues in their songs and represent Trinidad's social and cultural concerns from a female perspective.[3]

It remained for me to find out how far these social changes had progressed, and how these were intertwined with musical change and innovation in the context of the expressive culture of Trinidad and Tobago.

Women's sexuality is an ongoing source of controversy and debate within studies regarding music and gender in the Caribbean. Certain scholars recognize that a woman's identity is often embedded in her sexuality, and musical performance can serve in some cases as a form of male objectification (Aparacio, 1998: 173). Other studies suggest that Caribbean music offers women an important space to express their sexuality and play erotized roles that are repressed in everyday life (Daniel Miller, 1991; Cooper, 1993 and 2004; Manuel, 1998). Thus, while a number of musical examples are directly "political," some readers may find the "party songs" discussed in this manuscript somewhat limiting in their potential for social progress. However, I agree with the viewpoint that even the more eroticized styles of Caribbean music offer a space for female performers to voice their own viewpoints on what constitutes liberation, and for their audiences to celebrate sensuality in a controlled and artistically creative context (Manuel, 2006: 282–83). While there are certainly contradictions created within the context of Caribbean popular music, cultural performances can also be spaces to imagine the possible, thus taking a place alongside more didactic forms of musical activism.

The Caribbean holds a specific place in the cultural imaginary of Europe and North America. This is a region that conjures up images of relaxation, comfort, warm temperatures, and friendly people. To outsiders it is seen as little more than a popular tourist destination, a place to sip sweet rum beverages and hear the serenades of calypso or reggae singers. It is sold to members of the "First World" as a completely relaxing, non-threatening region, from which we can freely consume various types of leisure and recreation, including musical products. The Caribbean appears before us as an earthly paradise, created as a place that "turns sunshine into money" (Hagelberg, 1985). For academics who study the people of the region and their expressive traditions, the Caribbean is vast continent of islands, and of great social and cultural complexity. The money that could be gained from sunshine caused Europeans to fight for nearly five centuries over this region, making the Caribbean among the most contested areas of land on earth. Its role in a world economy that depended on the vast migration of people from various continents—slaves, indentured laborers, and various groups who more freely chose to settle in the region—resulted in communities that are among the most diverse in the world.

The Republic of Trinidad and Tobago is an island nation located at the southernmost end of the Lesser Antilles of the Caribbean. Trinidad, the larger and more heavily developed of the islands, lies seven miles off the coast of

Venezuela. Tobago, whose topography is allegedly the inspiration for Daniel Defoe's *Robinson Crusoe,* had little connection to Trinidad until the two were united as a British crown colony in 1889.[4] The indigenous peoples of Trinidad referred to it as "the Land of the Hummingbird"; Christopher Columbus christened the island La Ysla de la Trinidad (Land of the Trinity) for the three mountain peaks visible along the northern coast. The early Spanish settlers named the towns they built and the geographic features of the territory, but the island became largely French speaking during the late eighteenth century, a time when the kings who ruled Spain were the descendants of Louis XIV of France. The Cédula de Población issued by Charles III in 1783 granted free lands to anyone willing to swear allegiance to the Spanish monarch. In less than a decade the population of Trinidad swelled with planters and their slaves from French West Indian colonies, who were later joined by a number of Scottish, Irish, German, Italian, and English families. In 1797 the Spanish governor surrendered the island to General Ralph Abercromby, and Trinidad became part of the British Empire.

Due to its history as an international crossroads, Trinidad and Tobago is probably the most ethnically diverse nation in the Caribbean. As with other Caribbean colonies, Trinidad and Tobago grew into a plantation-based economy, made possible by the importation of African slaves. Following emancipation in 1838, indentured laborers from China, Portugal, and India were contracted to replace the Afro-Creoles who had left the plantations to pursue employment in the capital city, Port of Spain, or on plots of land in the countryside. The majority of the indentured came from India, with approximately 144,000 migrating to Trinidad in the period 1845–1917 (Brereton, 1981: 103). New arrivals from other regions resettled in Trinidad during the late nineteenth and early twentieth centuries, including migrants from other islands in the Eastern Caribbean, as well as Christian Syrians and Lebanese who sought relief from the religious persecution of the Ottoman Empire by resettling in the Americas. As of 2013, of the nation's 1.2 million citizens, 40 percent are Indo-Trinidadian, 37.5 percent Afro-Trinidadian, 20.5 percent of mixed ancestry, and the remaining identify themselves as "other" (including European, Syrian, and Chinese ancestry) or "unspecified." The sex ratio of male to female citizens at birth is 1.03, comparable to that of the United States. Approximately 96 percent of the republic's citizens live on the island of Trinidad; of that, 14 percent reside in urban areas.[5]

Trinidad and Tobago was ruled as a crown colony with no elected representation until 1925, when the first legislative council that would advise the governor was elected. In the years following World War II, universal adult suffrage was attained, and the colony moved toward self-rule. The People's

National Movement (PNM), led by Prime Minister Eric Williams, became the dominant political party, assuming full control of the government in 1956. Trinidad and Tobago became an independent nation in 1962, and a republic of the British Commonwealth of Nations in 1976. As of the 2010 election, women represented approximately 27 percent of the total membership of Parliament. More significantly, Kamla Persad-Bissessar, the leader of the United National Congress, became the first female Prime Minister of Trinidad and Tobago that year, and as of 2015 was still the leader of the Republic.[6]

During the late twentieth and early twenty-first centuries, Trinidad and Tobago has been an interesting place to look at how improving the lives of women could dramatically shape expressive culture. Various social movements, including several influential feminist organizations, had made it possible for women to make enormous gains in access to education, employment, and equal pay during the second half of the twentieth century. From speaking with Trinidadian friends and reading news stories from abroad, I also knew that Trinidadian women had experienced a backlash against their new freedoms, including verbal critiques by male journalists, scholars, and in some cases, popular singers. Several feminists in Trinidad noticed an increase in domestic violence during the nineties, and blamed that on men feeling inadequate because their women worked or more readily found work in a depressed economy because they would accept lower pay (Mohammed, 1991; Senior, 1991). Despite the many advances that the women's movement has accomplished in the region, feminist scholars often felt that they were severely misunderstood by the general public. "Ideological relations of gender are at their worst for Caribbean women: women now exist in a climate of hostile gender relations. This hostility is fed by men and women who argue that the Caribbean feminist movement exists to emasculate and marginalize men" (Barriteau, 1998: 204–5).

My own experience suggests more distrust and misunderstanding than outright hostility in gender relations in Trinidad. One contributing factor is that gender roles are still very conservative compared to countries in other parts of the world with a similar standard of living and rate of literacy among the general population. When I first came to Trinidad, I was amazed at the amount of work for which the average woman of the house is responsible: she might get up at 4:00 a.m. to cook lunch for the members of her family before running to catch a bus or maxi taxi to a full-time job, then return home to finish the housework begun in the morning. Weekends are typically filled with household activities such as laundry, cleaning, food shopping, and cooking in preparation for the Sunday lunch that is the centerpiece of the week for the average Trinidadian family. Many Trinidadian women work triple shifts, supplementing wage work with enterprises in the informal sector, while still managing to accomplish the aforementioned housework and childcare.

Other conservative aspects of Trinidadian life contribute to contemporary gender relations. Boys and girls attend separate schools after the primary level, giving them little experience with members of the opposite sex in an adult-supervised setting. Child rearing is also very gender biased. Even if they have a spouse or partner, the woman still is expected to run and supervise the home. While children of both sexes are to avoid bad influence from the street, girls in general are subjected to stricter controls on their movements and behavior than boys. Even though mothers may be more attached to their girl children, this is also because girls can act as "adult appendages" in helping with housework, younger children, and later on care for their parents' welfare in old age. Girls are responsible for far more household chores than boys, who are encouraged to play games and to allow their mother and sisters to cater to their needs. "Boys are fledgling kings of the farmyard, bound by few rules, while their sisters may wait on them hand and foot and patiently tolerate their wildest vagaries. Girls are reared to be put upon" (Senior, 1991: 35).

As a woman living in Trinidad, I did have experiences that made me uncomfortable, and they are similar to those I have heard from Trinidadian women. I could not walk past a group of male limers without drawing attention and comments, though as an obvious foreigner I probably received a different type of commentary than did local women. To me, it was on par with the kinds of lyrics one gets from construction workers in many North American cities. On several occasions, I was followed by young men who wanted to know more about me. I am not sure if they would have attempted this if I were a local woman. There is a saying in Trinidad that in addition to a wife, "a deputy is essential." The "outside woman" or "the bit on the side" is a residue of a colonial patriarchy that accepted the abuse of slave women as the bits on the side of the master/wife relationship (Mohammed, 1998: 23). Yet most Trinidadian women will tell you infidelity knows no color or social class. Many of my female friends made the following comments: "Trini men can't be trusted." "I would never marry a Trini man, they are too spoiled." "Don't fall in love with a Trini man, he is sure to horn you." However, I also noticed it was possible for a woman to find an "outside man" for the Carnival season, and in fact I had to end contact with certain male acquaintances because it was apparent that they were interested in my becoming their "deputy." My male friends countered that Trinidadian women cultivated an "ice princess" attitude. A woman would "pass them straight" if they talked to her on the road. "Girls always ready to leave you for the next man in the party, yes?" In short, women distrust men because they see them as childish "man-boys" who feel the need to assert their manhood by having many women. Men mistrust women because they fear being "horned" (cheated on), or abandoned for another man who is more attractive both physically and financially. Yet for men, having a wife (and a deputy, and other outside women) and fathering children is a sign of manhood, proof that one is not a "buller man" (homosexual). The complexities of gender relations have been summed up in many calypsos that have been recorded over the years. An excellent example is the following verse from Calypso Rose's "What She Go Do," from which this book takes its title:

> Every woman they want
> And using we at they convenience
> Then they turn and say
> They can't trust a woman today.[7]

Men's feelings of inadequacy may also result from the comparative success women have in finding work in a depressed economy. These jobs tend to be low-skill and low paying, oriented toward women's "natural" abilities, such as manual dexterity or a willingness to perform service duties (Reddock, 1998: 64–65). This forces many women to "respond with resilience and ingenuity in expanding their sources of livelihood" (Freeman, 1997: 82). Meanwhile, lower-class males accept the ideology of the feminist backlash, claiming that women have taken their jobs away. They turn to their "posse" on the corner or the rum shop, where they may be harassed by police but can assert their manhood by voicing male intent and desire "openly without regard for the embarrassment or discomfort they may cause to others, mainly women" (Lewis, 1998: 166). "Violence against women, children and society in general could become a way through which some men seek to revalidate themselves in their own eyes and over their peers."[8] Certainly, the more education a person has, the more likely one is to interact with members of the opposite sex as social and intellectual equals. University students are exposed to co-education both abroad and at home at UWI and UTT, and that tends to change interactions learned in childhood. Mass media from outside Trinidad exposes people to other kinds of gender relations, both positive and negative. Thus I found gender relations the most copasetic among women and men who were near my own age and who benefited from educational opportunities similar to my own.

Gender roles and relations have a significant impact on culture and expressive forms in the Caribbean. Some of the earliest research on Trinidad noted the important role that women play in the culture, especially *Trinidad Village*, the now classic study conducted by Melville and Frances Herskovits in the years just prior to World War II. In the small village of Toco, where the Herskovits studied the effects of sixty years of modernization upon local culture in order to test their theories of acculturation and syncretism in Afro-American culture, they observed that Afro-Trinidadian women are the principal exponents of culture: "they are the essential bearers of tradition, the primary agents in maintaining conventionally accepted modes of behavior" (Herskovits and Herskovits, 1947: 8–9). They saw women as the chief agents of socialization—not just the biological mother but also the grandmother and other female relations who play a role in raising children. Other important female figures included schoolteachers and family friends and neighbors, all of whom assist in the socialization of the younger members of the community. The Herskovits also noted that women "figure importantly in the economic life of the community, they are paramount in matters having to do with family affairs, they are predominant in the religious life, and in any concern with magic controls" (8–9). Subsequent scholarship on the West Indies has addressed the dichotomy of "respectability," often construed as the values of the colonizing power, and "reputation," or the internally generated value system that opposes and resists its opposite (Wilson, 1972; Abrahams, 1983; Miller, 1991; Burton, 1997). Respectability is the "inside" of culture, the home and yard, the church, school, and workplace, and is marked by self-restraint, industry, education, and respect for social hierarchies. In terms of gender, "inside" corresponds with the "female" sphere, although in truth few inside institutions are literally female-centered. Reputation corresponds to the world "outside" the control of inside institutions, and represents an external world of relations by which men secure their identity more or less separately from women (Wilson, 1972: 149; Safa, 1995: 47–48; Burton, 1997: 158). "Inside" corresponds with the bourgeois values of British colonialism and its inside institutions such as the Catholic and Anglican churches, government, and private schools. Women are "naturally" more willing to assimilate these values and pass them along to their progeny. "Outside" corresponds with the street and rum shop, the refuge where men escape the home environment for the company of men and "affirm and enhance their sense of their own value and identity" (Burton, 1997: 160–61). The processes by which this came about obviously intersect with other dualities such as nationalism vs. colonialism, authenticity vs. modernity, high vs. low culture, and so forth (Miller, 1991; Burton, 1997).

This dualist paradigm is one I still find to be useful for certain purposes. What is most important to this study is how dualism can be used to explain the intersection of music and gender within the Trinidadian context, and how changing perceptions of gender roles have opened up new musical opportunities for women in Trinidad's musical scene. In order to do so, many of the expressive forms discussed in this book had to shed some of their association with reputation-based practices and gain qualities associated with respectability. However, like anthropologists Daniel Miller and Jean Besson, I also theorize that the true opposition and resistance to colonial and post-colonial oppression may lie not in reputation-based practices but in the female-centered search for respectability, particularly in institutions such as the family, education, and other arenas for the attainment of long-term ambitions (Besson, 1993: 31; Miller, 1994: 263). Thus, I theorize that musical change could only come from wider social change and new attitudes toward the nation's culture. These changes were instigated by both Trinidadian nationalists and dedicated artists and musicians, and culminated in the cultural shifts that occurred as Trinidad and Tobago achieved independence from Great Britain. The result was an increasingly diverse music scene that greatly facilitated the participation of a wider selection of musical talent, which included women from various walks of life.

The West Indies in particular is an area well noted both for its ethnic diversity and the rich cultural heritage that developed over the course of its colonial and postcolonial history. Cultural production is one of the hallmarks of these islands, and in every decade performers generate new musical styles—calypso, ska, reggae, soca, dancehall, and so on. Trinidadians are the people who through creativity and determination invented and developed pan, the musical instruments that make up the modern steelband. The public celebrations that mark the social calendar of the Caribbean, in particular Trinidad's annual Carnival, have become familiar worldwide. Trinidad's expressive arts have inspired numerous scholars and intellectuals from a variety of viewpoints and methodologies, and enlivened the work of various regional writers such as V. S. Naipaul, Earl Lovelace, Merle Hodge, Derek Walcott, and Errol Hill.[9]

The scholarly literature on Trinidad Carnival is vast, and includes a large amount of research conducted by Trinidadian scholars. The earliest work sought to document local expressive forms and make them accessible to a wider segment of society. In these endeavors, the scholarship of Melville and Frances Herskovits was influential. For example, in their book *Land of the Calypso* (1944), Charles Espinet (journalist for the *Guardian*) and Harry Pitts (entertainer) were both strongly influenced by Melville Herskovits and his theory of acculturation and syncretism. They stressed how calypso expressed national unity and acknowledged the assistance of the Herskovits, who had met Espinet during the course of their fieldwork.

Alan Lomax went on a recording expedition to Trinidad and Tobago in 1962, the islands' first year of independence, and enlisted as his research assistant J. D. Elder, a Tobagonian graduate student at the University of Pennsylvania.

Together they recorded a number of examples of folk dances, Carnival songs, Midnight Robber talk, and calypsos, as well as the children's game songs that Lomax originally came to record. Elder used some of the material for his own dissertation *Evolution of the Traditional Calypso of Trinidad and Tobago: a Socio-Historical Analysis of Song-Change* (1966), which along with that of Melville Herskovits's student Richard Waterman (1946), were the first PhD dissertations to discuss the music of Trinidad and Tobago. Elder published a number of subsequent articles, and both the work of Lomax and Elder had a lasting impact. Lomax's sound recordings and the musical transcriptions Elder made of them became available commercially during my fieldwork and were remarked upon in the local press.[10] During my own fieldwork, I attended a lecture and book launching celebrating the publication of *Brown Girl in the Ring*, an anthology of the song games that Alan Lomax and Bess Lomax Hawes made with Elder throughout the eastern Caribbean. The event featured a performance by local schoolchildren whose teacher used the book to recreate these song games for this occasion.[11] Thus, the ethnographic work of Lomax and Elder now allows many Trinidadian musicians to learn and pass along their cultural heritage to a new generation.

Caribbean Quarterly, whose charter issue was published in 1949 via the Department of Intramural Studies at UWI, became an important platform for publishing research findings on the culture of the English-speaking Caribbean. In 1956 a special issue of *Caribbean Quarterly* was dedicated to Carnival. Particularly pertinent to my study is Barbara E. Powrie's essay on the role of women in Carnival as middle-class attitudes toward the festival changed in the post–WWII era (Powrie, 1956). Playwright Errol Hill conducted extensive historical research that resulted in the seminal work *The Trinidad Carnival* in 1973. Updated and revised in 1997, Hill's work serves as both a detailed analysis of the development of the expressive arts associated with the national festival and as a manifesto that urges citizens to embrace these arts as symbols of national culture and for the government to financially support artistic expressions of the highest order that can convey to the outside world the legitimacy of Trinidad as a social and cultural entity. During their lifetimes, two famous calypsonians, Atilla the Hun (Raymond Quevedo) and the Roaring Lion (Rafael De Leon), wrote essays on calypso and its history. De Leon wrote columns for Trinidad newspaper the *Guardian*, and later these columns were collected in the book *Calypso: From France to Trinidad, 800 Years of History* (1978). Atilla died in 1962, and his writings were published posthumously as *Atilla's Kaiso* (1983).

Since that time the literature on calypso has become fairly copious, with many studies focusing on calypso as a form of oral history and social commentary. Gordon Rohlehr and his student Louis Regis have written extensively on calypso music from the nineteenth century to the present, and their volumes remain the most important reference works on various calypsonians throughout history and the sociopolitical events and cultural climates that influenced them (Rohlehr, 1986, 1990, and 1998; Regis, 1999). The ongoing work of Rohlehr focuses on the vast repertoire of oral history contained in the calypsos from the early twentieth century to the present, as well as poignant analyses of contemporary trends in Trinidad's popular music scene. Much of his work addresses male/female interplay and gender roles within the calypso art form (Rohlehr, 1990 and 2004). Patricia Mohammed, director of the Gender and Development Institute at the St. Augustine campus of the University of the West Indies, has written several articles on calypso, and has been active in creating connections between feminist scholarship and the creators of local expressive forms (Mohammed, 1991 and 2003).

Until quite recently, women were absent from narratives about expressive culture in the Caribbean and/or women's contributions were marginal to these discussions. However, since the nineties there has been an outpouring of studies detailing the gendered aspects of Carnival and Caribbean music in general. These studies include the work of Pamela Franco, which analyzes the contributions of women to Trinidad's Carnival in the nineteenth and twentieth centuries, and relates them to the gender politics of their respective time periods (Franco, 2001 and 2007). Also pertinent to this study are the theoretical perspectives of contemporary scholars of Caribbean music, such as Carolyn Cooper, Peter Manuel, Deborah Pacini-Hernandez, Jocelyne Guilbault, and Shannon Dudley. While they have taken diverse approaches to gender, all have strived to avoid Eurocentric or essentialist interpretations of their various topics (Cooper, 1993 and 2004; Pacini-Hernandez, 1995; Manuel, 1998; Guilbault, 2007; Dudley 2008).

The soundscape of communities in the contemporary Caribbean is far denser than one finds in North America or Europe. Roosters do not confine their crowing to sunrise, but start their own lime sometime in the predawn hours. By sunrise other birds start to ramajay with the roosters, and neighbors are awake and doing household chores and preparing to go to work, or to shop in town if it is a weekend. Throughout the Caribbean, one can hear popular music of all kinds in a variety of public spaces. Walk down any main road in Trinidad and Tobago, and you will hear calypso, soca, and North American pop and R&B broadcast from the radios and sound systems of local shops. If you take a "maxi taxi" to travel, you will need to shout over the dub (dancehall reggae) the driver is playing. Walking through downtown Port-of-Spain, you will see at least one young man selling pirated CDs of soca, dub, "slows" (R&B

ballads), or whole albums by international stars such as Bob Marley or Buju Banton. Local radio stations, televisions tuned to the local music channel Synergy TV, or cable stations MTV or BET provide a constant soundtrack to a home's daily activities.

The typical Caribbean house contains walls that are nearly 50 percent windows and doors in order to accommodate a warm and humid climate where few homes have air conditioning. In urban and suburban areas houses are nestled close together, so sounds from neighboring houses blend with the cacophony of one's own household. It is easy to keep up with the neighbors' tastes in music and television programs. Sundays you might hear the man down the way running through his collection of classic calypso and steel pan recordings at a volume that can be heard for several blocks. You will always know when a crucial cricket match is in progress, as the sound reverberates through one's compound of flats if not the entire neighborhood. In these days of increased crime and insecurity about personal safety, nearly every yard has one or more hounds and bulldogs who howl and bark through the night at every passer-by. This can be overwhelming to the average North American, and the first few weeks in Trinidad one finds oneself sleep deprived and eager to become accustomed to the local soundscape.

For such a small country, Trinidad is media-saturated. There are currently three major daily newspapers and several more weeklies and tabloids, at least one of which most adults read on a daily basis. As of 2015 there were twelve local television channels (five broadcast and seven cable only), including the music channel Synergy TV. These compete with hundreds of foreign channels available via cable or satellite. Even very modest dwellings, with no running water, have electricity and cable television, sometimes tapped off a neighbor's line. For this reason, newspaper columnists have fretted for a number of years about the increased Americanization of the nation's culture and values through the influence of cable television. Nearly forty FM radio stations and two AM stations now compete for audience share in a nation of less than two million, featuring everything from local calypso and soca to American R&B, Indian film music, and alternative rock.

Sound in its various forms, including speech and personal interactions, is a constant presence in West Indian life. My experience has been that the women and men of Trinidad are keenly interested in self-expression of all kinds. From my initial fieldwork period to the present I have been amazed at the level of participation of Trinidadians in all sorts of expressive forms, which include various types of amateur music making, drama, fashion, handicrafts, fine arts, filmmaking, poetry, and literature. In terms of interpersonal communication, Trinidadians are passionate about voicing their opinions in the presence of an audience who can appreciate and participate in the debate. This results in a verbal culture that is remarkable in its vibrancy and creativity. Whether one expresses oneself through musical expression or "merely" conversing, the art of verbal expression and performing one's particular personality is a critical way for Trinidadians to share experience and observations that empowers its participants in various performative contexts.

Oral expression is fundamental to interpersonal relationships in Trinidad, and the desire for human engagement and sociability influences many aspects of daily life. Community spaces are constructed to offer opportunities for pausing and conversing with other people, an activity known as liming in Trinidad and Tobago. Of course, many situations and contexts are gender or class specific. People tend to lime with others their age, race, gender, and social class. Upper-class ladies do not lime with old men in rum shops, and schoolgirls don't linger to lime with the maxi driver unless they want to be called a "skettle" (slut). During Carnival, there are numerous opportunities to lime with one's social group: fetes, calypso tents, nightclubs, and the various rounds of Panorama all have space for "a nice lime." The fact is, people lime in different contexts for various reasons, but essentially the activity renews social networks and offers a performance space for participants to share knowledge and daily experiences. While it appears to be "the art of doing nothing," liming is an important way to reinforce social bonds or create new ones, and to gather news and information in the true West Indian fashion. In other words, doing any sort of research in Trinidad means learning how to lime (Erikson, 1990; Miller, 1991; Birth, 2008).

Once formal workplaces close, people will lime in town or at the central market before taking public transport home. The main maxi taxi and bus terminal, City Gate, is set up to accommodate after-work limers, as is Independence Square with its dozens of fast food restaurants and informal food and clothing vendors. Shopping malls such as the Grand Bazaar are constructed so that people may congregate to lime even when most shops are closed. In rural communities, many residents still have to carry water from a common standpipe, which provides yet another opportunity to pause and lime with neighbors. Most Caribbean houses and even one-bedroom flats have a substantial gallery (front porch), nowadays enclosed by burglar-proof gates and bars, that serves as a place for relaxing and conversing with family and neighbors. Thus architectural design is influenced by and continues to influence how Caribbean people interact with each other by creating spaces for socializing that are essential to homes and public spaces. There is, of course, a difference between being sociable and being "too fast" (curious) or a *maco* (relentless collector of gossip). Open windows in Caribbean homes are draped with sheer fabric so that the occupants may look out on the street but the neighbors cannot look in. If the family next door is having a domestic argument, which they may take outside for a piece of "street theater," everyone will hear it and embroider the story for friends and neighbors who pass by their homes.

Trinidad's small scale gives the country a small-town feel, and as in small-town America, gossip and scandal are a major source of entertainment. Having grown up in a small town in Vermont, it was easy for me to appreciate this taste for gossip, though it did get me into a few tight spots on occasion. Any lime in which I was a participant—whether at a neighbor's front gallery or at a local bar—drew much of its content from "minding other people's business." This included not only the neighbors' business but also major public figures, both local and international. In this intimate, personal, small-town atmosphere, politics (and sex and scandal) are real entertainment. Unlike the United States, where political fever breaks out only at election times, in Trinidad (and other Caribbean countries) it is an unending, year-round bacchanal. "Sexual scandal and scabrous political gossip: this is the name of the game. It is almost as if . . . the Caribbean were one enlarged, regional Washington D.C." (Lewis, 1985: 229).

Do not phone a Trinidadian during the evening newscast; unlike North America, the local news is aired during primetime and lasts an hour. More likely than not, he or she will be watching with family and any neighbors who have dropped by. It is, however, acceptable to visit in person during the news and join the lime. Each news item becomes the subject of commentary or *picong* (snapping satire) against the individual or institution in question. A story will often remind one individual of someone present in the room and he or she will direct picong at that friend or relative. Others will join in to *fatigue* the individual in question, as he or she fights back with a defending barrage of talk and wordplay. Generally, Trinidadians will not just watch television or view a movie but endlessly comment and debate with whomever is watching with them at the time, engage in one-sided conversations or sessions of picong with the onscreen characters, and spin anecdotes triggered by onscreen action and dialogue.

In addition to local news, Trinidadians are keenly interested in world events. The Bill Clinton/Monica Lewinsky scandal played out while I was doing my fieldwork, and it was an endless source of entertainment and commentary in Trinidad. My friends and even people I had just met asked my opinion on the situation. "How can Hillary stand her man horning her so?" Or they would comment, "Clinton is real man!" During the 1999 Carnival season several calypsonians parodied the situation and impersonated President

Clinton in the calypso tents. During the 2008 election, Obama fever reigned throughout the Caribbean, as it did in much of the rest of the world. Numerous calypsos, soca, and reggae songs were written in support of Obama's candidacy and to celebrate his election as the forty-fourth president of the United States.

Over my years of research it has been absolutely vital to keep up with the media-saturated environment that is Trinidad and Tobago. Usually I would buy both the Trinidad *Guardian* and Trinidad *Express* every day and cull relevant articles. The online versions of these newspapers have been valuable for ongoing research. I conducted research at the National Archives and the UWI libraries. I purchased many useful materials at the UWI bookshop, the Institute for Social and Economic Research, the Centre for Gender Studies, the UWI Festival Centre for the Creative Arts, and privately owned booksellers. Local television programs and radio broadcasts were tremendously valuable in providing me with information regarding musical performers, style, performance practice, as well as attitudes regarding local music and musical events. Audio and video recording are prohibited at most performance venues, largely because performers rely on the sale of professional audio and video recordings. Therefore, the only things I recorded myself were my own rehearsals, lessons, and interviews. Everything else I either purchased or obtained gratis from the performer. Other useful artifacts include programs from musical events, musical instruments, lead sheets provided by musicians and composers, as well as locally published books and pamphlets.

The Internet has been available in Trinidad for a number of years, and its use there has been the subject of several academic studies (Miller and Slater, 2000; Miller, 2011). During my fieldwork, it was a great comfort to be able to correspond with my husband and others I had left back home. After I returned from my initial fieldwork, my natural curiosity led me to consult the daily newspapers online at least a few times a week, a habit that continues. Various personal and professional commitments have limited my return visits to Trinidad. However, even though I was not physically there, I knew all of the local concerns and read updates on the local music scene, including interviews with various important musicians. I was able to listen to local radio stations and could hear the music discussed in the local press. By the time I was completing this book, I could also see performances of new music on YouTube and other sites providing video content. Additionally, a number of people I had met in Trinidad now were accessing the Internet at either at home or via Internet cafes. I found myself exchanging emails or messages via social networking sites such as Facebook, often on a daily basis, with friends I had not seen in nearly ten years. While it was obviously valuable to me personally to be able to reconnect with old friends, this also served as an immeasurable resource for staying connected to Trinidadian culture in a way I had not anticipated when I began this project. As many West Indians now live abroad, this is also how Trinidadians keep in touch with family, friends, and current musical trends when they are not able to visit home as often as they would like; so this in itself was not an oddity.

Most of the research for this study was conducted among popular musicians in urban Trinidad: interviews with popular singers and musicians (both female and male) and detailed observation of musical performances, rehearsals, and recording sessions. My fieldwork included participating as a working musician in various performance contexts in Trinidad, including the annual Panorama competition. I also assessed the reception and use of popular music through informal exchanges with audiences at musical performances and other social events. My primary interest regarding the musical expressions examined in this study is how particular singers meet the expectations of their respective genres. My focus is on the agency women are able to obtain through musical performance and how this affects their status in general. What interests me most is how music is transmitted, maintained, or changed due to the agency of particular artists. Like Victor Turner, I am interested in "how people get ready for performances to be" (Turner, 1987: 8). Interviews with performers focus on how they see themselves meeting the expectations of their particular musical genre and how their gender influences what they are able to accomplish artistically. I also solicited their opinions about how their music gives them various kinds of agency in changing the perception of women and enhancing and improving contemporary gender relations.

The fieldwork encompassed the time period December 1997 to March 1999, along with short return visits in 2001 and 2011. During my initial fieldwork, I lived first in St. Ann's and then in St. James, both neighborhoods of the nation's capital. While the greater Port-of-Spain area is the hub for Trinidad's nightlife and commercial music industry, quite a few of the people I worked with lived in other parts of the island, particularly in the southern urban center of San Fernando. I also spent a great deal of time at the University of the West Indies, which is located in the middle of the east-west corridor between Port-of-Spain and Arima. Therefore, my research was not conducted in any one place, but involved commuting between various locations to conduct interviews, observe studio recording sessions, sit in on university music classes, and take music lessons. When I had free time, I limed with various friends and acquaintances, and these conversations provided important insights into Trinidadian culture. I had only a little experience with the steel pan before I came to Trinidad, but I felt it was important to learn this performance tradition because the steel pan had developed in that nation and was a key symbol of national identity. I also wanted to learn about women's role in the development and maintenance of the steel pan movement, and knew that the most appropriate way would be to participate in it myself. While lessons at UWI were helpful, my learning curve progressed rapidly once a friend introduced me to the members of the Courts Laventille Sounds Specialists steelband. Despite my lack of experience as a pannist, they allowed me to perform in both the Pan is Beautiful festival of 1998 and the Panorama prelims and semifinals of 1999 (Courts did not make the Panorama finals that year). They also allowed me to be part of the rhythm section in their stage side performances at the Cruise Ship Complex. The reader should know that to perform in a stage side is a significant sign of approval, and probably would not have been extended to me if I had not already had significant musical experience.

My aim was to immerse myself in the local music scene in all its various aspects, and not merely document significant musical events. Although I conducted a number of formal interviews with musicians, both female and male, I eventually found it more useful to work closely with up-and-coming musicians than to rely on interviews with the major stars of the music industry. This allowed me to meet with musicians on a number of occasions, ask followup questions, and observe musical compositions as they evolve. Most of this aspect of my research was done with songwriter Abbi Blackman (daughter of the famous calypsonian Ras Shorty I) and her singing partner Shanaqua (Rachel Fortune). I was fortunate to receive lessons in singing calypso, soca, and jammu soca with Ms. Blackman, for which I reciprocated by playing flute in Abbi and Shanaqua's performance of "The Real Self" at the 1998 Caribbean Song Festival and on one of their studio recordings, "Love Life." I also found that the informal conversations resulting from being a member of the audience, volunteering to assist with the organization of musical performances, participating in rehearsals at the panyard, and sitting in on classes at UWI were even more valuable than formal interviews and surveys.

Thus, the ensuing chapters are based on various resources, from personal experience to journalist accounts, historical narratives, and so forth. I see this case study as part of my ongoing interest in the politics of popular music. Much of my graduate school writing dealt with validating the expressive forms that make up the everyday world of those who are not members of the dominant class of first-world nations or members of the academy. I see popular music as an important aspect of local and global culture that, for both musicians and audiences, is different from the culture learned in school and in books and thus has a life outside of these institutions. Popular musicians present a particular reality; the image musical personalities project, the acts they perform, the tone of voice they use, the language they choose, the relation they cultivate with the public, and the concert experience they bring all incite fans to react by adopting specific attitudes and developing various ideas about their identity and ways to apprehend the world (Guilbault, 1990; McRobbie, 1994). Hence, through various musical forms and performance contexts, a space is opened to suggest new ways of organizing social relations, empowering audiences to question the relations that cause domination in their own lives. Music thus becomes a platform for expressing new possibilities regarding life experience, including those that pertain to gender relations, and a motivational tool in forming fair and equitable social relations.

1

Woman Is Boss: Music and Gender in Trinidad's Cultural History

As a number of scholars have noted, it is impossible to discuss the Caribbean in any meaningful way without addressing its music. Music and the expressive forms that depend on music (such as dance and festivals like Carnival) play a pivotal role in the lives of Caribbean people, and are often central to their discussions about what makes them distinct from other peoples of the world. This is true both within their countries of origin and in cities in which people of the Caribbean diaspora have settled in North America and Europe. Many have argued convincingly that Caribbean music is more important to people who have emigrated, as it becomes a key symbol of their regional identity in the midst of ethnic and cultural heterogeneity (Manuel, 1988, 1998, and 2006; Pacini-Hernandez, 1995; Aparacio, 1998; Guilbault, 2007; Scher, 2007; Birth, 2008). This chapter provides an overview of the role Trinidadian women have played in the creation and maintenance of various genres of music and their related performance contexts. Women been involved with music and dance throughout Caribbean history, and there is evidence of this participation in the relevant literature. At times, various historical circumstances have facilitated women's participation in the public sphere; at other times the opposite has happened. In this region, the music world and public culture in general has been male-dominated, and for the most part this continues to be the case (Manuel, 2006: 279). However, in the music scene of Trinidad and Tobago, there has been remarkable progress in achieving gender equality within certain expressive realms.

Women have been instrumental in the maintenance and transmission of musical practices throughout Trinidad's history. At various times women's agency has been limited based on material circumstances, prevailing attitudes toward women's proper role in public life, and even legislation that banned or tightly regulated various forms of expressive culture. However, as these material conditions changed, so did the extent of women's contributions and their ability to initiate and maintain their creative roles in Trinidad's expressive culture.

As Marcia Herndon noted twenty-five years ago, "the study of music and gender is not simply a matter of describing the domains, styles, and performance types typical of male and female musicians in particular social settings. Rather, the focus on gender, as a methodological strategy, allows us to examine issues, problems, and interrelationships from a new point of view ... [including] the relationship between biology and culture in determining culture-specific musical behavior, thought and action" (1990: 11). Thus, gender is a culturally specific enactment, involving a complex of social roles, the gendered division of labor, and other variables based on one's age and status within a given society. In her study of Cherokee music, Herndon emphasizes that people acquire gender traits through the enculturation process, and the examples and rewards given by elders. In other words, biology does not determine the form gender roles take, and societies such as the Cherokee are quite different from how US mainstream culture constructs gender. These include balance between gender roles and the value of women's labor—all of which are expressed symbolically in colors, status, expressive performance, artwork, and music (Herndon, 1990: 11). Like Herndon and other scholars influenced by her work, I seek to do more than simply describe or recover women's musical traditions. I will also place Trinidadian women within the complex ethno-history of the nation, illustrating their roles as cultural agents over time. In their roles as performers, arrangers, composers, and music educators, they are like their sisters in other westernized countries who have, as Jennifer Post notes, "worked hard to erase the boundaries between public and private during the last few generations" (1994: 47).

Of course, the Trinidad context is fundamentally different from that of North America or Europe, and not all conditions or experiences are universally shared among all women in a culture as ethnically diverse and socially stratified as Trinidad and Tobago. I have aligned my approach with that of Caribbean feminists who recognize that feminism is both consciousness raising and activism, with one of the primary goals to bring about changes in real-life material conditions and gender relations. There is a long history of feminist scholarship and social movements within the Caribbean, resulting today in NGOs such as the Caribbean Association for Feminist Research and Action (CAFRA), and academic programs such as the gender studies programs at all three campuses of the University of the West Indies. This activism and research is based on the particular history of the region and various sociopolitical struggles relating to worker's rights, nationalism, universal suffrage, education, public health, and social welfare. In other words, the struggle for women's rights in the Caribbean has been closely tied to the struggle for civil and human rights in the region. While stimulated by European, American, and African feminist studies, Caribbean feminist scholars have also developed a theoretical stance and related research projects specific to their part of the world. "Caribbean women just did not fit received images and rhetoric. They were not 'marginalized' in the same way as their Third World counterparts, they could not be accommodated into private/public dichotomies which confined them to home, domesticity and motherhood, and, though constrained by patriarchal ideology and practice, they did not suffer the same subordinate status in relations with their menfolk" (Barrow, 1998: xi). In general, the women's movement in the Caribbean has been different in origin and orientation from that of its Euro-American counterparts. Feminist work and scholarship has overlapped with other social issues such as development, nationhood, and regional identity—topics largely absent from liberal feminism in North America and Europe. On the other hand, Caribbean scholars have tended to shy away from discussions of sexual orientation and other aspects of radical feminism, a fact that reflects conservative attitudes toward gays, lesbians, and bisexuals in the Caribbean region in general (Lewis, 2003: 5). For the past three decades, Caribbean feminist scholarship has grown rapidly, but as Patricia Mohammed explains in a special issue of *Feminist Review* devoted to the topic, the Caribbean is still distinctive from other regions of the world: "That feminism in general and the feminist movement in the Caribbean appear to be eclectic is that is has responded at the same time to the issues of class, race/ethnicity, nationhood, and to gender identity. Only the openness of the mid-twentieth century onwards has created both the global consciousness as well as the rapid spread of the ideas of gender equality, which were always part of the struggle" (Mohammed, 1997: 17). Mohammed has written several articles on calypso, which demonstrates the commitment of feminist scholars to addressing local culture and expressive forms (Mohammed, 1991 and 2003).

I also share the theoretical perspectives of such contemporary scholars of Caribbean music as Carolyn Cooper, Peter Manuel, Deborah Pacini-Hernandez, Jocelyne Guilbault, and Shannon Dudley. While they have taken diverse approaches to gender, all have strived to avoid Eurocentric or essentialist interpretations of their various topics (Cooper, 1993 and 2004; Pacini-Hernandez, 1995; Manuel, 1998; Guilbault, 2007; Dudley, 2008). Within the Caribbean as in other regions of the world, one can make certain distinctions between women's participation in musical performance based on their ethnicity and class. For example, working-class Afro-Caribbean women have had greater access to various genres of public musical performance than European or East Indian women in nearly every country within the region. As I will discuss below, there is evidence that working-class Afro-Caribbean women more closely shared men's genres in the distant past, and their relative disappearance from musical performance is a result of various aspects of colonization. Most pertinent to my work are studies that suggest that women played important roles in Trinidadian expressive culture during the post-emancipation period until they retreated from that sphere at the end of the nineteenth century, due to interventions from the state and church-based institutions (Cowley, 1996; Mohammed, 2003; Rohlehr, 2004b; Guilbault, 2007). Women in Trinidad have played an increasingly prevalent role in the popular music scene since the early sixties, when Trinidad and Tobago became independent from Great Britain and solidified a strong sense of national culture. This is in contrast to the Hispanic Caribbean, where the presence of female performers is a fairly recent phenomenon (Aparacio, 1998; Waxer, 2002).

What makes Trinidad somewhat striking within the region is the significant contribution of women to the country's musical culture and the rather unique space they have created to voice matters from a women's point of view. This does not mean that women's musical agency is not subject to patriarchal confines, and much of this book addresses these limitations within contemporary Trinidad in parallel to the work of other scholars of Caribbean music, who note that women have largely been confined to roles as vocalists with limited participation as instrumentalists, arrangers, and producers (Aparacio, 1998; Manuel, 2006; Guilbault, 2007).[1] As I will show, women have both maintained tradition and have been key musical innovators in the transformation of Trinidad's musical landscape. Depending on their circumstances, women have played an important role in public life, making themselves visible and their voices audible, creating aesthetics of performance compatible with their goals even in time periods when historical circumstances tightly regulated women's role in public life. They assisted in promoting the nation's music as a form of cultural capital[2] that benefited both themselves and the culture at large.

Trinidad is geographically a piece of South America that became an island when the Orinoco delta submerged during the last Ice Age. For many years, various Amerindian[3] tribes traveled from what is now Venezuela to hunt game in the rain forests and mangrove swamps of Trinidad. Members of the Arawak and Carib tribal groups eventually founded permanent settlements on the island. The indigenous peoples of Trinidad referred to it as "the Land of the Hummingbird," a prosaic term still in use today in history books and travel brochures. As the Spanish settled the island, most Amerindians perished. Those who survived were driven off their lands into mission towns in

Arima and Siparia, or intermarried with Spanish peons who came to work the land. Due to the rapid disappearance and assimilation of the indigenous population, little is known about their expressive culture (Manuel, 2006: 3).

The early Spanish settlers named the towns they built and the geographic features of the island of Trinidad, but the colony there became largely French speaking during the late eighteenth century due to the Cédula de Población issued by Charles III in 1783. Planters and their slaves from French West Indian colonies settled the island, and were later joined by a number of Scottish, Irish, German, Italian, and English families. In 1797 Trinidad became part of the British Empire when the Spanish relinquished governance to General Ralph Abercromby (Brereton, 1981: 13–14). Despite colonization by three different European language groups, the ethnic makeup of this new British colony was primarily Afro-Creole. These included both slaves and free people of color, the latter of whom were, like their white contemporaries, landowners and relied on slave labor for their economic pursuits. Under the first twenty-five years of British rule, the population of Trinidad doubled as the flow of immigrants continued from neighboring islands such as Martinique and Barbados, the Spanish colony of Venezuela, and North America, including freed slaves who had assisted the British in the War of 1812 (Hill, 1973: 9; Brereton, 1981: 50–51).

The legendary strength of Afro-Caribbean women to survive despite great odds has its roots in various structures and strategies that emerged during slavery and the early years of emancipation. Marriage and cohabitation were at various times forbidden or else tightly regulated under slavery, leading to the dominance of matrifocal kinship groups in the Anglophone Caribbean. While slave men were not absent from family life, they were prevented by design from fulfilling the role of family patriarch; marriage was the preserve of plantation owners and wealthy merchants (Reddock, 1994: 20–23). Subsistence farming, petty trading, and other income-earning activities were ways for slave women to gain a certain degree of independence and, in a number of cases, to purchase their freedom and that of their children. As they do today, matrifocal households within the Caribbean typically relied on a system of balanced reciprocity among kinship groups as well as among friends of long-standing relationships and strong emotional ties, otherwise known as "faux family" (Senior, 1991: 37).

Throughout the colonial period, residents of Trinidad celebrated various types of feasts and fetes to commemorate important events or for recreation during free time and holidays. Prior to emancipation, slaves were allowed to congregate during their days off and also for various life cycle rituals such as funerals and wakes. The French introduced elaborate celebrations for

Christmas and Carnival, and during these festivals slaves were "given license ... for dancing, feasting at the master's expense, some freedom of movement, and elaborate costuming" (Pearse, 1956: 18–19). Afro-Creole festivities are often described under the collective term "drum dance," as they most commonly used drums as the principal or sole musical instruments. Chroniclers of these events mention that women and men performed dances from their ancestral lands as well as those of their own invention such as the "bel air," "jhouba," and "bamboula" (Rohlehr, 1990: 18–24). Sometimes these festivities parodied the vain and ridiculous aspects of their masters' lives. On some plantations, the master would support the efforts of singers known as chantwells, who would sing improvisatory songs, often of a lewd and bawdy nature, accompanied by singing and dancing by the women and men in attendance. "Their songs were usually sung extempore and were flattering or satiric, depending on whether they wished to praise their master and his friends or berate his enemies. There were times when the singers would engage in a war of insults between two or more of their number" (Hill, 1972: 56–57). Chantwells often created songs that derided the estate owners and commented on various aspects of plantation life. However, slave masters were well aware of the motives that underlay satirical songs, and meted out punishments accordingly (Pearse, 1956: 144–50).

Role reversal is an ongoing theme in the cultural expressions of the English-speaking Caribbean, particularly in the case of Carnival celebrations. In the case of pre-emancipation Trinidad, the climax of the Carnival season for the planter elite and "colored" population were elaborate balls that featured masking and disguise. A common masquerade was the *negue jardin* (black field slave) for men and the "mulatress" for women. Elite women essentially masqueraded as the slave mistresses that their husbands desired, while their men enacted a parody of *cannes brulées*—the singing and drumming that gangs of field slaves performed as they controlled the burning of the fields prior to the harvesting and processing of sugar cane (Cowley, 1996: 20–21). Meanwhile, at their own entertainments slaves enacted dramatic rituals, sometimes referred to as dignity balls, in which they grouped in regiments of kings, queens, princes, dauphins, and dauphines and created elaborate costumes for royalty and the members of the court. Chronicles of the time period state that drummers and a chorus of brightly dressed female dancers provided music for these occasions. In general the focus was on fancy dress and decorum, part of a performance tradition popular throughout Afro-Caribbean culture (Franco, 2001: 83–84).

Though it was certainly a plantation-based economy, Trinidad never became a "mature" slave colony like Haiti or Jamaica, mainly because it was settled so much later and at a far slower pace than other Caribbean islands. Also, the British gained control of the island just as humanitarian movements back home questioned the moral justification of slavery and imperialism. By the first decades of the nineteenth century, abolitionists helped bring about the end of the slave trade in Britain's colonies. Trinidad became the experimental crown colony that tested new policies for improving the status of slaves and giving rights to free Afro-Creoles. In 1833 the British passed the Act of Emancipation, although full emancipation of the slave population did not take place until a period of "apprenticeship" ended in 1838 (Brereton, 1981: 74–75). Most former slaves chose to leave the plantations for other types of work, creating a severe shortage of agricultural labor in nineteenth-century Trinidad. At first the English attempted to solve this problem by introducing indentured laborers from West Africa, the Portuguese states of Fayal and Madeira, and immigrants from main land China. Eventually, the British would turn to India; already under British control, India offered a huge population already accustomed to agricultural labor in tropical conditions. By 1917, when the system of indentured labor ended, 143,000 Indians had come to the island. After completing their period of servitude—usually five to ten years—most opted to remain in Trinidad, settling in villages adjacent to the estates, which continued to provide them with employment (Myers, 1993: 14–15).

Some of the newly emancipated slaves chose to settle in the hills surrounding Port-of-Spain and vicinity, managing to achieve a fragile freedom from the plantation system in neighborhoods that surrounded the city. As novelist Earl Lovelace poetically describes this situation: "refusing to be grist for the mill of the colonial machinery that kept on grinding in its belly people to spit out sugar and cocoa and copra, they turned up this hill to pitch camp here on the eyebrow of the enemy" (Lovelace, 1979: 24–25). By the end of the nineteenth century, over one quarter of Trinidad's population lived in Greater Port-of-Spain (Brereton, 1981: 131). The rest of the Afro-Creole population remained in rural areas, and by 1869 they were finally allowed to buy land. These peasant farmers settled in villages east of Port-of-Spain and also along the Northern Range, where they established small agricultural holdings. Cultivation of cocoa, rice, tobacco, and citrus was the primary employment opportunity for rural laborers and peasants during this era (Brereton, 1981: 94–95).

This new black urban proletariat found work in various jobs available in the city, such as domestic service, messengers, petty traders, dockworkers, and various building trades. Often their work was seasonal, with segments of this population unemployed and falling victim to juvenile delinquency, vagrancy, prostitution, and petty crime. Working-class women seem to have fared somewhat better than men at making do in difficult economic times, largely through work in the informal sector (Brereton, 1981: 52–53; Johnson, 1996: 39). Afro-Creole women now had the freedom to form kinship ties and various permanent cohabiting relationships with the fathers of their children: however, only 15 percent of the Afro-Creole population was legally married and living as nuclear families by the end of the nineteenth century (Reddock, 1994: 23–24).[4] This does not mean, of course, that the lower classes did not aspire toward things like marriage and upward mobility, but the focus on economic survival made these goals less of a priority. In the pre-independence era, social progress was difficult for those born into poverty; for example, universal education did not exist in Trinidad and Tobago until the middle of the twentieth century. Thus, while Afro-Caribbean women did not develop the same dependency on men as did European or Indian women in the region, their legendary self-reliance was a result of circumstances beyond their control (Safa, 1995: 48–49).

The growing Afro-Creole population in Port-of-Spain caused considerable anxiety for the middle and upper classes. As the nineteenth century progressed, the urban proletariat was viewed as a seedy underworld of hustlers, prostitutes, and other criminals. This urban subculture was variously referred to as "jamets" or "jamettes"—a word that comes either from the French *diametre* or *demimonde*—denoting status below the line of respectability and association with the underworld of immorality and vice. The jamette woman was especially vexing in the post-emancipation social climate: ex-slaves who had toiled beside men in the plantations, these women found themselves in an urban environment that required ingenuity and skill to provide for their children. Prostitution did become one of method of survival; some women probably made a conscious decision to pursue prostitution as a career, others worked as "occasionals" in the trade (Trotman, 1986: 249–50). Enterprising women who ran inns and boarding houses that catered to the needs of single men were known as "matadors"— which in Trinidad became synonymous with madam or retired prostitute, since it was likely that these institutions made sexual services available to their patrons (Franco, 2001: 142). While the urban proletariat did include a criminal underclass, the middle and upper classes tended to paint the entire laboring population with the same broad brush, viewing the entire Afro-Creole proletariat as "jamettes."

Neighborhoods in and around Port-of-Spain formed around various ethno-linguistic groupings of the former plantations, as well as those representing communities that resulted from labor migration from the eastern Caribbean (Brereton, 1979: 110; Cowley, 1996: 43–45). Urban dwellings for the working poor during this time consisted of rows of barracks—essentially little more than sheds divided into rudimentary sleeping quarters, with many people sharing a common yard in which various activities such as cooking, laundry, vegetable gardening, the raising of chickens and goats would take place. This urban proletariat sought to continue their drum dances, wakes and funerals, and Afro-Caribbean religious services in their new urban surroundings, and it was at this time that they began to participate loudly and colorfully in Trinidad's annual Carnival. These activities dramatically changed the urban soundscape, and newspaper accounts from the time period are full of letters from the middle and upper classes complaining of the "hideous and untuneful music" of the laboring classes.[5] These collective celebrations for both sacred and secular events took various forms, and involved enthusiastic participation by both women and men of the community.

Drum dances of various kinds were held as communal events in barrack-yards in Port-of-Spain as well as in the countryside during the decades following emancipation. These dances combined African musical traditions of drumming and responsorial singing with various styles of choreography, gradually incorporating influences from styles introduced by European colonists, such French contredanses and quadrilles, as well as English reels and jigs (Donald Hill, 1993: 23). One of the more common dances of the time period that has survived to the present day is the belé, and it resembles various forms of Afro-Caribbean dance from the region, particularly the bel air from Martinique and the belé of Dominica. The dance gets its name from the *bel airs* (beautiful songs) that female chantwells composed to accompany the dances (Franco, 2001: 85, 88). In Martinique there are two distinct set dances known as belé (Cyrille, 2002: 230–31). These dances seem to have been introduced to Trinidad via inter-island migration in the eighteenth century (Franco, 2001: 85). In Trinidad, the dance has been typically danced on and around public holidays, with female dancers trying to outdo each other through flirtatious sweeping movements of their skirts toward the male dancers, whose movements are more intricate and athletic (Ahye, 1978: 44–45). The songs that accompany the belé, at least in the past, provided a platform for social commentary and satire. In the nineteenth century, the female chantwells gave news and gossip about the people in the village, composing songs full of saucy lyrics and picong (Elder, 1968; Hill, 1973: 57–58; Ahyoung, 1977: 47–48). In essence, the belé was a dance for women to demonstrate their beauty in dance and their skillfulness as "native improvisatori" (Hill, 1973: 58). "In the *Belair*, women were the premier dancers and singers, and men were the musicians and the women's temporary dancing-partners," each playing a distinct and complementary role (Franco, 2001: 92).

For accompaniment the dance employs the use of three traditional skin drums, two Fula and one Cutter or lead drum. The drummers are usually well versed in their art and the cutter drummer takes pride in his improvisations, while the fula maintains the basic rhythm. Shac-shacs are played by the Chantuelle and others, [who] dictate the style and tempo depending on the song chosen. Some songs sung in Patois or dialect are in 2/4 time and others are in 3/4 or waltz time, 4/4 and 6/8. This wide range enables the dancers to create many refreshing variations in their movements. (Ahye, 1978: 44)

The most infamous of Afro-Creole entertainments that emerged in the years following emancipation was a martial art called calinda,[6] a dueling sport played with long hardwood sticks by pairs, trios, or quartets of stick-fighters in the evenings as a form of entertainment. Gayelles were located in both rural villages and the city, but the most notorious ones that operated in the barrack-yards of Port-of-Spain carried fantastic names like "Hell Yard," "Cobeaux Town," "Le Trois Chandelle," and "Behind the Bridge" (Elder, 1966b: 193–94). Music was provided by a chorus of singers who sat in a circle around the gayelle,[7] led by chantwells versed in calinda songs and accompanied by the African doun-doun (Elder, 1966a: 91). J. D. Elder's informants recalled that women were involved in the battle itself: "some men who were stick-fighters taught the art to their wives who sometimes excelled them" (Elder, 1966b: 196). When fighters paused to take rest and refreshments, female chantwells would take center stage in the gayelle and sing carisos. These songs were exclusively the domain of women, and they were typically "lewdly erotic" or full of banter and gossip (Elder, 1966a: 91–92). Notorious chantwells of the late nineteenth century included Bodicea, who according to Andrew Pearse's informant Mitto Sampson "had a beautiful voice, a masculine face and was a wizard at extemporaneous verses. Her life was devoted to three things—singing, drinking and fighting" (Pearse, 1956: 160). When Bodicea learned that an obeah man had stolen the head of a recently deceased stickfighter, "Bodicea composed an impromptu ditty" that appealed to the crowd: "Congo Jack vole tet-la Hannibal / U vole la mo, gade bakanal" (Congo Jack steal Hannibal's head / You steal from the dead, look bacchanal).[8] The crowd loved the song so much that "they began to gyrate in the cemetery." When the "mirth-maddened carousers" refused the police's demands to the leave the cemetery, "Bodicea tore off her dress and waved it as a banner, still singing the captivating ditty" (Pearse, 1956: 160).

Both Raymond Quevedo (the calypsonian Atilla the Hun) and John Cowley discuss a jamette "matador" Sophie Mataloney,[9] a singer who popularized a song from Guadaloupe called "Pauline" or "Estomac-li bas." This song, also sung in French Creole, was the story of a young woman pregnant and abandoned by her lover:

> Pauline ma fils pas desoler-ou
> Vaut mieux c'est ca qu awiver-ou
> Deux mois loye a sous tete-ou
> Pas sa trouver papa ish-ou
> Estomac bas, bas, bas
> Pas sa touver papa ishe-la
> (Pauline my child don't worry
> Is the best thing that could happen to you
> Two months rent you have to pay
> And you can't find your child's father
> Her belly drop low, low, low
> And she can't find her child's father (Quevedo, 1983: 15–16; 169)

During her research on women in calypso, Anna Gottreich discovered a song from the turn of the century by an unknown woman that is a testimonial about prostitution:

> A year ago I was a girl
> A girl in my mother's house
> This year I am a woman
> Fighting to make a living for myself
> Ale Ale
> Shake your body and I will give you
> Naughty girl
> Shake your body and I will give you
> A hefty mister (Gottreich, 1993: 30)

Although these three songs attributed to Bodicea, Sophie/Sophia Mataloney, and an unknown jamette woman are not conclusive evidence, several things can be theorized from them. First, we can assume that up through the end of the nineteenth century, there were women performing songs of their own invention that were significant enough to be remembered many years later by other people in the environment, such as Mitto Sampson and Raymond Quevedo. Second, these women commented on the difficulties of daily life in the urban environment, and had an audience that sympathized with the commentaries that they made. Finally, we can see that they were voicing their displeasure at the injustices of the urban environment that were specific to women, including lack of support for unmarried mothers and the economic conditions that forced women into prostitution as a means of survival.

It is also possible that, in "Pauline" and the song by the anonymous woman, the singers were reacting against legislation directed specifically at them. In 1869 Trinidad enacted Ordinance 18, which "required women accused of common prostitution to register and to be periodically examined for venereal disease, and if diseased, to be incarcerated in a certified hospital ward" (Trotman, 1986: 251). Knowing that this population was poor and vulnerable, unscrupulous policemen exacted sexual favors from these women: those who refused were brought to court and forced to register as prostitutes (Trotman, 1986: 251). "This led to a public perception that prostitution was the main occupation of poor Afro-Creole women, a perception that they tried hard to resist. As Pamela Franco notes, they protested loudly as they went up en masse to the St. Ann's Hospital for their monthly internal examinations" (Franco, 2001: 169). Franco theorizes that Afro-Creole women "may have appropriated the Carnival arena to voice their discontent," specifically by using the *Pissenlit* masquerade of nightgown and menstrual cloth to "protest against the violation and unfair treatment of their bodies" (Franco, 2001: 169). It is not unreasonable to surmise that female chantwells, like female masqueraders, also addressed issues of social injustice in song, as the above examples seem to indicate.

The "unruly howling" of the lower classes eventually came under censure by the colonial government. During the 1880s public noise ordinances, such as Ordinance 11 of 1883, were passed[10] that tightly regulated when musical instruments, particular drums and other percussion, could be played and in what context. This decreased and tightly regulated performance contexts for both men and women, in particular the stick-fighting gayelles and drum dances that were an important part of secular life in both the city and countryside. Even music associated with religious worship and life-cycle rituals came under censure. For example, in 1917 the Shouter Prohibition Ordinance was passed to prohibit Shouters' meetings; the stated reason for the ordinance was the "noise" that Shouters made with their loud singing and bell ringing, and the "unseemly" expressive and emotional behavior of the worshippers (Henry, 2003: 32–34). Worshippers continued to practice in secret, often taking their services deep into the countryside in order to avoid fines and possible imprisonment.[11]

From the 1840s through 1890s, the street Carnival gradually became an annual celebration dominated by the urban proletariat, while the middle and upper classes retreated to private parties and masquerades exclusive to their social circle. The lower classes, labeled *jamettes*, celebrated the annual festival with exuberance but also continued their defiance of upper-class norms. Calinda stick-fighters appropriated the *negue jardin* mas and paraded through the streets during Carnival. They were accompanied by bands of followers enacting the cannes brulees with flambeau torches, led by chantwells who sang songs that challenged the other bands of revelers. These bands and their accompanying stick-fighters represented ethno-linguistic enclaves, and at various times, but particularly during Carnival, resorted to fighting one another when they believed it necessary to establish or maintain their territory (Cowley, 1992: 72). As the nineteenth century progressed, these bands of jamettes were critiqued in the newspapers as increasingly wild, noisy, and violent, with lewdness in costume, gesture, and song lyrics, cross-dressing by both men and women, and violent clashes between bands and individual stick-fighters (Cowley: 73–74).

"Imagine the assault on the upper class' sense of decency given the spectacle of jamette mas'; bands of prostitutes, stickfighting, drum beating, kaiso singing women who carried bottles, extra weapons, and food for the stickmen, chantwells and drummers."[12] As masqueraders, these jamette women were just as rowdy and uncontrollable as their men. Some would through open their bodices and expose their breasts. They marched in bands through the street, singing songs of challenge to rival bands they met on the road (Johnson, 1988: xv). Women of the urban proletariat formed dancing societies associated with their local community. The names were satiric or salacious— Black Ball, Dahlia, Don't-Care-A-Damn, Maribone, True Blue. They paraded in fantastic dresses and performed the elaborate choreography from their neighborhood drum dances in the streets and in yards along their parade routes. However, because these dancing organizations reflected linguistic and religious groupings as well as the territory their membership inhabited, like the male stickfighters, these women often had to do battle in cases of quarrels and physical confrontations with other bands (Cowley, 1996: 60–61).

This working class Afro-Creole culture caused considerable anxiety for white elites and the British colonial administration, but it also disturbed middle-class Afro-Creoles who aspired to upward mobility. These classes distanced themselves more and more from the Carnival of the streets, while maintaining their exclusive fetes and gatherings. Eventually, the white elite withdrew from public participation in the annual Carnival, critiquing the disorderly conduct of the jamette class (Pearse, 1956: 21–22). For years the elites pressured the government to censure or ban outright most of the cultural expressions of this grassroots class. This was both to appease the upper classes and to assert control over an "unruly" urban populace. The elites were willing to concede space during Carnival for inverting the social order because it allowed the lower classes to let off steam in a ritualized setting. However, the "therapeutic value and social control possibilities of carnival took second place to the very real potential of class and race revolt" (Trotman, 1986: 269). The infamous Canboulay Riots of 1881 and 1883, in which Captain Baker and his police force fought the crowds who marched with sticks and flaming torches, led to the passing of the Peace Preservation Act of 1883 and Ordinance 2 of 1891. This legislation restricted the street festival to a two-day period during daylight hours, prohibited the carrying of lighted torches, and outlawed carnival presentations such as stickfighting (Trotman, 1986: 269; Cowley, 1996: 120). J. D. Elder suggests it was at this time period that men shifted their focus from the outlawed stickfight to the topical songs of the women chantwells (Elder, 1968: 25). Eventually, the names of women fighters and chantwells faded into obscurity. "You playing Bodicea" became a term used to rebuke little girls showing wayward traits (Pearse, 1956: 161). Now, the former male fighters appropriated the feminine cariso that emphasized banter, gossip, and abuse, transferring the physical challenge of the calinda to the challenge of song. Thus, calypso "became increasingly and almost exclusively, a forum for the fiercely competing egos of male chantwells" (Rohlehr, 1990: 213).

The attitude of the Afro-Trinidadian middle class toward the cultural expressions of the working classes was often ambivalent. Like the white elites, they avoided mingling with the lower classes in the streets, but viewed Carnival as "an important season of festivity and sociality" and were "deeply resentful of any interference with Carnival by the government and . . . ready to use it if necessary as a means of indirect attack on the Governor and the upper (white) class whenever the tension rose" (Pearse, 1956: 23). Preferring to stay among their own kind during the season, their exclusion from the white upper class also forced them to organize their own activities. Upward mobility required conforming to the standards of British colonial life, accepting its institutions, succeeding in attaining what educational achievements were available to them, and so forth. At the same time, this class was invested in Carnival as part of their shared cultural heritage, as something that was distinctly Trinidadian. Eventually, members of the middle class took it upon themselves to enact dramatic changes to Carnival that would change the nature of the festival and help defend it from its detractors. "Towards the end of the century the festival re-emerged and began to move 'upwards' toward the position it occupies today, namely, acceptable to and practiced by all the main sections of the community" (Pearse, 1956: 35). While the more spontaneous expressions of the street carnival continued despite various ordinances—including old-time calinda songs and lavway accompanied by tamboo-bamboo or bottle-and-spoon percussion bands, instead of the banned drums and stick-fighters—they were tightly regulated, and unruly or obscene mas makers, both male and female, were fined or sent to prison (Cowley, 1996: 104–6). By the 1890s, prizes were being awarded by middle-class clubs, newspapers, and other businesses to costumed individuals and bands, thus encouraging good behavior and decency during the festival. "Bands representing socially mobile black creoles began parading in greater number than before. Likewise, this signaled a difference in musical values, with more genteel string bands taking the place of the drum that also been banned in parades" (Cowley, 1996: 133).

Like their neighbors in the Caribbean, Trinidadians began movements toward self-rule at the turn of the century. By this time, a middle class of Afro-Trinidadians had emerged that could challenge the French Creole and British elite. Educational opportunities had allowed this class to enter professions such as teaching, civil service, and other white-collar occupations. "Indeed, British colonialism, by providing a public education system, however limited, made possible the emergence of an educated middle class that would become increasingly politicized and would eventually turn against Crown Colony government" (Brereton, 1981: 128–29). However, educational opportunities in the early twentieth century were not class or gender equal. Upper-strata women received their education at parochial schools, such as Holy Name Convent and Bishop Anstey High School; curriculum at these institutions was oriented toward languages and the arts, subjects appropriate for bourgeois women of that generation. Working-class women had few educational opportunities past primary school. It would not be until the period following World War II that educational opportunities for women and men achieved near equality, regardless of social class.

Meanwhile, the women's movement in the Anglophone Caribbean was developing from various women's self-help societies that had been established in nineteenth century, including international organizations such as the YWCA. Although their original mission was economic support for women of reduced means, these organizations went on to campaign for women's political rights, girls' education, and legal reforms that would benefit women. Thus, they combined their concern for women's status with actions related to charity and social work, areas of activity that were not seen as selfish or challenging the status quo (Reddock, 1998b). Social work remained an important activity for upper- and middle-class women outside the home in the early decades of the twentieth century. The most important women's organization of this period was the Coterie of Social Workers, founded by Audrey Layne Jeffers in 1921. Their goal was to help the underprivileged through charitable work such as providing free lunches to schoolchildren and establishing hostels for "women in distress." Their long-term goals were to raise the status of girls and women via expanded educational opportunities, to improve the working conditions of women in professions such as teaching and nursing, and to enable women to enter politics (Reddock, 1994: 180–81). Jeffers's work among the impoverished working class so impressed Captain Arthur Andrew Cipriani (then mayor of Port-of-Spain) that he introduced legislation that allowed women to be elected to the city council. In 1936 Jeffers became the first woman elected to the Port-of-Spain City Council.[13]

Alongside the charitable work of the middle class, the working class initiated its own sociopolitical organizations. Throughout the West Indies, the first three decades of the twentieth century were filled with various labor movements and struggles to address rural and urban living conditions and other hardships created by a depressed world economy. The Afro-Trinidadian masses, though not allowed to vote during this period, contributed to ongoing reform through their confrontations between newly formed labor organizations in the sugar and petroleum industries and the colonial administration (Brereton, 1981: 168–69; Johnson, 1998: 46). The natural allies of the first wave of Trinidad's women's movement were in large-scale mobilization and organization for workers' rights, racial dignity, religious freedom, and national self-government. Both women and men participated in these struggles, and in fact, it was over the issue of divorce that the Trinidad Workingmen's Association was split into rival factions (Reddock, 1994: 131–32).

Several of the major labor leaders of the thirties were women, in particular Elma Francois and Christina King, founding members of the Negro Welfare Cultural and Social Association (NWCSA). Francois was the force behind many large-scale solidarity movements, including the Anti-Abyssinian War Agitation of 1935. "The Ethiopian crisis conditioned a deep and popular discrediting of the British Empire . . . (who) adopted a policy of appeasement toward Italian aggressors and hence were viewed as racist accomplices" (Neptune, 2007: 40). As Francois declared, the war was "a concern of Negroes throughout the world" (Neptune, 2007: 40). More radical ideologies were represented in the work of Christina King, who advocated that married women liberate themselves from husband domination in order to perform revolutionary duties (Reddock, 1994: 181). "From its very inception the NWSCA set out to attract women members. It was for this reason the words 'cultural' and 'social' were included in the name of the organization as these were the areas of work in which, they felt, women could initially be most easily incorporated" (Reddock, 1988: 17). In general, the NWCSA strove to improve the living conditions of the working class (both urban and rural) and ensure fair wages and working conditions.

Another product of this period was the intensification of race consciousness, and movements to instill within the Afro-Trinidadian community an awareness of its African heritage. The invasion of Ethiopia by Italy, and the lack of European response to the threat to the ancient kingdom of Abyssinia, was commented upon in the local papers and inspired racial pride among many middle- and working-class Afro-Trinidadians. Marcus Garvey's publication *Negro World* was circulated in Trinidad. The dockworkers' strikes of 1919–20 and the revival of the Trinidad Workingmen's Association were strongly influenced by Garveyism (Brereton, 1981: 161–62; Neptune, 2007: 38–43). The organization reactivated the observance of Emancipation Day, and sought to bring about solidarity with "the masses of oppressed people the world over in a struggle for the better welfare of the Negro people" (Neptune, 2007: 35–36).

As Carnival continued to be restructured and improved via the efforts of the middle class, the Fancy Bands that organized to participate in the festival constructed tents to hold practices for the bands' membership, which included composing and rehearsing the songs for performance on the road. "Songs were composed by the chantwell, and generally had topical themes. The chantwell sang the lead and the chorus was provided by the women members of the band.... Throughout the season, songsters would visit the tents of each other's band, assembling one night at one location, a second at another, and so on. They would compete against one another in song and in a group perform *picongs* or war" (Cowley, 1996: 137). Carnival tents gradually moved from being community organizations to professionally run music venues. The rivalry between neighborhood bands was transformed to rivalry between competing venues and their casts of singers. Eventually they became exclusively commercial ventures run by middle-class businessmen, who charged a set admission price to enter these "calypso tents," now housed in privately run establishments rather than the communal yards of Port-of-Spain. By the time calypso music began to be recorded around 1914, the old-time chantwells had come to be known as calypsonians. However, the move toward a professionalized setting for Carnival music did not make it easier for women to participate but rather did the opposite. While there is evidence of working-class women who performed in vaudeville and for visiting cruise ships, there is no record of female calypsonians before the mid-thirties (Rohlehr, 1990: 276). When women were hired as part of the cast of a calypso tent, they were usually part of husband-and-wife teams or were sisters of established calypso artists.

The reason for the lack of female calypsonians in the first decades of the twentieth century can be explained in several ways. Although she does not address musical performance specifically, Rhoda Reddock theorizes that by this time working-class women had been successfully "housewifed"—in other words, they accepted that upward mobility meant cultivating "good breeding" in their children and emulating middle-class ideals of femininity and propriety (Reddock, 1994). Pamela Franco reaches a similar conclusion regarding the transition from the communal setting to a professional setting: pursuing the path of the chantwell/calypsonian was the moral equivalent of being a public woman, a prostitute (Franco, 2001: 108). Of course, the dialectic of respectability versus reputation does not fully explain the paucity of female calypsonians during the first half of the twentieth century. Pure economics probably kept women out of these performing venues, because music has always been a very precarious financial undertaking. Women who might have had the talent or opportunity to pursue music as a career probably found they could make a better living performing in other types of venues, such as vaudeville, or from doing other kinds of work. Another explanation is that as this environment emerged as a battleground between men of words, it became a sort of "men's club" that was difficult for female calypsonians to negotiate. It is probably a combination of all these factors that explains why the female chantwell/calypsonian had disappeared by the early decades of the twentieth century.

As in Europe and North America, it was acceptable for middle-class women to cultivate musical skills as a sign of education and good manners. These women would have attended the mainstream churches and sung in their choirs. Private schools for girls offered musical education in the classical repertoire, and most young ladies of the middle and upper classes took piano lessons. Like the middle classes in the United Kingdom and throughout the British Commonwealth, these young women would have performed within the confines of respectable institutions, particularly the parochial schools for girls such as Bishop Anstey High School and Holy Name Convent. Those with exceptional talent and adequate financial resources would have been sent abroad to study at the Royal Academy of Music or similar foreign institutions, of course focusing on various forms of Western art music, perhaps returning to Trinidad to teach music privately or to become schoolteachers. Examples include Helen May Johnstone, the founder of the Trinidad Music Association and one of the chief forces behind the instigation of the biannual Music Festival competition in 1948 and the building of Queen's Hall in 1959.[14]

Despite the ambiguous relationship of the middle class to Carnival music, middle-class women did have an influence on the direction this music took. Bandleaders of the early twentieth century received their earliest musical training from their mothers, who typically had training in the classics. Lionel Belasco's mother, for example, had studied in Europe and toured the Caribbean as an accompanist for the concert singer Black Patti in the late 1880s. Belasco studied piano with his mother and later became a piano instructor himself (Donald Hill, 1993: 171–72). In addition to his work as a bandleader and in promoting calypsonians, Belasco cultivated a more genteel form of Carnival music for solo piano and small dance bands that eventually won favor as light entertainment in the homes of the Afro-Creole middle class. Belasco's compositions were some of the earliest forms of Carnival music to be recorded (Donald Hill, 1993: 175–76). Despite the fact that many women in Trinidad received advanced training in music, it would not have been acceptable for them to play music in the context of calypso tents or Carnival fetes. It would have been acceptable for them to perform West Indian songs in a concert setting, as Massie Patterson did with Lionel Belasco in the late 1930s (Donald Hill, 1993: 175).

Women did participate in mas in the first few decades of the twentieth century, but their activity was often tightly constricted by various factors. Female costumes typically included masks that could conceal the identity of the masquerader, in case a person's revelry might call into question her respectability. Women were clustered together in the center of the street bands, and surrounded by the men of the band, to avoid being "interfered with" (touched or pinched) by male revelers.[15] By the twenties and thirties, middle-class women who played mas rode on lorries hired for this purpose. These vehicles would circle the Savannah "bearing their jumping, singing group of girls and musicians" (Powrie, 1956: 99–100). This allowed the middle class to participate in the parade of bands, yet avoid unwanted physical contact with the revelers in the street (Riggio, 2004: 97–99).

Despite middle-class reforms and influence, satirical representation and commentary on the country's ruling powers continued to be a theme in Carnival—picong and fatigue writ large. These included military and naval masquerades, and characters such as Dame Lorraine that parodied the pretensions of the upper classes. Other revelers modeled themselves after figures of the underworld, such as various kinds of devils and demons, in which the masquerader covers his or her body with mud, molasses, paint, motor oil, or powder (Crowley, 1956; Pearse, 1956; Errol Hill, 1972; Johnson, 1988; Cowley, 1996). While these can be viewed primarily as venues to express male reputation, contestation, and camaraderie, there were also opportunities in mas for working-class women to express solidarity of various kinds. As Pamela Franco theorizes, the popular and highly visible Bajan Cook mas can be read as representing female domestic workers and their concerns that in the first two decades of the twentieth century were at the forefront of the trade union and labor movement in Trinidad and Tobago:

> Fabricated from such sumptuous materials as organza and lace, the dress belied the drudgery and hardships of the domestic's life. This fancy dress temporarily "transformed" the women from working class to upper class, the latter being the indicative of the social status of the leaders of the TWA. By doing this, the women symbolically "assumed" the mantle of leadership. More importantly, the dress assisted the women in visually constructing a corporate or collective identity.... The clothes convey a sense of corporate identity to the observer. Dressed in identical garments, the women presented a unified front. Finally, the white dresses, glistening in the tropical sun, insured that the Bajan Cooks would not be ignored or overlooked. (2001, 151–52)

By the mid-1930s the Bajan Cook mas was in decline: labor riots had created a climate of anxiety, and trade unionism focused more on the oil industry than on the cause of domestics (Franco, 2001: 153).

By the end of the thirties, Carnival was vastly "improved" by various entities, both commercial and governmental. Meanwhile, calypsonians Atilla the Hun (Raymond Quevedo) and the Roaring Lion (Raphael de Leon) had been venturing to New York City since 1934 to record for various labels, including Decca and the American Record Company (Donald Hill, 1993: 184). It is likely that they saw themselves as emerging stars on the road to upward mobility; after all, Atilla and Lion had been to America and sung on Rudy Vallee's radio program. However, prevailing attitudes toward calypsonians within the dominant culture in Trinidad were that they came from the lowest social classes. They acted as a mouthpiece for the common man, but calypsonians were not someone a person with class would want to associate with as equals (Donald Hill, 1993: 89–91). Thus, there was little change from the turn of the century regarding public opinion on the musicians who provided the music for Carnival, even as it had come to be performed in a more professionalized setting.

In 1940 the British colonial government signed an agreement that granted property to the US military for use as naval and air force bases in Trinidad.[16] American military personnel arrived to build the bases and to enhance the island's infrastructure, and to assist the British in defending the Eastern Caribbean from invasion by Axis forces. The American occupation of Trinidad instigated a love/hate relationship between Trinidadians and the "Yankees." The military provided thousands of civilian jobs on the bases, setting the example of American fair labor practices and decent wages. American military personnel boosted the local economy in a number of ways, and the influx of capital rapidly improved the general standard of living for those who benefited from these expenditures. Women labored to take advantage of the influx of foreign employers in Trinidad. This was especially true for the women who made a living cooking, cleaning, washing, and performing sundry domestic duties in other people's households. The new economic conditions allowed these women to struggle for material betterment and dignity among local employers. In the thirties, approximately 36 percent (10,000) of the island's wage-earning females were engaged in domestic work. As more North Americans arrived on the island, these domestic workers were able to leave depressingly dreadful working conditions with colonial employers and double or even triple their wages under employment of the new arrivals (Neptune, 2007: 99). The war economy also offered women legitimate wage-earning opportunities that they did not have previously. As in the United States, jobs previously dominated by men, particularly teaching and various white-collar clerical jobs, were successfully taken over by women. Female-dominated professions such as nursing and midwife professions expanded during the war years, and were now able to expand public health services into rural areas (Reddock, 1994: 205–6).

However, as historical Harvey Neptune notes in great detail, the American military presence also had negative effects, one of which was the exploitation of women. As indicated above, prostitution existed in Trinidad before the war years, but "the arrival of thousands of American men injected new vigor and profit into the local trade. Each day, according to one official source, between 600 and 700 prostitutes plied their trade in Port of Spain" (Neptune: 180–81). As with everything else in the nation's history, this became a source of commentary in many calypsos of the period, the most famous of which was Lord Invader's "Rum and Coca Cola (Yankee Dollar)." Various observers, such as writers Ralph Mentor and Jean De Boissere, noted that it was becoming common for working-class females in Trinidad to supplement their wages through commercial sex during the war years: they were "girlfriends," "occasionals," and "clandestines" who were "victims of circumstance" rather than professional sex workers. The politician Albert Gomes lamented the "uprooted and adrift" young women of the era, confronted by modernity and easy money, "girls only superficially successful in their search for independent womanhood" (Neptune, 2007: 188).

Even women who were not engaged in prostitution were vulnerable, as American military personnel took advantage of the desires of local women for financial support, and their dreams of marriage and emigration to the States. Locally based U.S. personnel had to get permission from their commanding officers to marry, and in most cases where the woman was nonwhite and the man was white, this request was denied. Moral panic ensued among locals as a result, as they commented upon the need to save women from temporary and illegitimate marriages to American military personnel. The only positive result of the encounter was the questioning of race relations that occurred during this period. "Liaisons between local women and American men frequently flew in the face of the combined forces of white supremacy, male domination, and class privilege, troubling precepts essential to the social order. Ultimately, the stories of these affairs, fraught with uncertain and undecided struggles over status, desire, and material ambition, composed the story of occupied Trinidad" (Neptune, 2007: 190).

On a more positive note, the US occupation was also a time of cultural exchange. USO bands and the US armed forces radio station WVDI brought American swing to Trinidad audiences. Jazz dance and music, along with the "jitterbug" fashion depicted in American films, became enormously popular among working-class Trinidadians. The street Carnival was suspended from 1942 to 1945,[17] but calypsonians were allowed to perform in nightclubs and calypso tents. They also performed for US personnel at the USO on Wrightson Road and were heard on WVDI (Neptune, 2007: 138). In response to fashionable dance music, calypsonians wrote songs that were more flexible in terms of poetic form, and calypso melodies became increasingly lively and tuneful. They also composed lyrics that addressed local concerns about the military presence. "Rum and Coca Cola" was not the only calypso in this vein; others include "Yankee Money" by Lord Beginner (Egbert Moore) and "No More Darling and Joe" by Growler (Errol Duke). However, as Neptune notes, such calypsos can be read as both anti-Americanism and "appeals to the ribald taste and, more important, rewarding pockets of U.S. personnel" (2007: 145).

At this time, several female calypsonians emerged as part of husband-and-wife teams. The most successful of these were Lord Iere (Randolph Thomas) and his wife Lady Iere (Maureen St. John), whose heyday was 1939–48. According to Hollis Liverpool, Lord Iere was failing to achieve success as a singer and brought his wife in to sing chorus with him (Liverpool, 2004: 82–83). Lady Iere also began singing her own songs in 1942, most of which projected a motherly love or good-wife image. This would have been in line with the general moralizing of the time period, which overall expressed a housewife ideology, even at a time when, at least temporarily, women had greater agency in pursuing wage work and a life outside the home (Reddock, 1994: 184).

Although there were few female calypsonians in the thirties and forties, women made important contributions to a cultural renaissance in Trinidad. Dancer and choreographer Beryl McBurnie was the most significant female contributor to these efforts. After training as a schoolteacher, she traveled throughout Trinidad as the research assistant of Andrew Carr in the thirties.

In 1938 McBurnie traveled to New York to attend Columbia University, where she studied dance with Martha Graham, but returned to Trinidad to stage productions throughout the war years.[18] After the war, McBurnie took up a position teaching at Tranquility Girls Government School and the Education Department.[19] McBurnie's dream of starting her own theatre was realized in 1948, when the Little Carib Theatre, housed in a structure in the backyard of her family home, formally opened with a program called *Talking Drums*. An impressive number of local dignitaries, politicians, and artists attended this performance. Paul Robeson, who was on tour in Trinidad himself, gave a dramatic reading of "The Freedom Train" by Langston Hughes. Dr. Eric Williams, who would become Trinidad and Tobago's first prime minister, in his newspaper column lauded the Little Carib Theatre as "the Albert Hall, the Carnegie Hall, the Opera of Trinidad." The evening closed with a performance by the Invaders Steelband led by Ellie Mannette, among the first occasions that pan was presented on stage rather than its traditional context of Carnival revelry.

After the war, McBurnie continued her dance research in the Caribbean and South America, and later compiled a book of various Afro-Creole, Amerindian, and East Indian dances, as did her protégée Molly Ahye (McBurnie, 1950; Ahye, 1978). In 1950 McBurnie was named Director of Dance in the Department of Education—a position created specifically for her. She was invited to London by the British Council to give lecture demonstrations on West Indian dance, and made research trips to various countries in Europe and South America to find cultural links with the West Indies. Her work in the UK was considered so significant that she was appointed OBE in 1959. The Little Carib Dance Company successfully toured throughout the 1950s, including festivals in Puerto Rico, Jamaica, Canada, and the United States. Meanwhile, the Little Carib Theatre nurtured developing talent, including poet and playwright Derek Walcott, who founded the Trinidad Theatre Workshop at the Little Carib Theatre in 1959. McBurnie turned her attention toward teaching children, and was the first among many schoolteachers to bring local music and dance into the school curriculum.[20] She collaborated on Carnival productions with fellow artists, including playwright and drama historian Dr. Errol Hill. McBurnie's efforts won her considerable critical acclaim. For her contributions to the arts, McBurnie was awarded the Hummingbird Gold Medal of Trinidad and Tobago in 1969, and her nation's highest honor, the Trinity Cross, in 1989.[21]

Another important figure of McBurnie's generation was Olive Walke. Educated at the Royal Academy of Music and Trinity College in London, she too researched folk music throughout the Caribbean. Olive Walke published her own collection of folk song arrangements and new songs in the folk idiom, including "Mangos" and "Every Time I Pass" (Walke, 1970). She is best known for founding and directing the folk choir La Petite Musicale in 1940. This was the first "serious" musical ensemble in Trinidad and Tobago to perform the region's folk music, and became a respected musical institution. This paved the way for future professional choirs such as the Marionettes Chorale, founded by Jocelyne Pierre and June Williams-Thorne in 1963, and Joyce Spence's Lydian Singers, founded in 1979.

As in the prewar period, the women's movement went hand in hand with nationalist ideologies and political positioning. Following the enactment of universal adult suffrage in 1946, the League of Women Voters was founded in 1949. At this time nonpartisan, the League's primary purpose was to interest women in matters relating to social, economic, and political conditions of the colony and to encourage women to exercise their right to vote. These changes paved the way for women's involvement in local politics as party leaders and candidates for public office. In the 1956 general elections, the People's National Movement, led by the charismatic Dr. Eric Williams, won the majority vote and Dr. Williams became the nation's first prime minister. Educated at Oxford and gaining his early professional experience in the United States at Howard University, Williams emerged in the fifties as an educator and orator extraordinaire, building his support through a series of public lectures on West Indian history presented in front of the Trinidad Public Library facing Woodford Square. The political platform developed by the PNM clearly emphasized public education, modernity and industrialization, nationalism, and a movement toward independence. Wisely, Williams quickly realized the potential of supporting the outburst of creativity in art, poetry, fiction, drama, music, and dance that poured forth during the forties and fifties. When he became prime minister in 1956, Williams continued to support Trinidadian intellectuals and their revival/reconstitution of the cultural heritage of the new republic of Trinidad and Tobago (Brereton, 1981: 233–34). As Williams said in one of his more famous speeches, "Massa" never invented anything of beauty; his attention was on finance and agriculture. It was the African slave and Indian indenture that kept alive agriculture and everything else, including artistic expression.[22] Williams felt that education was the great emancipator and part of his development plan for the newly minted nation was both artistic and industrial. He forged a campaign of popular education, including his own public lectures in Woodford Square, working on the native intelligence of the aspiring lower middle classes. Influenced by the Cuban ethnographer Fernando Ortiz, Williams was interested in the African origins of Caribbean music and folklore and encouraged scholarship in that area (Lamming, 1998: 731). The People's National Movement under Williams brought about vast cultural change and transformation within the new nation, as well as retention and renewal of the country's inherited complex of cultures. His own rise having come from education, he saw it as critical for Trinidad to become a modern nation. This education included self-betterment through a "re-enculturation" in local ways and customs, most of which had been diluted under British colonial rule.[23]

In the early years of its existence, the PNM enacted a number of changes that greatly increased access to secondary education. In 1960 the first state-owned secondary school for girls opened in Port-of-Spain. In 1962, the first year of Trinidad and Tobago's independence, the PNM granted free secondary education to all students regardless of gender or ethnicity. Along with other countries in the West Indian Federation, the PNM instituted a common entrance examination based on the British model to ensure equal opportunity to the most select secondary schools. The University of the West Indies, whose parent campus opened in Mona, Jamaica, in 1948, established campuses in St. Augustine, Trinidad, in 1960 and Cave Hill, Barbados, in 1962. Ultimately, these new educational policies would increase opportunities for women in higher education and success in many fields previously dominated by men, such as medicine, and law (Mohammed, 1991: 36).

In 1956 a special issue of *Caribbean Quarterly* was dedicated to Carnival. In her article on the changing attitudes of the middle class toward the annual festival, Barbara E. Powrie makes a number of observations about the role of women in Carnival at the time. She comments that the religious significance of Carnival is "highly significant for women" and that "it is their annual opportunity to do all that the Church and society condemns, and further, it encourages them to participate with so much feeling and outward show of devotion in the yearly religious climax of Lent and Easter" (1956: 97). Powrie also notes that, for the middle class, "Carnival is the one chance in the whole year when the socially embarrassing facts of inheritance can be used to advantage, freely and openly. Particularly for the females, the blessing of the Church (Roman Catholic, at least) upon Carnival behavior gives sanctioned release from mental tension" (1956: 98) She also notes that the emancipation of women that occurred during the war years gave them economic independence and thus the ability to pay for their own costumes and shape the direction that the look and themes of mas bands would take. Powrie comments that women brought a new style of movement to mas, bringing the movement of the dance floor to the streets: "This exaggerated and erotic dancing, known as 'wining,' no longer stands out as abnormal when performed in the streets under the public gaze" (1956: 102–3).

Beginning in 1963, the Ministry of Community Development has held the Prime Minister's Best Village Trophy Competition, in which community groups vie for prizes in folk literature, folk music, folk dance, local foods, and folk art. For fifty years it has been one of the main instruments by which various folk activities from earlier historical periods have been revived and renewed. As Gordon Rohlehr notes: "Fostering 'culture' involved the recovery and rehabilitation of the steadily waning pastoral folk culture, which had declined, with the spread of education in English during the last quarter century when the older languages of Creole French and Spanish went out of currency.... While dying languages could not be resuscitated, old traditional folk dances were rescued and taught to younger generations, albeit in stylized form" (1997: 868). Today, dozens of villages compete, and it is largely the members of the grassroots class who take part in the competition. Best Village has become a significant platform for young people, particularly young women, to perform and experience various performance traditions at times other than Carnival. Various folk dances are showcased, including representative styles from the nation's various ethnic groups. A major competition in Best Village is La Reine Reve, a combination beauty pageant/talent competition, which in recent years has come to feature women from both the Afro-Trinidadian and Indo-Trinidadian communities. Generally, Best Village and other heritage festivals in the region have kept alive various aspects of a common cultural heritage, despite their stylized form and competitive context. Most importantly, there has been a certain amount of crossover between traditional music and popular music, which seems natural given the country's small size. Calypsonians such as Singing Sandra and Calypso Rose told me that some of their earliest performance opportunities were as participants in Best Village. Popular performers and musical arrangers have been exposed to various aspects of Trinidad and Tobago's folk culture via these festivals, and this has allowed them to experiment over the years in creating interesting new types of songs and interesting musical arrangements (Bilby, 1985: 206–7; Guilbault, 2007: 237).

In addition to his regard for folk traditions, Williams was keenly interested in contemporary music. He was a great fan of calypso and the steelband, and the prime minister's popularity was constantly reinforced by calypsonians such as the Mighty Sparrow singing his praises from the stage of the Young Brigade Tent. Of course, Williams was also critiqued by Sparrow and other calypsonians when they were displeased with the People's National Movement and its leader. During the Williams administration, the Carnival Development Committee (later known as the National Carnival Commission) was established, and government support for various aspects of the festival was increased. This was both to enhance support for the PNM among the working classes and to attract tourists to Trinidad and

Tobago—for both purposes, Carnival had to be improved further via the establishment of new competitive contexts and the strengthening of existing ones such as the Calypso Monarch competition (Manuel, 2006: 224–25). The result of the efforts of Williams and the PNM was a tremendous change in how local arts and culture are perceived by the average Trinidadian. The middle classes could finally shed their ambivalence toward the expressions of the lower classes and embrace them as examples of national identity. The lower classes could take pride in their accomplishments in ways that they could not in previous generations, and were given new performance spaces to showcase their talents.

As women in the West Indies gained greater access to education and the professions in the sixties, a new form of feminist consciousness emerged. As in Europe and North America, this "second wave" of feminist thought and activism built upon the women's movements of the first half of the twentieth century. While many of the social welfare groups established earlier continued to operate, new organizations arose that adopted a more developmental approach. The first focus of these groups was providing solutions to the high level of unemployment among poor and rural women in the Caribbean and addressing women's low earning potential in general. Various work groups formed in the late sixties that organized income-generating programs in rural areas to increase women's earning potential. The second important issue of this time period was addressing concerns about abortion and rape and women's rights to have control over their own bodies. This led to the formation of various organizations in the Caribbean to address these issues, including Defense for the Rights of Women in Trinidad and Tobago. National Councils of Women were also formed in various countries to act as umbrella organizations for groups focusing on the rights of women (Ellis, 2003: 71–73).

As I will discuss in more detail in the next chapter, both the performers and content of calypso music changed as a direct result of the improved status of women and the vast expansion of the their role in public life. During the sixties, the new generation of calypsonians included a number of female singers, including the most enduring female calypsonian, Calypso Rose. The female calypsonians of Rose's generation addressed the many issues affecting the lives of women in Trinidad, but most often the issue of domestic violence. For example, Singing Francine made her debut with a song by the Mighty Sparrow that warned women to "Run Away" from men who humiliated or brutalized them. Singing Diane's response to "licks in de morning, in de evening" was "I Done Wid Dat," composed by arranger Ed Watson. Such song lyrics mirrored the efforts of feminist activists in Trinidad to advocate legislation to restrain men from inflicting bodily harm on their wives.

Throughout the post-independence period, Afro-Trinidadian women were active participants in developing a sense of regional identity and improvement of the condition of their race. But by 1970, lack of progress regarding development, an end to racial discrimination, and establishment of employment opportunities for working-class Afro-Trinidadians brought about massive strikes and organized marches to protest these conditions. This "Black Power Revolution" included intellectuals from UWI, political leaders from the newly formed National Joint Action Committee (NJAC), as well as members of the laboring classes (Ryan, 1995: 695). A crucial part of the Black Power struggle in Trinidad and Tobago was the National Women's Action Committee (NWAC), the women's arm of NJAC. They gave both moral and material support to the men on the picket lines, and visited their families to boost the morale of wives and children. "During the incarceration of the leadership when the state of emergency was called on April 21st 1970, a new leadership emerged to continue the struggle, [and] among them were women who assisted in conducting the affairs of NJAC, competently."[24] Despite minority support as a political party, NJAC, along with NWAC, have been important proponents of cultural change and revival. Since the late seventies they have sponsored a number of calypso competitions during Carnival season for various age groups, including the NWAC Calypso Queen competition. They support efforts throughout the year to reach out to youth in schools to enable them to strive to better their lives through their participation in Afro-Trinidadian culture. NJAC and NWAC are particularly visible during Emancipation Day celebrations, when they support cultural activities such as calypso competitions, performances of Afro-Caribbean dance, and fashion shows featuring traditional African dress and hairstyles.

Like Venezuela, Trinidad's south coast is rich in oil and natural gas, and proceeds from the oil industry are controlled by the state. During the energy crisis of the mid-seventies, the local economy experienced an "oil boom" in which the standard of living in Trinidad and Tobago changed rapidly and dramatically. Many new jobs were created due to the increased demand for and production of petroleum products, and the standard of living in the republic increased dramatically. Government investments included the building of new schools and expansion of existing educational programs, low-cost housing projects, and infrastructure improvements that expanded utility services. Urban growth was an obvious result, but even rural villages were rebuilt with brick and concrete houses replete with modern electrical wiring and plumbing (Miller, 1991: 32–33). Thus, the government was able to enact the changes demanded by the Black Power revolution at a time when other Caribbean countries were in deep recession.

The result for the women of Trinidad and Tobago was greater social mobility and participation in the labor force at many different levels. In general, the oil-boom period marked another period of urbanization of the population, as expansion of industrial enterprises caused a decline in agricultural production. Women who would have worked in rural environments were now pursuing blue-collar jobs in factories. Social mobility was also enhanced by educational mobility that allowed women to pursue professional, technical, and clerical jobs in greater numbers than they ever had before (Reddock, 1991). The United Nations Decade for Women (1975–1985) assisted in opening up space for further feminist work. For example, from 1979 to 1982 the Women in the Caribbean Project was conducted under the auspices of the Institute for Social and Economic Research at UWI. This project involved regionwide research carried out in several countries, covering issues as diverse as socialization and education, domestic and family life, sources of livelihood, and interactions with men and the wider society. While the study focused primarily on lower-class Afro-Creole women in the Eastern Caribbean, it did throw light on contributing factors to the feminization of poverty in the region, and the obstacles to women's advancement that remained (Senior, 1991).

The prosperity, optimism, and relative liberalism of the sixties and seventies set up the conditions for women to (re)emerge in Trinidad's expressive culture. Female calypsonians who emerged during this time added a female perspective that had been missing for generations. This included participation in the then new form of calypso called soca, which represented the optimism of the seventies and eighties and resulted in a party-fueled atmosphere that revitalized the local music scene. During these years, women revelers burst onto the masquerade scene with new self-confidence: Carnival became a forum for gender emancipation, at least in the temporary space of the festival. The move toward "pretty mas," or as some call it "bikini mas," was completely engineered by women, who wanted the figures they had shaped in the months before Carnival admired by the crowds and the international television cameras. By 1988 some mas bands were 80–90 percent women, and female masqueraders have continued to outnumber male masqueraders at a rate of five to one (Mason, 1998: 134). During the seventies and eighties, new styles of party music, collectively referred to as soca, provided an energetic soundtrack to mas bands and fetes attendees, as well as providing a new musical platform for female artists. The formalization of pan education in the schools as well as the formation of new steelbands, particularly for young people, all facilitated the participation of female musicians, leading to a "domestication of pan" that continues to the present day (Dudley, 2008: 249–53).

Although there have been several "oil busts" since the prosperous seventies and early eighties, Trinidad and Tobago continues to have one of the highest standards of living in the Caribbean. As of 2010, the literacy rate in the republic was 98 percent, a result of a system of free and compulsory public education from age five to sixteen. Children typically enroll at age three at an Early Childhood Care and Education (ECCE) school. Students are expected to acquire basic reading and writing skills by the time they begin primary school at age five. During the seventh and final year of primary school, students sit for the Secondary Entrance Assessment (SEA), formerly known as the Common Entrance Examination. These examinations determine which secondary school a student is allowed to attend, and the standards for receiving government assistance to support their attendance at the more prestigious institutions are rigorous and competitive. Secondary school consists of Forms One through Five, and most secondary schools are single-sex rather than coed. In Form Five, students take the Caribbean Secondary Education Certificate (CSEC) examinations, which are the equivalent of the British GCSE taken at the age of sixteen. Students who are academically qualified may opt to continue secondary school for another two years, at which point they may take the Caribbean Advanced Proficiency Examinations (CAPE), the equivalent of the British A-levels taken at age eighteen. Students are then eligible to enroll in tertiary education. As of 2015, tertiary education at the University of the West Indies, the University of Trinidad and Tobago, the University of the Southern Caribbean, and several other accredited institutions was fully subsidized by the government for academically qualified students.[25]

Along with advancements in education and quality of life, serious social problems emerged during the eighties and Nineties that continue to affect the daily lives of Trinidadians, including gang-related crime and violence, kidnapping and extortion, drug trafficking, domestic abuse, teen pregnancy, and HIV/AIDS. Upward mobility was often seen as a way to avoid or escape these social problems, but emigration for educational and employment opportunities also increased dramatically during this time, leading to a "brain drain" of talented individuals just as the nation needed them most. Grassroots feminist organizers formed organizations in the eighties and nineties to address the particular needs of women in their communities. These included Women Working for Social Progress (Working Women) and the Hindu Women's Organization. In general, these groups see the lower status of Caribbean women as a result of fewer education and work opportunities and the effects of adverse social and economic conditions (Ellis, 1986). Working Women in particular is concerned with labor issues and how they pertain to women workers. Meanwhile, permanent university programs in Women and

Development studies were created in 1993; their directors Rhoda Reddock, Eudine Barriteau, and Patricia Mohammed are leaders in contemporary feminist work in the Caribbean, each founding academic programs in Women and Development Studies at the University of the West Indies campuses in Trinidad, Barbados, and Jamaica, respectively.[26]

On April 2, 1985, an autonomous umbrella organization for feminists and women activists in the Caribbean region was launched. Named the Caribbean Association for Feminist Research and Action (CAFRA), the organization currently is headquartered in Trinidad, near the University of the West Indies in St. Augustine. The organization defines itself as "a regional network of feminists, individual researchers, activists and women's organizations that define feminist politics as a matter of both consciousness and action. We are committed to understanding the relationship between the oppression of women and other forms of oppression in the society, and we are working actively for change."[27] CAFRA is not just an ivory tower institution, nor one limited to a particular nation-state. Its outreach is to the entire Caribbean, though membership is predominantly activists from the West Indies, Guyana, and Belize. Like earlier organizations, CAFRA is also involved with cultural work. Every meeting of CAFRA T&T that I attended featured some sort of cultural presentation, including musical performances by Lady Gypsy (Lynette Steele) and the calypso duo Abbi Blackman and Shanaqua. CAFRA sponsored a calypso competition prior to the Fourth World Conference on Women in Beijing in 1995, and the prize for the winning calypsonian, Abbi Blackman, was a trip to Beijing to perform at a number of events sponsored by the conference. Patricia Mohammed has written several articles on calypso, and feminist scholarship in the Caribbean is deeply concerned with various aspects of local culture and expressive forms (Mohammed, 1991 and 2003).

In contemporary Trinidad, much of the local music is centered around production for the Carnival season. Carnival channels the energy of many creative women and men, most of whom do it for love rather than financial gain. Preparations for Carnival typically begin in the late summer, when mas camps hold fetes to raise money and give a preview of their band concept and costumes for the coming year. Late summer and fall are busy times for the local music industry, when new calypso and soca songs are recorded and released to radio stations and music distributors. Music sharing sites such as Sound-Cloud, Reverb Nation, YouTube, and Facebook have made it easy for artists to get their music directly to audiences well in advance of the Carnival season.[28] Auditions for the casts of the main calypso tents typically occur in October or November, and the schedule for the various competitions and fetes for the Carnival season is published in the local newspapers. Throughout the holiday season, new Carnival music is heard alongside seasonal music such as parang, soca parang, and local versions of holiday standards. Promptly on Boxing Day, radio stations switch to playing the music associated with the coming Carnival season. Shortly after Old Year's Night, steelband arrangers and their bands have selected their tunes of choice, and rehearsals for Panorama begin in the many panyards throughout Trinidad and Tobago. By mid-January audiences and critics have a good sense of what songs calypso and soca artists will be showcasing for the season in the calypso tents and Carnival fetes. By the last week of the season, masqueraders have a good sense what tunes they will hear played by DJs on the big trucks that accompany them during the Parade of Bands. On Carnival Monday and Tuesday, the most popular songs are played incessantly on the road to accompany the various mas bands, and a clear winner emerges for the Road March title.[29]

Interest in local culture reaches a peak around Carnival time; afterwards Trinidadians return to their more diverse musical interests. My husband and several friends visited me in Trinidad during Lent, and were disappointed in the lack of opportunities to hear local music. By that time the locals have had their fill of calypso and soca, and need a cool-down period. For some, this is a time of spiritual reflection, and thus there are a number of concerts of gospel music and visits by various fundamentalist preachers from Ash Wednesday to Easter. What fetes there are during Lent typically take the form of beach parties, with music provided by DJs who mix local and foreign music. There are also post-Carnival champions' shows and prize-giving ceremonies, but they are decidedly more low-key than the competitions during Carnival.

Because Carnival music is associated with a particular season, it receives less attention and interest at other times of year—although things today are a major contrast to earlier generations, when calypso was banned from radio airplay during Lent and Christmas; nowadays one can hear calypso and soca on local radio stations year round. However, aside from the Carnival season, radio programming is mixed between local and foreign styles. There are stations that play no local music; they are devoted to rap and R&B, soul, smooth jazz, rock and pop, or various types of inspirational music such as gospel. On stations dedicated to playing at least some local music year round, when Carnival is over the season's big hits are played less frequently, and programming goes into "back in time" mode, showcasing calypso and soca of previous decades alongside "slows" (ballad-style R&B) and conscious reggae and dub. Dancehall, R&B, and rap are played alongside local or regional soca songs on radio stations that cater to a younger audience. In a nation in which half the population is of East Indian heritage, there are of course a number of stations that play Indo-Trinidadian styles such as chutney soca, as well as music from Indian film soundtracks as well as Indian classical and religious music.

The most successful local artists spend much of the year performing throughout the Caribbean, North America, and Europe. While calypsonians such as Calypso Rose and Denyse Plummer give cabaret-type shows at the Hotel Normandie, Mas Camp Pub, or similar venues, local calypso and soca artists are generally taking a much-deserved break during this time to rest up for their foreign engagements. Following Easter, there are usually music festivals such as the Plymouth Jazz Festival in Tobago, which despite its moniker typically features various forms of soca, reggae, and pop. Local soca artists such as Machel Montano, Destra Garcia, Denise Belfon, Roy Cape All Stars, Kes the Band, and Imij & Co. are usually on the bill, playing a selection of recent soca hits mixed with popular reggae and R&B selections. However, the headliners are usually foreign pop or reggae artists, in recent years including Diana Ross, Elton John, Rod Stewart, LL Cool J, Shakira, and Sean Paul.

Most Trinidadians have been keenly interested in North American music for many years, due not only to the proximity of the two regions but also because many West Indians make North American cities their permanent places of residence. Additionally, there has always been an understandable affinity on the part of Afro-Trinidadians with various types of African American music. Today, most North American music is widely available in the Caribbean via radio, sound recordings, cable television, and the Internet. During my fieldwork, both female and male friends, classmates, and informants would indulge my questions about local culture, and then grill me about my knowledge of then popular entertainers such as rappers Sean Combs and Biggie Smalls (or rock groups such as Sugar Ray and Smashmouth, about whom I was embarrassed to know very little). I had lengthy discussions with friends and acquaintances of various ages about styles as disparate as hip hop, alternative rock, country and western, heavy metal, mainstream pop, and gospel. Due to the fact that my personal tastes ran toward world music, jazz, and the underground rock typical of the Austin music scene, at times I felt that I was an inferior informant regarding mainstream American music. In contrast, even Trinidadians who claimed that they were not that interested in Carnival knew details about the local music scene, the lives of important calypsonians, the history of the steel pan, and so forth.

According to the experts, calypso has been "dying" for many decades, and every year there are articles and panel discussions assessing the vital signs of the nation's art form.[30] Several times a month there are comments on various online forums regarding how local musicians are ruining the music by incorporating aspects of Jamaican dancehall or American R&B and hip hop. These may appear at first glance to be new debates, but in fact throughout Trinidad's history, local musicians have mounted responses to foreign music and received either applause or derision for doing so. As I have learned from my years of research on Caribbean music, every generation creates a new vision of what it means to be local, yet also expresses a local identity that is savvy to the possibilities of being a part of a larger global culture. Thus, appreciation of foreign music is an ongoing pastime for audiences in Trinidad. Foreign artists regularly tour the Caribbean, and in recent years Grammy award–winning performers such as Beyoncé and Maroon 5 have appeared in Trinidad.

Meanwhile, there are local artists who do not specialize in calypso music or any of its offshoots. Musicians such as Gillian Moor, Paula Obe, and Karissa Lewes were prominent in the nineties as exponents of an intimate singer-songwriter style of music. As Timothy Rommen and Robin Balliger note in greater detail, there is a small but lively alternative rock/metal scene in Trinidad. The rock musicians I met while in Trinidad, while from ethnically diverse backgrounds, were all from upper- and middle-class families who could afford to invest in fairly expensive musical instruments and sound systems. The events at which they played were held at middle-class clubs such as the Anchorage and Pier 1 in Chagaramas. Middle-class dominance as performers of rock/pop is is confirmed by Rommen's extensive research on the Trinidad rock scene (Rommen, 2007: 374). However, I found that the audience at these events is not homogenous, as a number of working-class young people of various ethnicities attended events such as the Anchorage Pop Music Awards, and enthusiastically supported their favorite bands. It is tempting to see Trinidad's diverse musical scene as a sign of social fragmentation in the face of globalization; in fact, this appears to be the conclusion of several academic studies (Balliger, 2001; Guilbault, 2007). However, I prefer to interpret this as part of a continuing process on the part of Trinidadians of appreciating and assimilating diverse musical styles. In the long run, this openness to new inspiration serves to reinvigorate local styles and gain the attention of both local and foreign audiences.

In contemporary Trinidad and Tobago, women play a crucial role in supporting and maintaining a variety of expressive traditions. Whether one is attending a soca fete, a Carnival tent performance, Panorama rehearsals and finals, or following the parade of bands on Carnival Monday and Tuesday, one will notice that women are visible in significant numbers as musical performers and musical supporters. Much of this is a result of number of initiatives created to foster interest and participation among young people in the musical expressions that originated in Trinidad and Tobago. In addition to activities supported by various government entities and the public school system, there is also considerable support from non-government organizations as well as private enterprise and entrepreneurship. Each Carnival season there are a number of competitions in calypso, soca, and steelband that involve hundreds of school-age children and young adults. Students participate in competitions at their schools and move on to national competitions. Musical training and coaching is incorporated within the school curriculum, and includes university level degrees in music, theatre, dance, and Carnival arts (Hope Munro Smith, 2013).

Thus, today it is far easier for women to pursue music as either a hobby or profession, and to do so in ways that are meaningful to them both as women and as citizens of Trinidad and Tobago. The importance of certain expressive forms to personal, ethnic, and national identity encourages women to participate in various ways and to take pride in their accomplishments. As I will show in the chapters that follow, some of the most successful calypsonians and soca artistes are women. Women pannists are present in significant numbers in most of the steelbands in Trinidad and Tobago, and several women have emerged as talented arrangers, including Michelle Huggins-Watts and Natasha Joseph. In terms of audiences, women make up over half the attendees at soca and chutney soca fetes during Carnival, and there are specific fetes marketed directly to women. Female masqueraders make up 80 percent of the popular "pretty mas" bands such as Tribe, Harts, Island People, and Legends. These large mas bands also feature all-women sections, which allows women to reinforce friendships and social ties in a fun and creative setting. This is in marked contrast to gender roles in previous generations, where men were seen as the primary agents of creativity and innovation in Carnival and its related musical expressions, and women were seen as mere participants with somewhat limited roles. As female masqueraders have become such a vital presence in Carnival, it is natural that they support the female musicians who reflect their changing roles and active participation in the annual festival. The increased participation of women in Trinidad's expressive culture that we see today is a revival and reinforcement of various roles they played in earlier time periods, and this has been facilitated by dramatic sociocultural changes. At the same time, new platforms emerged for expression of concerns that were specific to women. Women became prominent in public life in a way that could materially alter their lives, and this was enhanced and encouraged by various means, including the educational system and political movements that advanced women's rights.

Over the course of the cultural history of Trinidad and Tobago, musical practices that were based in communal spaces such as the gayelle and drum dances changed with the emergence of the professional calypsonians and became essentially male-dominated art forms. Since the middle of the twentieth century, the festival has developed in ways to allow women to emerge as vibrant and enthusiastic participants. Several moves had to occur for these developments to happen. First, there needed to be a widespread change in attitudes toward women as a group. This was accomplished through the tremendous social improvements that occurred during the country's transition from a crown colony to an independent nation. Second, there also needed to be changes in how Trinidadians regarded themselves as a Caribbean people, rather than as colonial subjects. Third, Trinidadians needed to change how they viewed their indigenous expressions, most of which had been historically associated with the lower strata of society. Thus, musical change could only come from wider social change and new attitudes toward the nation's culture. These second two moves were instigated by both Trinidadian nationalists and dedicated artists and musicians, and culminated in the cultural shifts that occurred in the fifties and early sixties. Finally, the increasing diversity of the music scene and the possibilities inherent in musical change greatly facilitated the participation of a wider selection of musical talent, which included women from various walks of life.

Of course, the nature of the contemporary festival and its music receives considerable commentary in both the popular press and academic circles, and these debates take several forms. One is the ongoing complaint that as the pretty mas favored by women has come to be the dominant form of masquerade on Carnival Monday and Tuesday—as well as a very lucrative commercial enterprise—it has pushed aside the traditional characters that were typically the domain of male masqueraders.[31] Today it may be more challenging for men to find a space in Carnival masquerade, and that is why they do not participate in the same numbers as women do. In earlier days, Carnival was a forum that men used to portray a political or social cause or reinforce their reputation and male camaraderie amongst their peer group. Mas still serves as a form of camaraderie and friendship for some men, even in the pretty mas bands. However, it is women who seem to have the largest physical and emotional investment in mas, and again this could be because they are the ones who most need to ease the pressure to conform to the standards of what is still a fairly traditional and conservative culture outside of Carnival.

Another factor is that today's mas costumes have become quite expensive, and men may prefer to put that money toward drinking and liming with their friends during Carnival. The expense of costumes also makes it difficult for working-class and grassroots people to play mas. Some might join smaller neighborhood bands that have inexpensive costumes: often these bands are associated with a steelband or other form of community organization or social network. Many people simply follow the mas bands and revel on the sidelines, listening and dancing to the soca music provided by the big trucks that accompany the streams of masqueraders. There are actually more revelers observing on Carnival Monday and Tuesday than there are participants in the various mas bands. During my fieldwork I did not play mas myself because I was living on a student budget and chose not to invest the money necessary to buy a costume. However, I enjoyed jumping up alongside the friends who did participate in bands such as Legends, Harts, and Peter Minshall's Callaloo Company. It was one of the few times in this urban environment when I felt I could "play myself"[32] openly on the streets in relative security and without negative commentary. Aileen Clarke, who was director of Gender Affairs for the Ministry of Culture and Gender Affairs in 1998, agreed with this when she explained to me that women in Carnival might take things to excess but perhaps they are overcompensating for the pressure to behave the rest of the year. Pamela Franco expresses a similar sentiment when she says that female masqueraders choose costumes that show their bodies as "a way of extricating oneself from the restrictions and limitations, in varying degrees, that society places on women throughout the year" (Franco, 2001: 190). Carnival also gives these women agency in artistic and beautiful self-expression, whether it be dancing and jumping up on the sidelines, or crossing the stage with a mas band in the Grand Savannah.

In the remaining chapters of this book I examine the efforts of various artists and performers whose experience and worldview has been shaped by the historical events described in this chapter. As in much of the world, it is in the realm of cultural expression that new models of Caribbean gender relations are worked out. Women's increased involvement in popular song, pan, carnival, and other expressive arts has benefited the overall culture at large, and made the performing arts an important forum for women to increase their cultural capital, and in certain cases their economic capital as well. The world of popular music in Trinidad and Tobago offers spaces to model new types of gender relations. As in the world of work, the expressive forms discussed in the following chapters allow both women and men a forum to improve gender relations in society at large. As in much of the developing and developed world, the women of Trinidad and Tobago are striving to make meaningful contributions to their musical culture, just as they have worked to attain basic human rights and equality within their everyday lives. As I will show in the remaining chapters, this was not only due to shifting attitudes and norms regarding gender roles, but also to changing musical styles that accommodated greater diversity in musical practice and supported the efforts of new generations of musicians.

2

Woman Rising: Women Find Their Place in Calypso Music

This chapter more closely examines the emergence of calypso music as a distinct form of popular music, and the role that gender played in the construction and conventions of the calypso art form. As I discussed in the previous chapter, the changing role of women as well as the improved status of local expressive forms helped create a space for women to participate in the cultural life of Trinidad and Tobago, just as they won a role for themselves in public life in general. Changing attitudes toward local expressive culture, which allowed it to be viewed as respectable rather than merely reputation based, also facilitated women's participation. However, as I will show, the musical change and innovation that happened as calypso music developed also enabled women to make more significant and lasting contributions to Trinidad's musical culture. As calypso became more diverse in both its poetic and musical structure, so too did the performers. Performers who learned music in other contexts were more easily able to transfer those skills to the calypso world, and in turn made lasting musical contributions to calypso as a genre.

Ideally, calypsonians express sentiments that concern and appeal to Trinidadians as a whole. Singers ridicule society and reveal its underlying absurdity, but they also offer analysis and alternatives. Their credibility is enhanced by the common belief that they are capable of recognizing, and unafraid of reporting, the unvarnished truth (Manning, 1990: 415). In every historical period, calypsonians have sung about serious social and political issues. However, they just as often address other favorite topics in Caribbean expressive culture: sexual innuendo and gossip, the public drama of the urban proletariat, as well as scandals from the lives of the ruling elite and burgeoning middle class. Throughout calypso's history, singers have also created and performed songs meant to accompany bands of masqueraders on Carnival Monday and Tuesday. These sorts of songs are meant to encourage the participation of revelers, and typically feature memorable choruses and call and response elements that allow audiences to sing along. In successive historical periods these calypsos have been referred to as calindas, lavways, leggos, or road marches (Liverpool, 2004: 84). Songs that encourage audience involvement and participation have are more appropriate for Carnival fetes and dances than are calypsos that focus on social commentary.

Thus, there are two main modes of calypso. As David Rudder sings in "Calypso Music," the songs have "lyrics to make a politician cringe, or turn a woman's body into jelly." The social commentary mode of calypso addresses the mind by telling a story and commenting on contemporary events. The "party mode" of calypso is simply the descendant of old-time calindas and lavways of the early twentieth century that accompanied the movement of mas makers down the road during Carnival. In these sorts of songs the singer establishes rapport with the audience, encouraging audiences to do and feel the same thing at the same time. Many calypsonians have sung in both modes, and this distinction between songs for the tent and songs for the road is maintained to the present day. Songs for the tent tend to be more oratorical in nature, focusing on storytelling and commentary. Songs for the road are meant to move the body rather than the mind, and to encourage audiences to enjoy participating in the pleasures of dance and Carnival revelry. Road/party songs are clearly intended to entertain fete goers and coordinate mas bands rather than convey serious sociopolitical commentary. These party songs have existed for many years in Trinidad, and since the seventies are usually referred to as soca, and have their own contexts for performance and competition.

Both male and female calypsonians sing on a variety of topics. While many of the famous female calypsonians have performed songs that address conditions specific to women, a number of them have addressed topics that are not gender specific, such as nation building, patriotism, ethnic pride, poverty, tributes to political figures or other musicians, parodies of current events, as well as the enjoyment of what Carnival has to offer. Thus, while social commentary is one of the main roles that calypso plays in Caribbean culture, many calypsonians use other means of communicating with audiences, including satire, parody, wordplay, and various means of encouraging audience participation, operating in different modes based on how they want to convey the subject matter of their songs. The topics of calypsonians are diverse, fueled both by their own interests and by what they believe audiences want to hear. New songs are composed by calypsonians themselves or in collaboration with other songwriters and musicians. Regardless of who composed a particular song, the calypsonian is accepted at face value as the author of a song's message, and songs are inextricably associated with the artist presenting them.[1] Between the calypso tents and the numerous song competitions, there may be as many as 300 calypsos written every Carnival season. However, only a small portion of these songs are recorded or played on the radio, and by the end of the season most have faded into obscurity (Mason, 1998: 33). The songs that live on through oral history and sound recordings reflect the concerns of their time periods and the musical tastes of the audiences that they entertained.

As I noted in the previous chapter, by the time calypso music began to be recorded around 1914, the old time chantwells had come to be known as calypsonians, and were largely performing as musicians for hire. Theoretically, calypso in a professional and socially sanctioned setting ought to have been a perfect vehicle for both women and men to express their displeasure with various aspects of life in Trinidad, including gender relations. However, as local music production coalesced around professional calypso singers during the first decades of the twentieth century, nearly all of them were male, which led to a situation in which a man's point of view completely overshadowed and marginalized that of women. Calypso tents became focused on the concerns of men, and that made it a world that was difficult for female performers to negotiate. When reading the various histories of verbal art and calypso, it is clear that this was a man's world, coded in masculine terms. As Errol Hill romantically points out, "the calypsonian has always identified himself with the warrior, defending the helpless, attacking the powerful, exposing the scoundrel, or merely upholding his own reputation and integrity" (Hill, 1986: 3). As Abrahams observes, the "man-of-words" in the West Indies must have a verbal repertory that "includes the ability to joke aggressively . . . to 'make war' with words by insult and scandal pieces, to tell Anansi stories" alongside the ability to "talk sweet and emphasize oratory and eloquence" (Abrahams, 1983: 57).

Meanwhile, the male calypsonian occupied a somewhat liminal position in the golden age of calypso. On the one hand, the calypsonian was thought of as a mouthpiece for the underclass, a performer who through his skillful use of wit and wordplay brings to light issues that concern society at large. Yet despite this well-defined role as a social and political commentator, the stereotype attached to the calypsonian was that of a shiftless character, not much better than a common street hustler (Donald Hill, 1993: 90–91). Calypsonians saw themselves as professional entertainers, but their singular efforts to secure singing jobs fostered the attitude that they were hardly men in search of serious work. It did not help that the many calypsonians cultivated the image of "a 'sweet man,' a macho man in 'control' of several women . . . a man who lived in the barrack yard and could therefore impart intimate knowledge of its comesse, scandal, and bacchanal" (Rohlehr, 1990: 214). Additionally, calypso tents were, and still are, adults-only venues, where audiences expect bawdy humor and sexual double entendre as part of the evening's entertainment.[2]

In the twenties and thirties it was not respectable for a middle-class woman to attend a calypso tent performance (Donald Hill, 1993: 188). Female musicians who aspired to respectability would not have felt comfortable seeking work as entertainers in this type of environment, due to its association with "smut" and "scandal." It is likely that women were present in the tents to help collect fees and to sell food and drink to patrons, as they did in the days when calypsonians were more closely connected to particular Carnival bands (Donald Hill, 1993: 68–69). Gradually women found roles as backup singers and dancers, and this change was facilitated largely by musical change, in which calypso arrangements became more elaborate and required larger musical ensembles and a greater visual spectacle to entertain audiences.

It is little wonder that, in this male-centered environment, recurring topics among calypsonians were, and still are, themes of male/female interplay, humor and fantasy regarding their sexual conquests, as well as gossip, scandal, and sexual innuendo regarding the lives of other people. As lawyer and feminist activist Hazel Thompson-Ahye puts it:

> Many are the women who have been immortalized by the calypsonian: "Netty, Netty," what you really had in your belly girl? Matilda, you really take Radio "money and run Venezuela?" Jean and Dinah, Rosita and Clementina, all yuh real like the Yankee dollar, yes. Mae-Mae, did Sparrow really make love to you on the beach? Maria, Blakie love you real bad, girl. Dorothy, you are a perennial favorite. Stalin and all believe in you. Melda, and one-foot Vizzie, you really wanted a wedding ring so badly? Stella, you made Nelson cry, girl. He love you Stella. Tiney Winey, Audrey, Mable, Ethel, Emily, all of you have something in common, and now Chanchanee[3] join the lime. (Thompson-Ahye, 1998: 55)

Calypso, of course, is not the only Caribbean musical genre that deals with the topic of gender relations in a controversial manner. As Peter Manuel observes, male singers from a wide range of genres, including rancherea, bolero, plena, bachata, salsa, merengue, compas, and reggae, denounce women for their alleged unfaithfulness and moral degeneracy even as male sexual conquests are celebrated. Women are denounced as prostitutes, practitioners of black magic to tie down a man, liars, cheats, and abusers. Although sexist themes are not the only ones explored in Caribbean music, they are plentiful enough to inquire as to their social significance and whether they are a true reflection of gender relations in the culture that produces them (Manuel, 1998).

Calypso scholars offer several explanations as to why calypsonians continually "sing on women." Keith Q. Warner proposes the male marginalization theory: slavery and its socioeconomic aftereffects seem to have "left its mark on the male psyche," with the Caribbean woman developing "a strong moral fiber to compensate for the weakening of the male." The result has led to a "desire of the man to do her down, to put her in her place, to safeguard his manhood threatened by the authority of the female upstart" (Warner, 1999: 115). Warner further suggests that Afro-Trinidadian men have been emasculated by slavery, the crown colony system, and the American presence during World War II. Gordon Rohlehr offers a more nuanced explanation, detailing aspects of manhood that have been transmitted from generation to generation, which includes the maintenance of reputation via competition with other men, which naturally includes rivalry over women. The archetype of this male hero is the stickman of the calinda battle, whose kingship covers his ability "with stick, with fight, with woman, with dance, with song, with drum, with everything" (Rohlehr, 2004b: 327). Patricia Mohammed, along with Rohlehr, surveys the culture of survival present in the working-class environment out of which the modern calypsonian emerged. During the economic hardship of the twenties and thirties, men often had to rely on women's labor—as domestics, workers in the informal sector, and in some cases prostitution—for day-to-day existence because they could not themselves find work (Mohammed, 2003: 158). "Hunger was the evidence that the male provider could not provide: that the bourgeois ideal of the household or family age earned exclusively by a male bread-winner had not been attained" (Rohlehr, 1990: 219–20). Bringing down women, through harassment, physical domination, and verbal art, were some of the few sources of power and domination available to the working-class man. This does not justify the behavior, of course, but does explain the socioeconomic hardships that caused the calypsonian to turn to women as a scapegoat for problems created by forces larger than the individual (Mohammed, 2003: 158).

In the urban environment from which calypso emerged, a certain class of man, eventually known as a "sweet man" or "saga boy," created in the fictional world of the calypso a space where the women of his social sphere supported him financially, emotionally, and sexually. However, when the woman demands that he repay her generosity by surrendering his libertine ways, he must escape or lose face with the other saga boys (Rohlehr, 1990: 233). Despite the middle-class origins of calypsonians such as Lord Executor and Atilla the Hun,[4] the professional calypsonian presented himself as a man with street knowledge, and because he pursues music as a career, respectable people did not view him as a social equal, even as they appreciated his viewpoints on politics and social conditions.

In the fictional world of the calypso, the singer as "sweet man" has unmatchable skill when it comes to attracting women of all kinds to serve his needs, and then discarding them when they become a problem and/or he loses interest. In the real world, going with a calypsonian was not a path to social mobility, and a middle-class girl would have had considerable trouble convincing her parents that a calypsonian was a suitable match (Mohammed, 2003: 133). One type of ideal woman for the calypsonian is the white woman, either Caucasian or Latin, typically a foreigner who is unaware of the social norms of Trinidad, and one who is quite wealthy and can support the calypsonian financially (Sierra, 2009: 74–76). The female tourist, usually from America or Europe, enhances the status and finances of the calypsonian and offers the possibility of travel and upkeep, another form of survivalism through women (Mohammed, 2003: 158).

Next in the hierarchy is the high brown woman: she is closer to the calypsonian in terms of social class, but can be both a status symbol and a possible source of light-skinned children for her man. Songs of this nature include Atilla's 1938 calypso entitled "My High Brown," in which he happily sings "I got a high brown working for me / That's why I'm happy as can be / The acutest depression can't trouble me / I have a high brown working for me" (qtd. in Rohlehr, 1990: 249). On the other hand, the high brown "demands a high style of living, is expensive, deceitful and unfaithful" (Rohlehr, 1990: 250–51), as depicted in Growler's 1939 calypso "No High Brown Again" (Mohammed, 2003: 160–61). Another good example is the classic calypso "Matilda," in which King Radio (Norman Span) laments that "Matilda, she take me money and run Venezuela."[5]

Realizing the limitations of lives with women above their station, calypsonians also express preferences for dark women, ugly women, or older women—all of whom are so desperate to keep a man that they will treat him nicely and put up with his infidelity or ill treatment. An example is "Ugly Woman" by Roaring Lion (Rafael de Leon): "A pretty woman makes her husband look small / Is mean, and very often cause his downfall ... / Therefore from a logical point of view / Always love a woman uglier than you."[6]

During World War II, calypsonians responded to the gender relations that resulted from the American occupation. Although Carnival street processions were suspended from 1941 through 1945, calypso tents were allowed to open during Carnival season. After Carnival, calypsonians also found work entertaining military personnel at nightclubs and at the USO building on Wrightson Road. Savvy singers produced lyrical stories that—in their minds—Yankees desired to hear. Women and their sexual relations with the Yankees are a common topic throughout this period. Examples from the time include the well-known songs "Rum and Coca Cola" by Lord Invader "Marjorie's Flirtations" by Lord Kitchener. These songs discuss how the romantic aspirations of local men are thwarted by the Yankee interlopers, largely due to the allure of the economic resources the Americans can provide. King Radio got back at the type of woman represented in "Matilda" by recasting the folk song "Brown Skin Gal" as the story of a local girl abandoned by her American lover: "Brown skin gal, stay home and mind baby [repeat] / I'm going away on a sailing boat / And if I don't come back / Stay home and mind baby."[7]

Calypsonians also sang about the cuckolding of local men. Beginner's "Yankee Money," Growler's "No More Darling and Joe," and Atilla's "News From the Bases" all provided commentaries about local women lost to sailors, officers, and aviators. Although these songs can be interpreted as deep local discontentment with the American presence, these songs were also great favorites with the Yankee patrons of the calypso tents. Hence singing of military men's sexual exploits were also vehicles for calypsonians to pursue their own Yankee dollars (Neptune, 2007: 148).

The calypsos of the postwar and the post-independence periods are well-regarded for the political commentary provided on the new PNM government and the social issues with which it dealt. However, calypsonians continued to sing about their own accomplishments, including their sexual conquests. "The stickman as phallic hero, dancer, and boasting celebrant of his own prowess metamorphosed into the saga boy and the cocksman, a prominent figure in post-1945 calypso" (Rohlehr, 2004b: 340). Many calypsos by the Mighty Sparrow in his early career explore the theme of sexual prowess and conquest. In his first road march winner from 1956, "Jean and Dinah," Sparrow bragged how the girls in town would have to return to their old saga boy crowd, now "the Yankee gone and Sparrow take over now." In "Mr. Rake and Scrape," he portrays himself as a "sexual scavenger—not the man who heaves the bag of rubbish onto the truck, but the man who scrapes up the remnants of garbage that have escaped the diligence of the main scavengers" (Rohlehr, 2004b: 341). In "Village Ram," recorded in 1964, Sparrow is the stud for hire who offers his services to anyone unable to satisfy his woman (Warner, 1999: 115–16): "I eh boasting, but ah know I got due ability / And if a woman ever tell you that I / Ever left her dis-satisfy / She lie, she lie, she lie." The following year, in "Congo Man" Sparrow created another sexual fantasy, which returned to an earlier theme of the white female traveler as the ultimate sexual conquest: "I envy the Congo man / Ah wish ah could go shake he hand / He eat until he stomach upset / And I, ah never eat ah white meat yet."[8]

Such sexual double entendre was not the sole preserve of the Mighty Sparrow, of course. Many calypsonians of his era and beyond used this technique to great advantage. In "Bedbug," the Mighty Spoiler (Theophilus Philip) expresses the desire to be reincarnated as a bedbug so that he can "bite the young lady's bumper / like a hot dog or a hamburger."[9] Examples from Lord Kitchener's oeuvre include "Dr. Kitch" (1963), in which the singer relates how his female patient "can't stand the size of the needle," and "My Pussin" (1965), in which the lady argues that Kitchener is interfering with "my pussin' / take off your hand from she / don't touch me pussin at all."[10]

Metaphors for genitalia and the sexual act abound in calypsos from the postwar era to the present. Euphemisms for the phallus include wood, snake, devil, brush, plantain, banana, bamboo, iron, needle, pole, wire, knife, watering hose, black pudding, roast corn, cock, totee, boy, son, cricket bat, yard broom, and whip. Pussy and cat, of course, migrated from standard English as euphemisms for female genitalia; others include tooney, pum pum, nanny, craw, hole, mango, food, honey, saltfish, purse, lolly, as well as various puns on "cunt" such as country, mudda country, contents, yuh mudder come, and so forth (Rohlehr, 2004b: 343–44). Calypso is only one of many Caribbean genres in which sexual double entendre abounds. They should be seen as part of a long history of erotic puns and clever wordplay within Caribbean music (Manuel, 2006: 234–35). Bawdy humor has been common for years in the calypso tents and nightclubs, and audiences have come to expect sexual double entendre as part of the evening's entertainment.[11] As several Caribbean scholars have noted, these types of songs serve to contest the moral imperatives dictated by conventional standards of decency, puritanical restraint, responsibility, and controlling desire through work and economic productivity (Cooper, 1993 and 2004; Rohlehr, 2004b). However, these songs also contributed to a musical war of the sexes, as they contained certain elements of sexist objectification or degrading insult that remained from the thirties and forties. The difference between the first half of the twentieth century and the period since Trinidad's independence in 1962 is that male calypsonians had to function in a steadily changing context. By the beginning of the seventies, Sparrow, Spoiler, Kitchener, and their contemporaries were sharing the stage with various female singers who voiced their own viewpoint regarding gender relations and sexuality (Rohlehr, 2004b: 362).

As discussed in the previous chapter, many individuals inspired both a political and an artistic nationalism to reinforce Trinidad's transition toward independence. The result was a tremendous change in how local arts and culture were perceived by the average Trinidadian. Before intervention by state patronage, it was rare to see a woman as a soloist in a calypso tent. As time went by, most made their way in as backup singers, particularly as musical arrangements became more elaborate and required larger musical ensembles. Other female calypsonians were part of husband-and-wife teams put on the bill as an added attraction, or were sisters of established calypso artists.

Calypsonians responded to changing musical tastes. In the twenties, rowdy call-and-response calindas of earlier generations gave way to more formalized calypsos. While calypsonians still used aspects of responsorial calindas and other creole folk songs, increasingly they "came to rely on a set of familiar, major-key stock tunes that were essentially English in character" (Manuel, 2006: 222). This allowed singers to emphasize their verbal artistry but did not facilitate musical innovation.

Meanwhile, traveling entertainers from Europe and North America, including minstrel shows, jubilee choirs, and ragtime bands toured throughout the Caribbean during the late nineteenth and early twentieth centuries. Throughout the history of calypso music, the musicians who accompanied calypsonians[12] in tents and who played at Carnival fetes earned their living by providing fashionable dance music in a variety of performance contexts. In the late nineteenth and early twentieth centuries, string-based dance orchestras, based on Venezuelan ensembles, played at various functions during Carnival and at other times of the year. The instrumentation included piano, flute, violins, guitars, cuatro, and later clarinet as well as chac-chac. Presented with this musical challenge from outside their shores, bandleaders such as George Bailey Lovey, Lionel Belasco, and Walter Merrick performed and recorded ragtime and jazz melodies popular in Trinidad. This in turn had an effect on calypso's musical aspects. By the thirties, bands in which brass and woodwinds predominated replaced the string orchestras of the early twentieth century in both the calypso tents and forms of entertainment and dance outside of Carnival.[13]

As calypsonians ventured outside their sphere, particularly as they traveled to New York to record and to perform in nightclubs in the thirties and forties, they became aware of new audiences for their music, and the musical challenges to which they had to respond. The primary innovators during this time period were the Roaring Lion (Rafael De Leon), Atilla the Hun (Raymond Quevedo), and Lord Invader (Rupert Grant). "Lion brought showmanship to calypso. He introduced new melodies to the basic kit of ten or twelve tunes that Executor once told Atilla were all the melodies used in calypso. Lion liked American popular entertainers, especially the Mills Brothers and Bing Crosby, whose rich vocal stylings he emulated" (Donald Hill, 1993: 108). By this time, the most common poetic forms were the single=tone and double-tone calypsos.[14] The single-tone calypso contains four lines per stanza, over the course of eight measures. The chorus of a single-tone calypso is also four stanzas. Many of the calypsos Lord Invader recorded fall into this category, including his most famous composition "Rum and Coca Cola." The double-tone form, as the name suggests, contains eight stanzas per verse over sixteen measures. This musical and poetic form creates a more complex verse structure that allows the songwriter to tell a more complex story about specific events—hence another name for this form, the oratorical or oration-style calypso.[15] In some double-tone calypsos, the first one or two lines of the verse, usually only the first verse, are repeated immediately, sometimes with a slight variation. An example of a double tone calypso is Atilla's "Woman Is Not the Weaker Sex": "If there is a thing that gets me vexed / It's to hear a woman called the weaker sex [repeat] / The modern girl is developed physically / Some of them could even fight with Joe Louie. . . ."[16] Innovation upon the poetic and musical structures within calypso tended to increase the popularity of certain calypsonians, and in general fostered an environment in which new talent could be cultivated.

According to most historical accounts, Thelma Lane, performing under the sobriquet Lady Trinidad, was the first woman to join the cast of a calypso tent. She had gotten her start in music as a member of a group of comedian/singers called the Matchless Boys, who would go aboard visiting cruise ships to entertain tourists. Calypsonian King Radio (Norman Span) saw Lane perform, and suggested that she learn to sing calypso under his guidance. In 1935, she made her debut at age nineteen as part of the cast of the Crystal Palace Tent on Nelson Street, singing the calypsos "Advice to Young Women" and "Old Man's Darling."[17]

Both "Advice to Young Women" and "Old Man's Darling" are cautionary tales about the opposite sex, but presented from the female perspective. In "Advice to Young Women" she offers the following: "I'm advising every young woman to be careful of the young men of this island [repeat] / First they pretend that they love you true . . . / But when they get you as a lamb, baby / Is then they does make you see misery." In "Old Man's Darling," Lady Trinidad states her preference for an older man, who will be a responsible economic provider: "I don't want no young man today / To bear with and put me out of my way [repeat] / I want an old bull for food and rent / And when he work will bring home every cent." Lewis took her own advice and married Hamilton Lewis, leaving the calypso arena to raise two sons and a daughter.

Essentially, both calypsos "warn young women not to be taken in the by the guile of faithless young men" (Rohlehr, 1990: 276). These young men would, ironically, include Lady Trinidad's fellow calypsonians, who (at least in song) would have expressed a preference for a woman with sufficient economic resources to maintain them in the style they felt they deserved. Hence, Lady Trinidad is warning against the dangers of going with a man like the typical calypsonian, something that her audience may have found both hilarious and in agreement with their own viewpoints. Both songs are also congruent with the social concerns of the day. During the tough economic times of the thirties, young girls were leaving the countryside for work in the city, lodging in girls' hostels, and were susceptible to being hustled by more savvy urbanites or even falling into lives of prostitution. Lady Trinidad's cautionary tales are thus based on the harsh realities of life in the Depression-era Caribbean.

Lady Trinidad was somewhat successful for her time period, and opened the door for other female calypsonians. Audiences enjoyed seeing attractive women onstage, and tent managers saw a new opportunity to increase revenues. In 1936 Lady Baldwin (Mavis Baldwin) and Lady MacDonald (Doris MacDonald) appeared in the tents for Carnival season. Allegedly, impresario Eduardo Sa Gomes wanted to send Lady Trinidad to New York City with Atilla and Lion to record for Decca. Lion advised him, however: "look at how beautiful she is—if she go away some man will fall for her, she'll get married and you'll lose your money." Instead, Lady Trinidad recorded her songs live onstage in Trinidad for the Akow Company. During that session she also recorded a duet with comedian Rass Kassa entitled "I Can't Live on Macafouchette." Neither the recording nor the lyrics have been preserved, but it is thought that the song was a dialogue between a man and his girlfriend, who works as a domestic. He complains to her that he cannot live on the macafouchette (leftovers) she brings him from the rich man's table (Mohammed, 2003: 152). Since the dalliances of upper-class men with working-class women were well known to Trinidadian audiences, the double entendre in this song would have been quite apparent.

Other female calypsonians of the thirties and forties were part of husband-and-wife teams. The most successful of these were Lord Iere (Randolph Thomas) and his wife Lady Iere (Maureen St. John), whose heyday was 1939–48. According to Hollis Liverpool, Lord Iere was failing to achieve success as a singer and brought his wife onstage to sing the choruses with him. Lady Iere began singing her own songs in 1942, most of which projected a motherly-love or good-wife image (Liverpool, 2004: 82–83). An example is "A Warning to Mothers": "A warning to mothers! / Keep your eyes on your daughters [repeat] . . . / Don't let them out of your sight / These force-ripe men we have are too bright." However, her most famous song, "Love Me or Leave Me," departs from the good-wife model to comment on a man's infidelity: "Love me or leave me / Or go live with Miss Dorothy / These times too hard / To be living with a man that's bad."

Lord and Lady Iere created their duet routine in 1943 for "Ice Cream Block," a song about frozen ice cream on a stick, a novelty introduced to Trinidad that year. The song's musical structure, credited to Lady Iere, changes the four-line single-tone calypso to a verse-chorus structure with a four-line verse and eight-line chorus; it is thought to be the first calypso of this type. Thus by bringing his wife into his act, Lord Iere helped further musical change in calypso (Liverpool, 2004: 84). Lord and Lady Iere continued to perform as a duet, and Lady Iere as a solo act, throughout the war years, performing at the USO building and other nightspots in Port-of-Spain. In addition to performing with her husband, Lady Iere recorded duets with other singers such as Growling Tiger, and toured as a backup singer with Peggy Daniels for the Muttoo Brothers Calypso Orchestra during WWII (Liverpool, 2004: 82–83). Her song "Love Me or Leave Me" was heard on the radio for many years, and was re-recorded on the cast album for Rawle Gibbons's theatrical production *Sing de Chorus*.

During the "Yankee occupation" of World War II, USO bands and the US armed forces radio station WVDI brought American swing to Trinidad audiences. Jazz dance and music, along with the jitterbug fashion depicted in American films, became enormously popular among working-class Trinidadians:

> Undoubtedly, the appeal of the jitterbug among young Trinidadian trendsetters derived in part from its provenance in the brave, antiestablishment, black American youth culture.... it went with the hottest swing music of the time and demanded of the male-female pair superb displays of coordination, athleticism, and energy. As a social dance, jitterbugging was a joyful expression of youthful creativity that helped to maintain various solidarities, from community to street gang. (Neptune, 2007: 114)

Local dance bands responded by learning the latest dance tunes, either by ear or via the scores provided to cinemas along with the latest American movies (Guilbault, 2007: 139–40). Arrangers in the forties developed one of the key structures of calypso performance: the "band chorus" or instrumental interlude between verses, influenced by the melodic materials of the vocal part of calypso songs. The band chorus helped familiarize the audience with the melody of the calypso and served the needs of the vocalist to enter and depart the stage. As calypsonians started to create more excitement for their audiences by dancing or doing various antics between the verses of their songs, the band needed this instrumental chorus on which to vamp while the calypsonian acted up onstage. In response to fashionable dance music, calypsonians and arrangers composed songs that were more flexible in terms of poetic form, and melodies became increasingly lively and tuneful. The call-and-response of the old calinda songs was revived in the form of a strong chorus that the audience could remember and respond to. To the present day it is the interjection of these chorus responses at strategic points in the song that enhances the drama of a calypso performance and allows for audience participation and excitement. Again, musical innovation created an atmosphere in which greater diversity among calypsonians, including gender diversity, could more easily flourish.

In addition to the tents, radio and sound recordings became increasingly important in drawing attention to local music and musicians. In 1947 Radio Trinidad became the first locally run radio station, first as a rediffusion service and then as a station that blended foreign and local original programming. The National Broadcasting Service followed several years later, and by the early seventies each had an AM and FM frequency, for a total of four radio stations in Trinidad and Tobago. Only a fraction of daily programming was devoted to local music; the remainder was made up of BBC news reports, soap operas, and the like. Until 1967 calypso was banned from the airwaves during Lent, and even after that reform it was only sporadically heard alongside various forms of foreign music and cultural programming (Guilbault, 2004: 56–57). Still, this was an improvement over earlier generations. Calypsonians could now focus on making recordings for the coming Carnival season to generate excitement about their work, and in addition to recording in New York and London, musicians were able to take advantage of several local recording studios that were established in the late forties and early fifties (Errol Hill, 1972: 56).

One of the major innovators of the postwar generation was Lord Kitchener (Aldwyn Roberts), who started the Young Brigade calypso tent in 1947. Its very name suggested that it catered to the youth who had experienced the jitterbug craze and that demanded interesting musical arrangements driven by lively rhythms and memorable melodies. Even after Kitchener left Trinidad for new career opportunities in England, the fifties saw the Young Brigade tent launch the careers of a number of innovative calypsonians, including Kitchener's main musical rival, the Mighty Sparrow (Slinger Francisco).[18] Arrangers of this new generation, such as Art de Coteau and Frankie Francis, recognized the need to respond to music from other regions of the Caribbean and North America, including jazz, rhythm and blues, mambo, and rock and roll music.

It was in this climate of musical innovation and desire for variety and novelty that a space was created for women to make a more significant contribution as professional calypsonians; a climate that encouraged flexibility of musical style and poetics in calypso also facilitated women's participation as calypsonians. Women who had experience in other styles of music, such as church singing or amateur productions such as La Petite Musicale and the Best Village Competitions, could transfer that mode of performance to calypso without breaking the rules, since audiences now expected the excitement, drama, movement, novelty, and creativity that had been pioneered by the Young Brigade generation of calypsonians. Also, audiences were more diverse—women could go to calypso tent and feel that they were supporting local culture rather than endangering their social status. As with many the male calypsonians of their generation, female calypsonians were mentored by experienced singers who brought them into the tents, such as the Mighty Sparrow and Lord Kitchener. As I discuss below and in the next chapter, these women had to be persuaded that calypso was something that they could perform—and as women had a duty to perform—in order to express concerns that a growing female audience wanted to hear, as well as to set examples for women in public life that were worth admiring and emulating. Also, calypso as a musical genre had become more accommodating to different performance styles and vocal types, and this greatly facilitated the participation of women in the art form.

The life and career of Calypso Rose (McCartha Lewis) will be covered in greater detail in the next chapter, but she was clearly the role model for most if not all the female calypsonians who followed her. Like her predecessors, Rose was mentored by established calypsonians, first the Mighty Spoiler, then by Lord Kitchener when he returned from England in 1963, and eventually the Mighty Sparrow, who dominated the calypso arena for three decades. Calypso Rose has been composing and performing songs of her own composition since the age of fifteen. With this material, she has managed to sustain a successful career in the music business for more than fifty years.

At least initially, female singers of Rose's generation tended to avoid recasting the masculine myth of warriorhood and sexual prowess that which is reflected in their choice of sobriquets. Most women chose stage names that emphasized musical talent: along with Calypso Rose there was Singing Francine (Francine Edwards), Calypso Princess (Veronica De Labastide), Singing Dianne (Dianne Davenport), Lady Excellence, and Lady Divine.[19] This does not mean that women singers avoid topics of sexual fantasy, humor, and the use of sexual double entendre. However, when they did address these topics, it was not in the full battle mode taken by the male singers. As a group, female calypsonians have not attempted to project themselves as superior to other women. Most do not degrade men, at least not to the same extent that male calypsonians have with women and their male contemporaries over the years (Warner, 1999: 127).

Rose and her contemporaries who entered the calypso arena did have to conform to certain expectations set by the popular male calypsonians of the time. Rose patterned her performance style on that of the Mighty Sparrow, in whose Young Brigade Tent she sang throughout the sixties and seventies. She presented her songs with similar gusto and bounce, and sang on similar themes (Rohlehr, 2004b: 362). As she acted as the female counterpart to the male singers of the time, she was in those early days dubbed the "Queen of Smut" by both the Trinidad *Guardian* and *Evening News* (Ottley, 1992: 5). By the late sixties, Rose was writing songs that were targeting the phallocentricity of earlier calypsos through her own songs that celebrated female sexuality and freedom (Rohlehr, 2004b: 345). She was also doing so at a time when women in Trinidad were beginning to experience these freedoms—hence her music is not just female sexuality on display for male voyeurs, but songs to be appreciated by the more liberated women of her generation.

Very early in her career, Rose created a persona that gave voice to the stock female characters of earlier calypsos.[20] In "You Must Come Back to Rose," she is the vengeful woman who uses obeah to tie down a man: "When ah take a piece of me clothes / And boil it up in spice and cloves / And ah pass the scent by your nose / You bound to come back to Rose."

In "What She Go Do," Rose presents the case of the unfaithful woman, the topic of many male calypsonians who fear being "horned" (Warner, 1993: 122). When one lives in a culture in which men say "a deputy is essential," it is only natural that a woman would want the same benefits: "I could understand why a woman must have an outside man [repeat] / A man does want to run like rat / And have his wife to abide by that / And every night he having a ball / And when he reach home he ain't kissing his wife at all.... /

No satisfaction. So you see a woman must have an outside man." Rose also offered a female response to the "smutty" calypsos of Sparrow and his generation. In "Sweet Pudding Man," Rose explains she has eaten from Chinese, Indian, and Portuguese "pudding men" but has developed an uncontrollable craving for black pudding. "It is different from male phallocentric calypsos in that its focus is one woman's response" (Rohlehr, 2004b: 367). In "Pallet," Rose plays the role of a vendor of ice cream lollies, and in the chorus she joyfully invites customers to "buy and suck her pallet." In these and other songs of the time period, Rose joins the "sexual revolution" of calypso spearheaded by Sparrow, by bringing female response and female desire into the open.

Other female calypsonians of Rose's generation followed suit with challenges to male machismo. Examples include "I Want a Good Husband" and "We Jamming" performed by Calypso Princess (Veronica De Labastide), and Lady Excellence's "Master Johnny" (Rohlehr, 2004b: 368). The woman as sexual rebel would become a recurring theme in calypso, and later soca, during the seventies and eighties, most commonly expressed through various dance metaphors: break away, give me tempo, kakalaylay, dingolay, play myself, wine down, wet me, and more.

Like Sparrow and Kitchener, Rose also has written in social commentary mode, depicting the empowerment of women using the persona of various female heroes who kick out drunken, abusive husbands and take control of their own destinies. "Repeatedly, Rose's calypsos of the late sixties and early seventies deconstruct macho notions of masculinity by portraying men as weak, impotent, parasitic, and brutal" (Rohlehr, 2004b: 364). "Rosie Darling," written in 1969, is the first calypso to protest against employers who require sexual favors for women to get work—a theme that Singing Sandra would return to twenty years later in "Die With My Dignity." In songs such as "Lemme Lone," "How the Bed Break Down," and "Bend Down Low," Rose is the warrior-woman who dismisses men who beat or sexually abuse their wives. In these early years, Rose constructed her version of the female hero "deconstructing in the process the prevailing masculine version of both the cocksman-lover and the noble breadwinner. The men of Rose's calypsos were drunkards, tricksters, crooks, and women beaters, whose violence was a sign not of control at all but of compensation for the dreadful uselessness of their lives" (Rohlehr, 2004b: 377).

Other female calypsonians of Rose's generation address the many issues affecting the lives of women in Trinidad, but most often the issue of domestic violence. Singing Francine used Sparrow's lyrics to warn women to "Run Away" from men who humiliated or brutalized them. Singing Dianne's response to "licks in de morning, in de evening" was "I Done Wid Dat," composed by arranger Ed Watson. Such song lyrics mirrored the efforts of feminist activists in Trinidad to advocate legislation to restrain men from inflicting bodily harm on their wives. The reader may wonder why these artists would sing lyrics composed by male songwriters rather than their own words. However, male calypsonians have frequently been the mentors of younger calypsonians, including women. Calypso Rose showed that it was necessary to give voice to women's concerns, and thus these men projected in their own lyrics how they thought women would feel about a particular situation. Of course, the male singer could have sung his own lyrics, but a great deal of the impact of a calypso performance comes from the vocal conviction of the singer as well as the physical gestures and movement. Providing support to women in the face of male insult, misbehavior, and brutality required a woman's voice and presence to lend the performance the necessary credibility with audiences and the judging panel of the calypso tents. A man singing what was basically a women's protest would not have gone over with a tent audience, especially if that calypsonian had expressed the opposite viewpoint in earlier years.[21]

Male calypsonians could not return to the raw misogyny of earlier days. They too were caught up in the political climate of the seventies, one that included Trinidad's Black Power movement. Whereas Lion sang of the ugly black woman in the thirties, the new generation of calypsonians celebrated the Caribbean woman in song. She who had been so denigrated by the calypsonian over the years now was praised in order to "inculcate a sense of pride and dignity in black womanhood in the face of constant competition from Eurocentric norms of beauty" (Warner, 1999: 132). An example would include "Black Is Beautiful," which won the Mighty Duke (Kelvin Pope) the Calypso Monarch competition in 1969.

The women's movement and changing attitudes regarding gender relations undoubtedly affected the creative output of calypsonians who began performing in the seventies and eighties. There were a number of calypsos in which the singers recognize the errors of earlier ways of treating women, particularly regarding the issue of domestic violence. Songs of this nature include "Think About the Children" by Merchant (Dennis Williams Franklyn), "That Kind of Love" by Explainer (Winston Henry), and "Homegrown" by Brother Resistance (Lutalo Masimba).[22] Other examples include progressive songs written by Black Stalin (Leroy Calliste) such as "Wait Dorothy Wait" (1985) and "Stay Giving Praises," a duet with Ella Andall. David Rudder, one of the first calypsonians to decline using a sobriquet, "consistently characterizes women as strong, even stubborn, sensual and complete people."[23] Songs of this nature include "Bahia Girl" (1986), "Bachannal Lady" (1988), and "Carnival Ooman" (1992). Rudder often portrays women as a metaphor for the nation as a whole, as in "Calypso Music" (1987) and "Trini to the Bone" (2003).[24] Although these enlightened viewpoints are not universal, they are far more common than they were in earlier generations.

As noted above, calypso has always been sung in different styles, based on specific performance contexts. However, in the seventies a new style of calypso, soca, emerged that many musicians and fans saw as a true break with the past. There are competing origin stories regarding this new musical style and the name that was used to describe it. Some say that the term comes from calypso's fusion with American soul into a hybrid genre known as "soul-calypso": soul + calypso = soca. Warner suggests that this stylistic affinity reflects the similar struggle for civil rights and expression of Black Power in both Trinidad and the United States. Also, the Black Power movement made it evident that there was a generation gap between singers who supported the PNM's increasingly conservative platform and those who felt unsatisfied with all aspects of the older generation, including its music (Warner, 1993). However, it is too reductive to say that soca is a blend of North American soul and calypso music. The true origins of the style are somewhat more complex and involve the multi-ethnic makeup of the nation of Trinidad and Tobago. Soca was a response to other Caribbean musical genres that were becoming hugely successful abroad, particularly reggae. At a time when adventurous musical fusion had become the norm, and coinciding with renewed interest in hot "Latin" sounds in the States, soca emerged during a particularly optimistic time in Trinidad's history; and with the oil-wealth of the seventies making many Trinidadians "feel to party," a new musical innovation was inevitable. A natural result was a proliferation of music in which "the rhythm rather than the voice leads the songs, which clearly address the body rather than the mind" (de Ledesma and Broughton, 1994: 508–10).

One of the key innovators of the soca style was Lord Shorty (Garfield Blackman, later Ras Shorty I) along with his musical arranger, Ed Watson. In many interviews, Shorty has said that at the time he felt calypso was "dying" and wanted to renew and reinvigorate calypso in order to compete with foreign dance music such as reggae, funk, and soul (Guilbault, 2007: 172–73). Shorty expressed the desire to blend Indian and African rhythms, suggesting to Ed Watson that he add East Indian percussion instruments, particularly the dholak and dhantal of Hindu folk and popular music, to his musical arrangements. Shorty called his new style "sokah" in order to emphasize the Indian contribution, and introduced it to the world with his song "Indrani" in 1973. In addition to the Indian rhythms, this song and others of the same period are clearly influenced by Hindi film music, which were broadcast on local radio stations for short periods each day (Niranjana, 2006: 141–42). These innovations were met with negative criticism from both the Afro-Creole and Indo-Trinidadian communities. Afro-Trinidadians felt that Shorty was ruining calypso, and Indo-Trinidadians assumed that "Indrani" was meant as a parody of their culture (Guilbault, 2007: 173).

Shorty responded by asking Watson to change his arrangements and transfer the Indian rhythmic patterns to the drum set, iron, and congas of the calypso rhythm section. The result was the single "Soul Calypso Music," released in 1974, which most likely led to the current spelling. The new sound, which along with the extra percussion foregrounded the bass, Hammond B3 organ, and electric guitar, struck the interest of other musical artists. Shadow (Winston Bailey) and Blue Boy (Austin Lyons) rode to success with arrangements by Art de Coteau that featured the melodic and rhythmically active bass line typical of reggae of the time along with Watson's other innovations (Guilbault, 2007: 160–61). Although initially resistant to the new musical innovations, older calypsonians such as the Mighty Sparrow (Slinger Francisco) and Lord Kitchener (Aldwin Roberts) realized its popularity with young people, and wrote songs with the soca sound in mind. One of the most successful soca songs during this time period was Lord Kitchener's "Sugar Bum Bum," arranged by Ed Watson, and released in 1978. While not usually referred to as soca songs, the musical arrangements that Pelham Goddard wrote for Calypso Rose's "Give Me More Tempo" and "Leh We Jam" clearly reflected the influence of new musical trends of the late seventies.

As musical arrangements became more exciting, soca lyrics generated much criticism from academics, journalists, and older Trinidadians who found the music "tata" (crap) because it did not have the "meaningful" lyrics of older forms of calypso. There were also objections to the sexual nature of lyrics, the most extreme example being Shorty's "The Art of Making Love," and the obsession with the female derriere in songs such as "Sugar Bum Bum" and "Tiney Winey." Those who upheld the standards of "true kaiso" complained that these "wine and jam" songs were bringing the culture down, celebrating decadent bodily display rather than elevating the mind. The new style placed far less emphasis on creative use of words, and what lyrics singers retained, so the critics continue to complain, are little more than aerobics instructions, or vastly unsubtle descriptions of male-female sexual interplay. It is true that soca songs are far more frivolous than other forms of calypso, but "frivolous lyrics have always helped people break away from their daily troubles, and to 'break away' is one of the main purposes of carnival" (Mason, 1998: 46). The musical artists who embraced soca knew their history: topical calypsos had never been very marketable abroad because of their specificity to local concerns. Soca, on the other hand, had much more potential for a worldwide market. Soca musicians began to see themselves as potentially having an international appeal along the lines of Bob Marley and the Wailers. The development of soca was the result of a largely successful attempt to respond to a world music market that demanded songs with international appeal. The biggest market is, of course, West Indians living abroad, who often prefer party music from back home rather than social and political commentary.

Ultimately, soca is a contemporary form of calypso that coexists with earlier styles. In a typical Carnival season, there are many artists performing in various styles of calypso and soca, addressing a wide variety of themes in their lyrics and utilizing arrangers and musicians who utilize varying performance styles. There are different performance settings for calypso and soca, though in the calypso tents and competitions it is very common for calypsonians to perform what are essentially party tunes. The reverse is usually not the case: audiences at fetes and Soca Monarch are not interested in hearing moral lessons or political commentaries when the whole purpose of fetes are to offer a place to "break away" and escape the pressure of daily life.

By 1972 there were enough women participating in the calypso arena to warrant an event separate from the Calypso King competition, which had never featured a woman participant let alone a female "king." In that year, several businessmen in the southern Trinidad city of San Fernando inaugurated the National Calypso Queen Contest. In addition to assisting in the promotion of female calypsonians, these entrepreneurs wanted to offer southerners the experience of a major calypso competition, because up to that time all the competitions were in Port-of-Spain. At the time, the main professional singers in the calypso tents were Calypso Rose, Singing Francine, Twiggy (Ann Marie Parks), and Calypso Princess. Thus, there were a number of "part-time" female calypsonians who were paid $50 each to appear in the contest and fill out the evening's program. However, from 1972–81 the show was largely a contest between Singing Francine and Calypso Rose; Francine won in the first year of the competition as well as in 1973 and 1981, and Rose won five consecutive titles from 1975–78 (Ottley, 1992: 180–81). It is likely that neither one of them competed in 1979 or 1980; in 1979, fourteen-year-old Abbi Blackman, the eldest daughter of Ras Shorty I, won with "Young and Moving On," and in 1980 Singing Dianne won the title. Eventually, the Calypso Queen competition and growing success of artists such as Calypso Rose highlighted the fact that the nation's main calypso competition needed to be renamed. Thus, in 1977 the Calypso King competition became the Calypso Monarch competition. Serendipitously, Calypso Rose took the title in 1978 with "Her Majesty" and "I Thank Thee," songs that addressed the fact that she had won the Road March title the previous year.

As Trinidad entered the recession period of the early eighties, it became difficult for the original promoters to continue the Calypso Queen competition, even with corporate sponsorship. The show was abandoned for several years, and in 1985 the National Women's Action Committee (NWAC), the women's arm of NJAC, acquired the rights to the show (Ottley, 1992: 181). NWAC has hosted the competition since 1985, by which time Rose and Francine were living abroad and no longer interested in competing. Thus, other calypsonians began to win titles, including the "part-timers" of earlier years. The first was Twiggy (Ann Marie Parks), followed by Lady B (Beulah Bob) and Singing Sandra (Sandra Des Vignes). Denyse Plummer, who made her calypso debut in 1986, came in second that year, when the competition was entitled "Women Rising" in honor of its fifteenth anniversary. Plummer went on to dominate the Calypso Queen competition, winning for the first time with "Women Is Boss" in 1988. Like Calypso Rose, Plummer eventually decided to move aside for other performers. As she explained to me: "I won it eight times so you think it's time to give someone else a chance. Also, you don't fool yourself, someone going to come and dethrone you eventually. Leave while the going's good."[25]

From its inception, the National Calypso Queen Competition has greatly facilitated women's ability to find work in the calypso tents and to be taken seriously as musical artists. More importantly, earning a title, whether it is the NWAC show or another competition, guarantees that a performer will find work at North American events such as Caribana and Labor Day Carnival, as well as engagements in other foreign countries. As Denyse Plummer explained to me: "The title makes a world of difference. They don't care what you look like, they are prepared to hire you immediately. Sometimes we say the prize money not that great and the prestige is not so great but it does so much for your career and you. And you have all the trophies and the monuments and you have them for life, for you to know you made a difference along those lines."[26] The NWAC competition has become one of the main platforms for women to express strong social commentaries on a number of important issues. In recent years, the winner of the National Calypso Queen competition is almost guaranteed to advance to the Calypso Monarch semi-finals, and is usually successful in making it to the finals of Calypso Monarch held on Dimanche Gras (Carnival Sunday).[27]

When I was doing my fieldwork in 1998, I attended what was billed as the 14th Annual National Calypso Queen Competition.[28] Many relative newcomers were competing alongside more successful artists such as Shirlane Hendrickson,[29] Karen Eccles, Shanaqua (Rachel Fortune), and Melanie Hudson. I had heard from Gordon Rohlehr, with whom I was taking a class at UWI, that Shirlane Hendrickson was favored to win, as her sister Lady Wonder (Dianne Hendrickson) had the previous few years. The audience at the show filled most of the Queen's Hall, and was largely friends and family of the competitors and serious aficionados of the calypso art form, alongside various invited dignitaries and government officials. The event began as many public ceremonies do in Trinidad and Tobago, with the national anthem and an opening prayer, this one given by Deacon Gloria Waldron. Calypso Rose was invited to the stage to give some opening remarks; as usual she was a formidable public speaker, and eloquently described her trajectory to success and gave words of encouragement to the competitors for that evening. The first part of the program finished with performances by two former winners of NJAC's junior competitions, six-year-old Stechelle Hazell, and Heather McIntosh, the nineteen-year-old daughter of calypsonian Short Pants (Llwellyn McIntosh), who sang a humorous calypso called "Mouse in the House" that was a thinly veiled commentary on controversies in the UNC government.

The program was a long one; fifteen competitors performed two songs each, one in each half of the program. I was expecting the competitors to perform songs on issues pertaining to women, and indeed there were quite a few that fell into that category. Pat Gomez performed a calypso called "Neither Brother Nor Man" that addressed the topic of sexual abuse; Lynda Byron addressed the topic of incest, based on the true story of a case between a mother and son. However, there was considerable variety in the topics presented. An example was the first song on the program, a calypso called "The Message" that was performed by Claudia Johnson. The song's author, Christophe Grant, later told me that the purpose of the song was "to heighten the self-esteem of every little black girl who sometimes mistakenly see themselves negatively because they are looking from a perspective set up by another race."[30] Shanaqua's first tune was "Unruly Police," in which she dressed as a female police corporal and sang "we don't want no unruly police / or the bandits win the war for sure." In the second half of the program, both Shanaqua and Melanie Hudson performed pan tunes,[31] "Pan for Carnival" and "Clear De Way," respectively, which had already received considerable radio airplay and were being arranged for several steelbands for Panorama.[32] Another recurring topic was the type of patriotic song that fall loosely into the category of nation-building calypsos. One of my favorites of the evening was Karissa Lewes's rendition of "Oh Trinidad" by Ray Holman with lyrics by Merchant (Dennis Williams Franklyn). In her stage presentation, Lewes brought out different representatives from the varying ethnic groups present in Trinidad, until they were all onstage dancing together, while she sang of a desire to return to a more harmonious way of life free of the divisions of political separatism and the discord it brings: "I wish that we could be once again / Fun loving and free, like we used to be . . . / Oh Trinidad, so beautiful / Could we ever learn to love again?"[33] Ultimately, Gordon Rohlehr predicted correctly; Shirlaine Hendrickson won that year's competition with two calypsos that she had written herself. The first was "Understanding," a song that expressed a sentiment similar to that of "Oh Trinidad," with actors portraying the three different leaders of the UNC, PNM, and NAR parties, and Hendrickson persuading them to find common ground. Her second song "African Renaissance" returned to the theme of racial pride that carries great importance in a setting such as the NWAC Calypso Queen Competition.

During Carnival, there are numerous fetes for various types of clientele. The music for these fetes is party-oriented tunes, including soca music and its various offshoots. Soca is also the dominant music that accompanies mas bands on Carnival Monday and Tuesday. Once Carnival is over, the tents close down and calypsonians perform in different types of venues. As in earlier times, calypsonians perform in nightclub settings such as the Mas Camp Pub, or similar venues that have sprung up along Ariapita Avenue.[34] The more successful calypsonians such as Calypso Rose, Denyse Plummer, and David Rudder give concerts at places such as the Hotel Normandie, Jean-Pierre Complex, and other venues with ample seating for attendees. As in earlier times,[35] calypsonians perform in nightclub settings and music festivals in North America and Europe—in fact, Calypso Rose, the Mighty Sparrow, David Rudder, and several other performers live in North America and only return to Trinidad for professional engagements at Carnival and perhaps one or two other occasions during the year.[36]

During my initial fieldwork, men still greatly outnumbered women on the casts of the calypso tents, although the casts in the government-run tents tended to have more gender balance. Several people commented to me that they would like to see more women in the tents, and thought the reason there were so few was because female calypsonians have gained a reputation for singing about social issues that people might not want to think about when going out for an evening of entertainment. Christophe Grant gave me the following thoughts on the matter:

> Tent managers and producers tend to be mainly male, and they have a fixed attitude of employing a female if she is going to come and sing a very suggestive number—a saucy number; if she's probably going to come and sing a party song. If she's coming to sing a strong female message they are going to be very wary because they feel somehow that the male patronage of the tent isn't going to want to hear any sermon from a female. The men hear enough of the women nagging them in the household, they only come out in the night to enjoy themselves and put their feet up and hear some bawdy tent humor. The last thing they want to hear is a woman again telling them they aren't treating their woman good. This is why the tent management, again in a very patriarchal society, tend to put their foot down against a woman singing a very strong anti-male anti-man songs as they call them. Strangely enough, the majority of the patronage [at the tents] is women. But somehow they think that the one who is paying is the man. He has to pay and come and hear more nagging.[37]

However, when Singing Sandra won the Calypso Monarch title in 1999, the first time a woman had won the competition since Calypso Rose in 1978, there was a seismic shift in the Carnival music scene. It was as if promoters suddenly realized that a major portion of their clientele were women, and to have a vast gender imbalance on the calypso tent casts, and the resulting skewing of the gender makeup of Calypso Monarch semis and finals, was not going to be profitable for them. The NWAC Calypso Queen competition was not sufficient to accommodate emerging talent, or even to offer a showcase for established talent, as many of the successful female calypsonians had retired from competition. Several entrepreneurs created events featuring women artists that had a female audience in mind. One of these was Rudolph Ottley, author of *Women in Calypso*, who noted that "each year there must be about 50 women coming for auditions, and if five are selected then it's a miracle."[38] Pooling resources with Margaret Gittens, Lynette Quamina, and Lisa Wickham, Ottley launched Divas Calypso Cabaret at the Mas Camp Pub during Carnival 2004. During the 2005 season, the star of the Cabaret was the newly crowned NWAC Calypso Queen Abbi Blackman, along with the Calypso Queens of St. Vincent, St. Lucia, and Miami. It also had a predominantly female calypso orchestra led by Chantal Esdelle on keyboards, American trumpet player Kelley Bolduc, Natasha Joseph on guitar, and Police Band members Ginelle Hamilton and Kurl-Ann McEachnie on saxophone.[39] With the exception of 2008, the Divas Calypso Cabaret has continued to run during the Carnival season, with occasional guest appearances by established artists such as Calypso Rose.

Another event that had its debut in 2004 was promoter Randy Glasgow's Ladies Night Out, an all-inclusive fete held at the Jean Pierre Complex. This is a decidedly more party-oriented event, hosted by comedienne Rachel Price, that often features bawdy entertainment such as "the men of muscle" (the local equivalent of the Chippendale dancers) and contests for the sexiest hard-working man in Trinidad.[40] Most of the bill is oriented toward party music, featuring popular female soca artists such as Denise Belfon, Alison Hinds, Destra Garcia, Sanelle Dempster, and Fay-Ann Lyons, However, every year Calypso Rose, Denyse Plummer, and Singing Sandra have performed at this event in recognition of their contributions to calypso and soca, and also because of their enduring popularity with audiences. Various male performers have appeared at this event over the years, including David Rudder, Iwer George, Shurwayne Winchester, Bunji Garlin, and Machel Montano. Showcased as an all-inclusive fete, Ladies Night Out is far more commercially successful than the Divas Calypso Cabaret and tends to appeal to a more diverse clientele.

Ultimately, the increased presence of women in the calypso arena has strengthened their role in musical culture and given voice to various issues that affect the lives of Trinidadian women. One thing that has certainly changed is how men portray women in song; in general men sing more sensitive lyrics than they did in previous generations. While double entendre is still a part of the calypso canon, the difference in contemporary times is that women finally have a space in which they can perform themselves, their identities, values, and concerns. If they wish, they can even "do dem back"[41] in their own use of clever wordplay and sensual dancing. Female fans now recognize themselves and their concerns in the messages expressed by the female calypsonians whose shows they attend. As I indicated earlier, musical and textual innovation have also benefited female calypsonians. In an atmosphere of musical creativity, there was more freedom to experiment with new ideas, and this benefited various women who chose to perform in the calypso arena. In the next chapter, I examine in detail the careers of the three most successful female calypsonians in contemporary Trinidad: Calypso Rose, Singing Sandra, and Denyse Plummer. Their achievements as musicians mirror the achievements of women in other social and cultural domains, and in many ways these musical artists have come to serve as role models for their contemporaries and as cultural ambassadors for the women of Trinidad and Tobago.

Calypso Rose performing at the Hotel Normandie, Carnival 2009. Photo by Jason Gardner.

Calypso Rose performing at the Hotel Normandie, Carnival 2009. Photo by Jason Gardner.

Singing Sandra performing "Equalizer" at the Kaiso House Calypso Tent, Carnival 1998. Photo by the author.

Singing Sandra performing "Ghetto of the Mind" in the Dimanche Gras Calypso Monarch Finals, Carnival 2009. Photo by Jason Gardner.

Denyse Plummer in concert, Carnival 2009. Photo by Jason Gardner.

Denyse Plummer in portrait. Photo by Jason Gardner.

Shirlaine Hendrickson, NWAC Calypso Queen Competition 1998. Photo by the author.

Alison Hinds performing on the Square One music truck, Carnival 1999. Photo by the author.

Sanelle Dempster performing on the Blue Ventures music truck, Carnival 1999. Photo by the author.

Destra Garcia performing at the International Soca Monarch Finals, Carnival 2009. Photo by Jason Gardner.

Denise Belfon in performance, 2011. Photo by the author.

The author with the members of Courts Laventille Sound Specialists, Panorama 1999. Photo by the author.

3

From Calypso Queen to Calypso Monarch

This chapter explores the careers and performance strategies of the three most successful women in calypso: Calypso Rose, Singing Sandra, and Denyse Plummer. Each has had to overcome the sexism inherent in the Caribbean music business, as well as the critiques of the media and audiences, in pursuing a musical career. The story of each woman's life and career reflects many of the issues addressed in previous chapters regarding those of Trinidadian women in the post-independence era, as well as the balance between the worlds of reputation and respectability that female artists have negotiated in the Trinidadian music scene. Experiencing calypso music in its various contexts, one is reminded how the genre is much more than tune and text; it is a nuanced performance that convinces the audience that the identity of the calypsonian is identical to the persona enacted on stage. In a successful calypso performance, there is a blurring of the stage persona and the personality of the singer because the persona "is so psychologically credible and consistent that he/she is accepted as real" (Regis, 1999: 212).

As in many forms of popular music, the performance of calypso involves expressive strategies used by singers in interpreting lyrics. Singers collaborate with instrumentalists to create song arrangements. With assistance from costume and set designers, calypso singers stage elaborate presentations that are integral parts of their musical expressions. Calypsonians bring together personal opinion, public persona, and various aspects of musical performance practice to create commentaries upon the contemporary moment. Over the course of a Carnival season, they create emotional bonds with their intended audiences and, along with other possible topics, they show that an alternate way of organizing gender representations and inter-gender relations is possible. All calypsonians take on a mask, usually one drawn from real life, and then make it a bit larger. Male artists often choose masks of reputation: the stickfighter, Sparrow's "Congo Man." Women artists often choose a role that stresses responsibility. They might use the banner of motherhood to protest unfair social conditions, or portray an old Baptist lady, a grandmother, or a concerned schoolteacher. However, performers may also choose to portray *dramatis personae* at the other end of the spectrum from those they have portrayed in the past. Sugar Aloes and Super Blue, among others, have portrayed Baptist preachers leading their flocks; Calypso Rose often appropriated the warrior stance from Sparrow and Kitchener, both her mentors and her direct competition for Calypso Monarch. Denyse Plummer frequently takes on the role of a party girl or a cultural cheerleader, depending on the material she has chosen for the season, but in other circumstances she opts for a more serious stance as an upholder of cultural and moral values. Calypso performances are enactments of the many contradictory gender roles found within Trinidadian society rather than an ideal type of what constitutes male or female identity. Thus the calypso arena allows performers to mirror and at times challenge the gender roles of contemporary society.[1]

Calypsonians play roles that match the topics at hand, usually created through weeks of rehearsal prior to the Carnival season in preparation for auditions for the calypso tents, and for various competitions that occur outside of the tents. Calypsonians prepare songs they have written or have contracted with songwriters to sing for that season. For the audition process, calypsonians must provide their own accompaniment, or use a backing track to which they perform the songs that they are auditioning. If he or she is successful in earning a spot on a calypso tent cast or for a calypso competition, a score must be created for the purpose of live performance. This cost usually comes out of an artist's appearance fee, and in these days of fifteen- to twenty-piece calypso orchestras, the cost associated with arranging and printing the scores for the musicians who will accompany them can add up. Through rehearsals and input from the calypso tent's musical director, most calypsonians and songwriters will make changes to lyrics and song structure, and eventually the final version of a song will take form. This can incur additional costs if new parts have to be written out for the band. If artists want to have recordings available for airplay, they have the choice of a handful of studios in Trinidad, or recording their songs abroad in Miami or New York. Even recording in a local studio is costly: many artists simply choose not to incur the expense, or will make a recording at the end of a successful season to meet audience demand.

Once a calypsonian is hired for a tent, each night is another audition. Artists are still polishing their acts and management is still trying to decide if the less experienced performers will work out. Working in a tent is a means to a more lucrative end: being invited to participate in Calypso Fiesta, the semifinal round for the Calypso Monarch competition. Because of this, calypsonians tend to focus their efforts on a limited number of songs, perhaps only two or three, for the entire Carnival/calypso season. If calypsonians are not giving good performances, they might get "benched" for a few nights until they put in more rehearsal time with the house band and improve (Mason, 1998: 31). Thus the tents struggle between preserving the art form of calypso and meeting their economic needs of bringing in audiences and making a profit. This is true even of the government tents, though these are somewhat more lenient because they need to retain an adequate number of singers on their roster. In other words, calypsonians, who sing some of the most politically oriented song forms in the Caribbean, must face the same commercial hurdles that performers of other types of popular music do.

Over the course of rehearsing and performing during Carnival season, calypsonians try out different types of gestures, phrasing, staging, and related dramatic aspects of the musical performance. This is known as "packing the calypso"—rehearsing it to the point where lyrics, melody, rhythm, phrasing, and pantomime cohere into a complete work of art, and the finished calypso is identified with the personality of the singer (Hill, 1973: 65). If the audience approves of a song, they will request an encore, during which the singer is expected to sing more verses; the reaction of the audience may thus cause changes to the original form of a calypso. In most cases, it takes a performer the better part of the season to solidify his or her songs into compact dramatic packages. As I noted in chapter 1, Trinidadians love antics along with their storytelling; in fact, that is one of the expectations that must be met for a successful performance. The calypsonian merely brings to life a larger character in a structured, professional setting, with a formal and elaborate acting out of an assumed role. It is through this reenactment over a season of performance events that such songs gain their rhetorical power.

As in any dramatic performance, costumes must be elaborate, and they become more so for the major Carnival competitions. Certain singers have become known for their stage attire. Denyse Plummer has invested in some of the most elaborate stage attire in the business, and her costumes for the Calypso Monarch competition have been created by mas designers such as Peter Minshall. Singers with an Afro-centric orientation, such as Ella Andall or Singing Sandra, appear resplendent in elaborate African formal wear. When singing soca or other party songs, performers such as Destra Garcia, Alison Hinds, or Fay-Ann Lyons wear fashions created by local designers such as Meiling and Peter Elias. On Carnival Monday and Tuesday, these soca artists wear more elaborate versions of the pretty mas costumes worn by female revelers in Parade of Bands. Of course, this is expensive, and many performers hold down costs by designing their costumes themselves and either assembling them at home or hiring a local tailor or seamstress.[2] There is no such thing as an advance in this business, and artists themselves must raise cash for costumes and all other expenses for Carnival season.[3]

The music scene of Trinidad and Tobago is very competition oriented. There are musical competitions for every age group, from young children to adults, in a variety of musical styles that include calypso, soca, steelband music, chutney soca, and various popular and inspirational musics. Calypso competitions are held for students in primary and secondary schools, who go on to compete for the Junior Calypso Monarch title. Many local businesses and government offices sponsor calypso competitions for their employees—there is even a calypso competition at the women's prison in Golden Grove.[4] One of the more prestigious competitions for female calypsonians is the National Calypso Queen Competition, discussed in the previous chapter. Professional and semi-professional singers who perform in the calypso tents hope to be invited to participate in Calypso Fiesta, the semifinal round for the Calypso Monarch competition. Over the course of several nights, a panel of judges visits each calypso tent to evaluate the various performers and make their recommendations on who should advance to the semifinals. Because of this competitive environment, calypsonians tend to focus their efforts on a limited number of songs, perhaps only two or three, for the entire Carnival/calypso season. Each performance becomes more elaborate as the singer goes various rounds of competitions.[5] If a singer is lucky enough to reach the semifinals Calypso Monarch or Calypso Queen competitions, he or she has worked out an elaborate staging of the issue their work addresses. Calypso Fiesta typically has forty competitors, out of which eleven finalists and one reserve are selected to compete against the previous year's Calypso Monarch. For the Calypso Monarch finals, it has become common for calypsonians to develop elaborate playlets starring local actors, or employ groups of dancers and masqueraders to create visual interest and fill the enormous stage in the Grand Savannah. This also assists in keeping audience interest and enthusiasm, which is crucial because it can help sway the judges in a singer's favor.

There are other calypso competitions during Carnival, such as the Young Kings Competition and the Calypso Queen competition. Achievements in these competitions help performers when auditioning for the tents the next season. Titles also strengthen a performer's international prestige, enabling one to earn engagements outside of Trinidad and Tobago once Carnival season concludes. The Calypso Monarch competition is the pinnacle of achievement for a calypsonian, and also carries a considerable cash prize.[6] The first female calypsonian to win a calypso competition in Trinidad was Calypso Rose, who won the Road March competition in 1977 with "Give Me More Tempo" (also known as "Going Down San Fernando"). The following year she took first place in the newly renamed Calypso Monarch competition with "Her Majesty" and "I Thank Thee." As I noted in the previous chapter, the winner of the National Calypso Queen competition is almost guaranteed to advance to the Calypso Monarch semifinals, and is usually successful in making it to the finals of Calypso Monarch held on Dimanche Gras (Carnival Sunday). However, since 1978, only three women besides Calypso Rose have won the Calypso Monarch competition: Singing Sandra, Denyse Plummer, and Karene Asche. As I discuss below, the women who have won the Calypso Monarch competition had to be persuaded that calypso was something that they could perform and as women had a duty to perform in order to set examples for their audiences.

Ask Trinidadians to name one of their most beloved calypsonians of all time, male or female, and Calypso Rose will be among the top ten. Female calypso and soca artists of every age consistently list her as one of their key influences. While not the first woman to sing calypso professionally, she is by far the most successful and the one with the longest career. Rose's contributions are recognized by every musical artist in Trinidad, female and male. Although she has not competed in Carnival competitions for many years, she is typically an invited guest at many performance venues, from cabaret-style shows at the Hotel Normandie and the Mas Camp Pub to soca fetes. At age seventy-five, Rose continues to tour extensively and to record and promote her own songs. In fact, it took some time for me to be able and sit down and talk with her, via telephone, as Rose was constantly traveling to one foreign engagement after another, including recording her latest album in France.

Calypso Rose was born in 1940 and named Linda McCartha Sandy, her middle name derived from that of General Douglas MacArthur. Called "Cartey" by her family, she was one of eleven children of a Spiritual Baptist preacher and his wife, whose parish was in the village of Bethel in Tobago, Trinidad's sister island. If little Cartey had remained in that one-bedroom house with her parents and ten siblings, her life would probably have taken quite a different turn. Instead, her father's brother and his common-law wife, who had no children of their own, offered to take one of the Sandy children to live with them in Barataria, a village in greater Port-of-Spain. This practice of informal adoption, known as "child shifting," is common among working-class Afro-Caribbean families. Rose recalled the experience for reporter Deborah John: "Well you know they wasn't really married, she was living with him, but he sent her over to choose one of us and my mother put all of us to stand up in a line. I was little and in those days I used to suck my finger. I used to stammer, and she saw me standing there and said 'darling, what is your name?' and I said 'c...c...c...c..artey'. She took my hand and said, 'you want to come to Trinidad with me?' The next day we went on the boat."[7]

Although it was difficult to live apart from her family, nine-year-old Rose soon came to appreciate the benefits of her aunt and uncle's generosity. She would have the opportunity to receive a better education than she would in Tobago, and be exposed to the vibrant culture of the country's capital city. She was enrolled at San Juan Government School, and on Sundays attended services at a Seventh Day Adventist church with her aunt and uncle. On school vacations, she returned to her father's house in Tobago, and attended Spiritual Baptist meetings with her family. It was in the enriched environment of her uncle's home, however, that Rose's gift for music blossomed. She learned to sing by participating in the school choir and taught herself how to play cuatro and guitar. By the time she was a teenager, Rose was writing her own songs. Her own listening tastes, and even her performing style, were strongly influenced by the gospel music she heard in her home growing up:

> I grew up listening to mostly gospel because my father was a Spiritual Baptist and in Tobago, where we came from we didn't have streetlights in my time. When radio was being introduced all we used to get was Nashville, Tennessee, Texas, and all those country-western stations and hillbillies. And when I started listening to phonograph records, Mahalia Jackson was my idol. Now I have more gospel music in my house than calypsos. American gospel. And then I start writing gospel from 1969 and recorded them. So I have two gospel CDs out. The first gospel CD is called *Jesus Is My Rock*. And the other CD that I wrote is just called *Jesus*. So the Baptist and gospel style has influenced my singing and my music.[8]

Throughout her childhood, Rose performed at school concerts at San Juan Government School and at various events in her home village of Bethel. In 1956 she was asked to sing for the recently elected Eric Williams when he came to Tobago. As she recalled (humorously imitating the prime minister) for filmmaker Kavery Dutta, Williams told her "you are very good. You should go to Trinidad and sing in a calypso tent."[9] Both her adoptive family and her father were very much against the idea. "When my father heard of me singing calypso, he was deeply annoyed, knowing the background I come from" (Ottley, 1992: 4). Thus the first obstacle for Rose was the viewpoints of her religious community. However, she had also been baptized in the Spiritual Baptist faith, and she believed that God had given her a gift that she was obliged to carry out. As she recalled during our interview together:

> I started in 1955 when I was fifteen years of age, which was very hard for a female to be a calypso entertainer. Because these folks in these years thought in these years that beating a steel pan and singing calypso was something derogatory and

degrading, especially for women. So I hung in there and showed them that this is an art and a talent and I would not let anything disrupt me from getting on the stage. And which I stood up and fought a lot of church groups, especially the women. I stood up and I fought them and then they realized in 1963 where I was really coming from. And I kept banging on those doors, until those doors flung wide open for me.[10]

The encouragement of the Prime Minister himself certainly worked in Rose's favor in getting her family to accept, albeit reluctantly, her writing calypsos and performing them professionally. In 1957 she successfully auditioned for the Mighty Spoiler's Original Young Brigade Tent. Despite her religious upbringing, Rose was an aficionado of calypso, and admired the stage personality of the Mighty Spoiler and Lord Kitchener. Her first calypso, "Glass Thief," was her eyewitness account of a man stealing an old lady's glasses and running away through the Croisée market (Ottley, 1992: 5).

While the young singer had chosen the calypso sobriquet Crusoe Kid, alluding to her origins in Tobago and her youth, Spoiler persuaded her to take the name Calypso Rose. Initially she was "helper" in the Young Brigade tent; in other words, she was not a contracted singer but received an appearance fee of $5 on the nights she was allowed to perform rather than sit on the "bench." This was common practice in the tents in those days regardless of one's gender, as young singers had to earn the right to appear before an audience. When she became a contracted singer, Rose made a weekly salary of TT$100 (Guilbault, 2007: 106). Needless to say, Rose continued to live in her uncle's house (she was after all, still a teenager and unmarried) and her income from the tents was probably welcome support in the running of her adopted family's working-class household.

As discussed in the previous chapter, Rose entered the calypso arena on the terms dictated by the dominant male singers of the time. However, like Lady Trinidad and Lady Iere before her, she was a special attraction and male calypsonians knew they needed to offer her their guidance and protection. "They could make money because there's a woman singing in that tent, and we wanna go and see that woman" (Ottley, 1992: 7). Thus, they called her "sister" and "tantie" and respected her because she maintained herself in a way to be respected, when she likely could have used the opportunity to advance her career via trading sexual favors. While Rose offered a female response to the "smutty" calypsos of Sparrow and his generation, her stage persona never carried over to real life. One fact about her personal history that Rose had kept from the public for many years was that in 1958, at age eighteen, she was brutally beaten and raped by three men while returning from a PNM meeting.

This experience was first related in detail to filmmaker Pascale Obolo, who directed the documentary *Calypso Rose: Lioness of the Jungle*. As Rose relates in the film, and the subsequent publicity surrounding the film's release, "I have never been to bed with a man since I was raped to now, because I'm still afraid."[11] With this in mind, one must regard with amazement Rose's ability not only to carry on with her career, but also to write songs that so brilliantly address women's experiences in various forms.

Many of Rose's songs express female sexual desire, and use double entendres to discuss sexual situations, thus representing a female response to the ribaldry of her male contemporaries. Some early examples were collected on Rose's first LP *Calypso Rose: Queen of the Calypso World*, released in 1968.[12] One example is "The Bicycle," in which Rose asks her neighbor for a ride on his bicycle: "Jump on Rosie, jump on / I jump on the bicycle and I gone / but before he pedal I had to jump off / because the tire run soft." Rose offers her advise on how to fix the man's equipment, including "some oil to grease down the ball," but regardless of Mr. Russell's efforts, the "tire is too soft for me." In another song from the same period, "Palet," Rose describes her intention to sell this frozen treat: "From Sunday to Monday, And public holiday / I selling me palet, Me ain't have no limit / Any time that you thirsty / You could suck a palet from Rosie."

By 1963 Rose had achieved sufficient status in the business that she was selected by Guyanese promoter Cyril Shaw to make a tour of the Caribbean, which would conclude with the Virgin Islands Calypso King competition in St. Thomas. Although Sparrow decided against making the trip, Rose went up against eleven other male calypsonians and won the title, making her the first woman to win any sort of Calypso King competition (Ottley, 1992: 6–7). However, Rose told me that she feels her true breakthrough moment was with the song "Fire in Meh Wire," a song she wrote while on another tour of the Caribbean a few years later in 1966:

> When I wrote that calypso "Fire in Me Wire" it was written in three separate islands. The first verse and chorus was written in St. Croix Virgin Islands, the second verse and chorus was in Barbados, and the third verse was in Trinidad. And I think that was the tune that broke the barrier right through. I think it is the melody and the lyrics. Because I was incorporating the Indian and I am a Negro. The way I visualized this calypso was to write this old lady was living alone and the only neighbor is a neighbor by the name of Ramsingh. And the Indians went with that tune. And that tune broke wide open.[13]

The tune was so successful, and created so much audience demand, that Rose was asked to perform it two consecutive years in the calypso tent, 1967 and

1968, something no other artist had been allowed to do. The song was popular with steelbands and masqueraders too, and nearly won the Road March competition of 1968.

"Fire in Me Wire" tells the story of an old Spanish lady, who runs out of her burning house to seek the assistance of her neighbor Ramsingh: "Fire fire, in me wire papa / Ay ya yeye O yo yoye / Fire Fire Ven aca papito / Da me mucho agua, Heat for so." As the story unfolds, Rosie, and the audience to which she sings, soon learns that the "fire" is of a different sort. The neighbor Ramsingh comes running, but thinks it must be a joke because "he didn't see no smoke." The woman bawls "come over Ramsingh, unreel the hose and let go the water to out the fire." "Fire in Me Wire" has grown to be one of Rose's best-loved songs, and no concert is complete without her performing this song with great sauciness and her unique style of wining her waist. As she continues to perform the song over the years, the "old lady" in the story seems to have become Rose herself, as she sings out to the neighbor Ramsingh to "bring the water to out Rose's fire." At the same time, she encourages the audience, to "bring the fire, play with fire" and enthusiastically sing along with the chorus and variations upon it that Rose creates in performance.

Other calypsos that Rose has written over the years depict independent women who have control in their relationships because of the contributions they make to the economy of the household. "It is she who owns the house or pays the rent, she who leaves for a year to fulfill contracts abroad, who dictates when the man can come visiting and when he can spend the night, and it is she who dismisses him as an expendable object when she is through with him" (Rohlehr, 2004b: 376). One example is the calypso she debuted in 1967 entitled "A Man is a Man," in which Rose advises two young girls that men are in essence interchangeable: "A man is a man / No mind his face like a frying pan / Obeah man or manicou man / Any man could give you satisfaction." Another example is the song discussed several times already, "What She Go Do," written in 1973. In light of her personal history, I see this song as Rose's "modest proposal" to take things to the extreme to highlight the ridiculousness of the male example: "If he picks up an outside woman / Just show him you could pick up two outside men / And that's the only way / A woman should get some respect today."

In 1977 Calypso Rose became the first woman to win the Road March competition, which is essentially a people's choice award that recognizes the calypso played most frequently during the Parade of Bands on Carnival Monday and Tuesday. Rose's song that year was "Give Me More Tempo (Going Down San Fernando)," in which she uses the then new soca style to persuade masqueraders to try an alternative to mas in Port-of-Spain: "We going down

San Fernando, down there have plenty tempo / They have a steel orchestra jamming sweet / We going to join San Fernandians, and roll down Coffee Street / So give me more tempo." Rose won the Road March again the following year with another soca tune, entitled "Come Leh We Jam." In this song, Rose enthusiastically embraces the new form of dance music: "I can't take this feeling / My heart is reeling / So hold me tighter / Let's dance the soca, come dance the soca."

Calypso Rose's strong presence in calypso competition, and the emergence of other female artists following her example, most likely inspired the changing of the name of the national calypso competition from Calypso King to Calypso Monarch. But as Rose likes to tell to the story:

> When Trinidad and Tobago became a republic nation, they could have no kings nor queens. So they had to come up with an idea to change the Calypso King competition and call it Calypso Monarch competition. So 1977 was the first year that Trinidad and Tobago had the name Calypso Monarch. And I, yours truly, won the Calypso Monarch in 1978. I won the Road March first, I won the Road March second, and I won the Calypso Queen. I took all the prizes in 1978. And I bow, I say I thank thee, and I got out of competitions. And no one have never beat me because I did not contest my crown for the following year.[14]

Thus, Rose was the first woman to win the Carnival Road March competition, and was Trinidad's first female Calypso Monarch. Her song of choice when she won in 1978, "I Thank Thee," pays tribute to everyone who helped her reach that point: "I thank my mother, my school teacher, my neighbor, my brother, the Government, the Mighty Sparrow, the panmen, the brass men, my fans, and everything" (Ottley, 1992: 8–9). Like her road marches, "I Thank Thee" was not about women's issues, but rather topics with which many different people could identify. This is also the case with the other female monarchs discussed below, whose winning songs were about widespread social problems that addressed the nation as a whole rather than one segment of the population.

Despite her successes, Rose also experienced the frustration created by gender biases in calypso judging in Trinidad. Several times in the sixties and seventies, when Kitchener's songs dominated the Road March competition, Rose's songs came within one or two points of winning. Kitchener passed away in 2001, and several years later the NCC went back and recognized that Rose actually won the Road March four times. Waiting nearly thirty years to be recognized for these achievements was a clear indication of the gender biases of calypso judging:

The NCC came out two years ago and said that Calypso Rose had four road marches, but they only gave me two. The first one was "Fire in Me Wire." The second road march was 1975 with "Do Dem Back." They came out and said that Lord Kitchener beat Calypso Rose by one. Then two years ago they came back and said we have to give you an apology. You really won four road marches. But they could not give me that in front of a male, you see. So in 1977 with "Give Me More Tempo" or "Going Down San Fernando"—I beat them. It was too blatant so they couldn't hide it. Then I came down in 1978 with "Come Leh We Jam." And then I just bow. I say I thank thee. I concentrated more on the international level of music.[15]

It is clear that Rose's frustrations with the sexism of calypso judging contributed to her decision to retire from competition. However, by the time she hung up her crown in 1978, she was in demand as an international artist and no longer had anything to prove in the realm of calypso competition, and thus retired from that aspect of performing in Trinidad and Tobago.

Rose's career also underscores the fact that political commentary alone cannot sustain a musical career in Trinidad; one must also be able to sing in the language of the fete. In fact, it is clear that Rose's popularity was due in large part to her gift for writing upbeat party songs suitable to inspire audience participation. Rose's stage presence is also a contributor to her popularity: she was in essence, the first "winer woman" as she matched the dancing styles of Sparrow, Kitchener, Shorty, and other male calypsonians of her time. Of course, she faced condemnation for this in the seventies, as her prizes were accumulating, to which she responded in her usual blunt manner: "These days they saying I too vulgar. Vulgar, me foot. When I get on that stage and I hear the bass-pedal drumming and the bass strumming, I does just start to move. I tell you I find myself doing some steps on that stage that I swear I know nothing about. The music just takes over me body and Rosie on the move."[16] By today's standards, Rose's wining of her waist is more playful than vulgar. On the occasions I have seen her in concert, I have found that the most enjoyable aspects of Rose's performances is when she "catches the spirit" and inspires the women in the audience, especially those close to her in age, with her youthful enthusiasm. In a recent interview, Rose was asked how she is able to exude such sensuality onstage despite the traumatic experience of her youth; she responded: "I love my audience, I embrace them. They give me themselves and I open myself to them as I am."[17]

For many years, Rose was the major breadwinner for her family. In 1966 she married Aubrey Lewis: this arrangement seems to have been to provide a mother figure for Lewis's daughter and to give Rose the opportunity to live in the United States. Aubrey Lewis passed away in 1982, and this left Rose fully responsible for her stepdaughter and grandchildren. Her decision to remain in New York rather than return to Trinidad benefited her family economically, and also facilitated her international career.[18]

Rose's spirituality is an ongoing force in her life and part of who she is as a person and a musical artist. She has surprised several people by saying she dedicates all her songs to the Lord, even her sex songs (Rohlehr, 2004: 365). In 1987 she became an ordained Spiritual Baptist minister, following in the footsteps of her father, who had been "deeply annoyed" at her singing calypso. As indicated above, Rose has consistently defended her music against the protestations of church groups by emphasizing it is a gift from the Lord Himself, and as He said in His Sermon on the Mount, she would not hide her light under a bushel. She also stresses the African origins of the music, and its importance to Afro-Trinidadian culture as encouraged by various political and cultural leaders. Thus, Rose uses the institutions of respectability to defend her decisions as a musical artist.

However, Rose recognizes that there are significant obstacles to women performing calypso, based on her own experiences but also on the nature of the music business in Trinidad. When I asked her why it took over twenty years for another woman to be crowned Calypso Monarch, she remarked it is because that most of them do not write their own music and until recently did not have access to the kind of writers who could write material suitable to win the Monarch crowd. When I asked her why there are so few women writers, she said that she has tried to counsel them in this direction:

> I keep telling them all the time, we have 365 days in a year. You could take a whole year to write a song. All you got to do is to use your imagination and create. So many things are happening in the world today. So many things are happening in the country and on the islands. You could take that same story and put it together and put it into song. I keep telling them that calypsonians are just like a reporter. Because we report our experiences into song and lyrics. And put it out there. We are the eye-opener. A calypsonian could build a country, could break a country: because they could write something against the government and make the government fall. They could write something to enhance the government and build the nation. We are the reporters. So once you give the public something that is appreciative, they could go with it and that could be a big battle.[19]

Unlike more conservative voices, Rose sees soca as an important vehicle for women in contemporary Trinidadian music:

> What I have been seeing is a lot of more female have been coming out. In the soca, not the calypso now because things have changed. And what I see is a lot of female come out not only in Trinidad about the whole Caribbean. The structure of the bass and the rhythm of the drums, with the modernized music that is being brought out now: the samplers and things. It's become a wide-open scope and as it becomes wide open the females are jumping in. I expect by 2010 we'll have a lot more coming in. And don't be surprised if the females will be in a larger number than the males. Because when I go to the schools in Trinidad during the Carnival season, the amount of young kids from the schools are singing calypso, especially the females. I say "this will be trouble!"[20]

Rose constantly collaborates with young artists, who also recognize her significant contributions to contemporary Caribbean music. For example, in 2003 she collaborated with Machel Montano, one of the most successful soca artists in Trinidad and the international scene, on the song "What She Want." Other soca artists have requested to cover her songs, and she is often an invited guest at soca fetes and competitions. During Carnival 2009 she joined Fay-Ann Lyons onstage at the Soca Monarch finals to shake her "bumpa" as a contributor to what would be Lyons's winning performance of "Heavy T."

Carnival 2009 also found Calypso Rose promoting a new album she had recorded in France just before I interviewed her in 2007. Simply titled *Calypso Rose*, the CD was released on the Harmonia Mundi/World Village imprint, the same label responsible for reviving the career of Omara Portuondo. In fact, Rose met Portuondo and discussed possible collaborations with her when the CD was launched in Marseilles at the Fiesta des Suds. "The arrangements on this album are open to a wider scope of listeners," said Rose in an interview after she appeared at New York's GlobalFest. Unlike many cheaply produced calypso CDs, produced for quick sale following Carnival, Rose's CD features new arrangements of her own songs and several covers, crafted by a young group of musicians that combine calypso and soca with reggae, ska, and Caribbean jazz.[21] The same year, Pascale Obolo and her film crew traveled to Trinidad to film a documentary on her life.[22] As usual, Rose had planned a number of foreign engagements in Europe and North America that would take her through the rest of the year.[23] Most years, Rose returns to Trinidad and Tobago to participate in various shows related to Carnival season. In 2015 she was back home to participate in a number of events. She was part of the cast of the Barrack Yard Tent Experience, an experimental calypso tent combining music, comedy, and theatre held on the grounds of the National Academy of Performing Arts.[24] Calypso Rose has endured long past any derogatory critiques of her and her work to become one of the most important ambassadors of Trinidadian music and culture, male or female, in the contemporary Caribbean music scene.

Sandra Des Vignes: Singing Sandra, and a "United Sister"

During Carnival 1999, the second season I experienced during my fieldwork, the Calypso Monarch competition was again won by a woman, something I was not anticipating but that was serendipitous for my study. Singing Sandra was that monarch, and as of 2015 she is the only woman to win a second time, in 2003.

Born in 1957, Sandra Des Vignes was raised by a single mother in various neighborhoods "behind the bridge," including East Dry River and Laventille, before settling into a government housing project in Upper Morvant. When I asked to interview her, just after the 1998 Carnival season, Sandra requested that I come by this very apartment, where she now lives with her husband and her mother. This area suffers from precisely the blighted urban decay about which Sandra would sing in "Voices From the Ghetto" the following year. As I traveled up there, even the taxi driver became nervous: although we were on his route he was uncertain which building I was looking for and was reluctant to leave a female foreigner alone in this part of the city until he knew I would reach my destination safely. Finally he recognized some people he knew, and found someone to guide me up the hill to Sandra's building. It was one of the more memorable trips I made during my fieldwork, but my worries were laid to rest once I was welcomed into the Des Vignes home for our interview, and assured that I would not have been asked to come up to this neighborhood if she felt I would not be safe in the daytime.

Unlike Calypso Rose, Sandra did not spend her teen years writing calypsos. In fact she says she never imagined she would be a professional singer at all. She left school at age fifteen, working various low-wage jobs to help her mother maintain the household, as did many young women of her social class. However, she did have opportunities to develop her musical talent from a young age, including singing in the Spiritual Baptist church. Her mother was not as strict as other women of her faith, and made sure to take her daughter to the calypso tents every season. Both mother and daughter liked to listen to calypso on the radio or sing it around the house. Sandra also had an uncle who sang in the tents in the forties, and thus was exposed to calypso as something that was positive and acceptable to pursue as a livelihood (Ottley, 1992: 127).

Sandra's was the first generation to benefit from the Best Village competitions initiated by the PNM in 1963, and this was her introduction to performing opportunities, for which she won Best Actress three years in a row as well as Best Chantuelle and Best Calypsonian.[25] Sandra proudly emphasizes that she is a product of Best Village, as are other calypsonians of her generation. She strongly believes it is a competition that continues to help underprivileged youth:

> It was really created for people to be more aware of their community and appreciate their community more. Because Best Village isn't only for performing. It's environmental, sanitation, handicrafts, athletics. Whatever type of art you can do. For exhibitions they put out their display. But it creates happening to keep the youths much more occupied. You know, because some of them are not academically inclined but they can learn to make something. You might be amazed what they can do with a drum or dance or have beautiful voice. Once you have the right motivators within this program, a lot will come out of it. Because we women and men in calypso are products of Best Village.[26]

Like Calypso Rose, Sandra's transition from Best Village to the calypso tent was due to the mentorship of experienced male calypsonians. In 1984 the calypsonian Dr. Zhivago (Felix Scott) approached her with two songs he wanted a woman to sing, "The Raper Man Coming" and "Pan For Independence": "I said, why not, I would try it. And he took me to the auditions and I was selected at Sparrow's Young Brigade. Sparrow had never heard me, but on the opening night after he heard me, he told me that he couldn't promise me that I'd be the next Calypso Rose, but from what he saw I'd be a force to reckon with. He said things to me like, I hope you're not in this just for the money, because if you are then you wouldn't last and you wouldn't learn the artistry of it."[27]

Although Sandra does not write her own songs, she does work very closely with her songwriters to make these compositions her own. Several years after she sang Zhivago's calypsos, she worked with Tobago Crusoe (Orthniel Bacchus) to create a statement about sexual harassment of women in the workplace. This became the feminist anthem "Sexy Employers (Die with My Dignity)," with which Sandra easily won the NWAC Calypso Queen competition in 1987. In her lyrics and delivery, Sandra loudly condemns the kinds of bad behavior women have experienced with male employers, in trying to find and keep jobs. Sandra's answer to sexual harassment and abuse is expressed clearly in the song's chorus: "Well if is all this humiliation / To get a job these days as a woman / Brother they go keep their money, I go keep my honey / And die with my dignity!"

The first time I saw Singing Sandra perform live was a memorable experience. It was at the government-sponsored calypso tent Kaiso House, where a friend took me one evening to experience a cast of calypsonians who were well known for social and political commentary and included a lot of female calypsonians. My favorite this evening was "Equalizer," in which Singing Sandra recommended the ultimate price for men who rape and abuse women: "For all their twisted desires / Give me a pair of old rusty pliers . . . / I have a license to circumcise / I come out to equalize." Despite the seriousness of her subject matter, Sandra added aspects of humor to her performance. This included dressing in full constructor-worker garb and brandishing an enormous pair of bolt cutters (rather than the old rusty pliers mentioned in the song) that were visible from the back row of the theatre. When we talked shortly after the Carnival season of 1998, we discussed the genesis of the song "Equalizer":

> I was on my way back home at two in the morning, and just as we were coming to Morvant junction I saw this young woman running down the street covered in blood. She was being pursued by a man, and he just had on his underpants. She was just running to cars and asking for help. She was bloody. We took her to the Morvant police station and left her there. I got home and I called Christophe and I told him about this experience and said I must address this. It was a terrible sight. If it had been me, one of us would have been dead. Because I'm not running, I am going to stand and fight. You know me, I am not one of the women who says he's bigger than me. God give him strength, and I will fight with you. I'm not running away. So I was very pissed. And I told Chris, I'm very bitter, and I want this song to be bitter. I told him that I wanted to go to castration and everything, that depth. Again, having to listen to the news every day and every time I open the newspaper I see some woman has been battered, some woman has been raped. And the incest, little girl children being molested. And just keep getting angrier and angrier and angrier. That is how the song "Equalizer" was born.[28]

Singing Sandra has always worked closely with collaborators to ensure that the songs she prepares to perform accurately reflect how she would express the feelings or opinions the songs embody. This is how she described working with Christophe Grant on the songs he has composed for her:

> Well, I am totally satisfied with Christophe's work. Because if I give Christophe an idea—like "Equalizer" was my idea—I would tell Christophe how far I would like to go with this song or how deep I would like to go with this song. Because this song actually becomes me, and I am the one bringing the song to life. The thing is with Christophe is that he will sit and discuss with you the littlest detail of how

you feel about it. Even if the song is his idea, I will go over the song with him if there are certain things I don't understand. In the attack that he is making I will ask him to explain this attack to me. If I feel it, I go with it. If I don't feel it then I will tell him, "well I don't feel it, and I feel the attack this way." And will say, "Ok, you are the one that's doing the song." Once you know it doesn't take away from the song you attack it that way. So it becomes a marriage between Chris and I. I can't speak for the other people that he writes for, but I say that I'm totally satisfied with working with Christophe.[29]

Like Rose, Sandra also ran up against gender bias in calypso judging in earlier competitions. For example, although "Sexy Employers" easily won the NWAC Calypso Queen Competition in 1987, it did not make even the semifinals of Calypso Monarch (Ottley, 1992: 121). When we spoke in 1998, Sandra was upset that she had not made it past the semifinals with "Equalizer," which I felt was one of the best songs I had heard that season:

I'm STILL angry, even more so for the way the song was treated by our so-called adjudicators, some of which were women. That they didn't see it fit enough to put the song in the finals so people could have heard. Because it's a cry of women, and not just women of Trinidad and Tobago—domestic abuse, incest is an international issue. Any man and woman anywhere could have identified with the song. If you have nothing to brutalize a woman with ... and the first man you make an example with the other would be scared because no man wants to be castrated and nobody wants to lose a limb. That's the way I think with no apologies! I don't know what is too strong or too weak for the judges. They are doing their job. Right? But, my philosophy is that God will do His job, in His time so they don't bother me. Because I know there's One greater.[30]

We continued to discuss how the song "Equalizer" had remained popular with audiences. Several weeks previously, I had seen men react quite positively to the song when she had performed it at the Mas Camp Pub. Like Rose, Sandra's Spiritual Baptist faith informs her decisions on how to perform her material, and the effect it will have on her audience:

Wherever I go to perform the song, men are asking for me to perform the song sometimes more than women. They tend to show us that we still have a lot of good men. But they are also afraid because they fear what they hear in the song. Because I sing it with everything in me and I sing it with rage. . . . But some of them, he hit his women and when he sees the rage in me it must come back to him. The time he did that. And if there's a heart in him, self will talk to self and he would say somewhere you were wrong for doing that. And God would be with him. But I want God to tell me to deal with them for him.[31]

Sandra has also been accused of "man-bashing" in "Equalizer" and "Sexy Employers." She said she refuses to take such people on, because she is confident that her lyrics are addressing a certain kind of man who should stop the mistreatment of women. She also feels she has an important role to play in bringing these issues to light and giving solutions to various social problems:

> In "Die with my Dignity," what I was saying to women is to be strong and stand up and say no to a man. If you have qualifications you shouldn't have to do that and still be subjected to advances from the bosses. You're in line for a promotion because of the work you do. But he would hold you back because he wants to interfere with you and you won't let it happen. You say no. But when you say yes now, then you get the promotion it makes no sense. It means you don't value my work, you don't value me. If I've taken time to go to school and taken time to better my situation in life I shouldn't have to be subjected to your stupid advances and harassment all the time. I should be able to stand and tell you I am simply saying to women, "Stand up for your rights."[32]

This led to a natural digression as to why Sandra felt that these social problems existed in Trinidad. Her answer again reflected her spiritual beliefs: when she was growing up, she recalled, adults instilled spiritual values in their children and gave them guidance in life. In her neighborhood, she now saw parents who were still children themselves, growing up with little guidance, and emulating the models of behavior they were seeing on cable television. She theorized that this was the reason there were so many abandoned children in the poorer regions of the city: "If you are a God-fearing person you know you don't leave your children to the elements of the earth. You keep your children in whatever weather. If you get a bread, you make sure your children get that bread and you stay hungry because you are responsible for their lives. You don't just put them down there. You might get someone to hold them for you until you get something to do, but you don' t just abandon them all over the street. Madness!"[33]

The topics of poverty and child neglect that Sandra discussed with me were ones that she would take later that year to songwriter Christophe Grant to create the songs "Voices from the Ghetto" and "Song for Healing." In these songs Sandra also implored the nation to take notice of the people who must survive in the ghetto and suggest that those who are better off could provide some material assistance to social problems. Sandra herself has also given back to her community in various ways, such as participating in programs that assist homeless children. When Singing Sandra took the Calypso Monarch crown in 1999 with "Voices From the Ghetto," popular opinion agreed that this was "true kaiso"—in other words, it was everything a powerful calypso performance ought to be. When I did an informal poll the day before the competition, several people said that Singing Sandra would win "first, second, and third" for this song. In her dramatic presentation for "Voices From the Ghetto," Sandra enacted the role of a senior citizen—most likely based on one of her neighbors at the national housing project in Morvant that she still calls home, despite years of international success. She was dressed as if she just returned from an Orisha or Spiritual Baptist religious ceremony (both of which form Sandra's own spiritual practices). Sandra transformed herself into one of the strongest voices of the ghetto, the elderly Afro-Trinidadian woman "stronger than a wall" yet crying in despair at how her land is changing: "Life does rape dignity and pride / 'Til is only bitterness there inside ... / One night is in bed you sleeping, next night is a wake that you keeping / Pray to win the lotto, not to hear voices from the ghetto, crying, crying." Behind the mask of the older woman the audience sees Sandra herself, who is a product of the very ghetto she portrays in song—a fact she emphasizes in the song's concluding lines, sung almost as an aside: "I was born and bred in the ghetto / I know what I talking about / I from the ghetto."

Like Calypso Rose and many other calypsonians, Sandra enjoys diverging from social commentary mode to speak the language of the fete. In 1991 she joined forces with three other female calypsonians, Lady B (Beulah Bob), Tigress (Joanne Rowley), and Marvelous Marva (Marva McKenzie), to form the group United Sisters. The original purpose for the group was to enter the Caribbean Song Festival with a composition by Lady B. Although they lost that year, they won the following year's Caribbean Song Festival with Lady B's "Ambataila Woman," a powerful tribute to the strength of Afro-Caribbean women (Ottley, 1992: 101–3). Meanwhile, the group decided that this was also an opportunity to masquerade as bacchanal women and performing upbeat responses to some of the latest soca songs. Their first song in this mode came out in 1992 and addressed the question "Why Can't a Woman Win a Road March"—an obvious one to ask since no woman had won the competition since Calypso Rose did in 1978. The following year they answered Ronnie McIntosh's "Donkey Dance" with a song called "Whoa Donkey." The song was so popular it came close to defeating Super Blue's "Bacchanal Time" in the Road March competition of 1993. Another answer song in this vein is "Four Women to One Man," a reply to Sparrow's "The More the Merrier."

Sandra explained that her United Sisters persona is a departure from that of Singing Sandra:

> United Sisters Sandra and my individual Sandra are two different personalities. Singing Sandra loves lyrics—she loves to stand and deliver—she loves the social commentary. United Sisters Sandra on the other hand would like the little uptempo, or medium pace music that will get on the stage and dance and get a little gyration for you. She loves to hear her bass and her drummer. I don't like to work with the drum machine. Because I like to interact with my audience, and I think you could see that in my last performance. I like to get you totally involved with me, be a part of what I'm doing, sing the chorus with me and whatever. That is me.[34]

United Sisters disbanded when Lady B passed away in 2001. However, Sandra still goes into fete mode during Carnival: she typically participates in Ladies Night Out, an all-inclusive fete held at the Jean Pierre Complex that typically features the major "divas" of calypso and soca music. In 2009 Sandra opened the show and shared the bill with Calypso Rose, Denyse Plummer, Sanelle Dempster (who won the Road March the same year that Sandra earned her Calypso Monarch title), and Denise "Saucy Wow" Belfon.[35]

Singing Sandra remains the most successful woman singing in social commentary mode. She has made the Calypso Monarch finals six times, and has won the title twice. In 2009 there was considerable speculation that Singing Sandra would achieve a third win in the competition with a sequel to "Voices from the Ghetto" called "Ghetto of the Mind," again co-written with Cristophe Grant. Another encouraging aspect of that year's competition was that it included five women, more than any time in its history. In addition to Singing Sandra, the finalists included the reigning Calypso Queen Twiggy (Ann Marie Parks-Kojo), Tigress (Joanne Rowley), and Karene Asche and Kizzie Ruiz, who as youths had won the Junior Calypso Monarch competition. It was a surprise to me that Sandra placed sixth, but she was probably pleased to see fellow United Sister Tigress place second (barely behind Hollis "Mighty Chalkdust" Liverpool), and Kizzie Ruiz fifth. Clearly, the competition had reached a turning point, and Sandra deserves credit for assisting in creating the gender balance of recent years.

Denyse Plummer: Woman Is Boss

When I first arrived in Trinidad, I was greatly looking forward to seeing performances by Denyse Plummer, whose recordings I had enjoyed listening to back in the States. I had the opportunity to see her perform her previous year's hit "Misbehave" at an awards ceremony during my second week in Trinidad, with the over-the-top antics for which she is known. When the calypso tents opened in January, I made sure to visit Kitchener's Calypso Revue, where Plummer has performed since she began her career in calypso in 1986. That season Denyse was performing an emotional tribute to her mentor, whose health was in decline, called "A Legend (Lord Kitchener)." She had also prepared a more upbeat composition she wrote with Calypso Rose called "Carnival Queen," which she recorded in both calypso and chutney soca style. Later in the season, Denyse would go on to perform in her first appearance in the Chutney Soca Monarch competition, an unusual career move for a calypsonian at that time.

The biography and career trajectory of Denyse Plummer[36] could not be more different from that of Calypso Rose or Singing Sandra. In fact, her life story is atypical not only of female calypsonians but calypsonians in general. Denyse Plummer was born in 1953 to a middle-class family. Her father, Dudley "Buntin" Plummer, was a white Trinidadian; her mother Joan Plummer was a light-skinned Afro-Trinidadian. Denyse Plummer's fair skin and blue eyes signify that she is white by local definitions, and Plummer identifies herself as white rather than Afro-Trinidadian. She attended both Holy Name Prep and Holy Name Convent, which along with St. Joseph's Convent and Bishop Antsey High School are among the most exclusive parochial schools for girls in Port-of-Spain. However, as she indicated in her interview with me in 1998, Plummer was exposed to local music and culture from an early age:

> I was born and raised on top of the College rum shop in St. James. My father was one of the founding members of one of the greatest folk groups we had in Trinidad, La Petite Musicale. The only white man playing guitar in La Petite Musicale. We lived in St. James and every Hosay at five o'clock in the morning we were on top of the porch to see Hosay. So I was born into that, I was born in an Indian area. My father was deep into folk music of Trinidad and Tobago and calypso was played in our house. Everything I learned about calypso was from Calypso Rose and Mighty Sparrow in my home growing up.[37]

Largely due to her father's influence, Plummer developed a strong interest in music. In an interview with Rudolph Ottley, she said that at age fourteen she told a nun, who scolded her for bad grades that she would be a famous singer and travel all over the world (Ottley, 1991: 86). She sang in the folk choir at Holy Name Convent, and won a number of music competitions for children and teens, including "Scouting for Talent."

As I have indicated earlier, a woman of Plummer's ethnicity and class may have enjoyed listening to calypso, but would never have considered singing calypso professionally. Plummer trained as computer operator at Colonial Life, and worked at several white-collar jobs until her mid-thirties. When she decided to pursue music professionally, Plummer followed her father's example and did so in a way that was appropriate for someone of her class and ethnicity. While working days as a computer operator at the Tatil Insurance Company, she sang pop standards four nights a week, first at the Baron Pub and then at the Chaconia Inn and Steak House. Of the remaining nights of the week, two were spent in rehearsals with the house band. Eventually, Plummer decided that her double life was unfair to her co-workers at Tatil, and she left her day job to plunge into the entertainment business full-time.[38] Between 1977 and 1983, Plummer made recordings of the popular songs she sang onstage, including the album *Natural,* arranged and produced by Carl "Beaver" Henderson in 1978, and the reggae single "Sweetest Thing," written for her by Francis Escayg in 1980.[39]

By 1985 Plummer had married Patrick Boocock, and they were expecting their first child. It was then that Len "Boogsie" Sharpe, the arranger for the steelband Phase II Pan Groove, asked her to be the vocalist on the recording of two calypsos he had written with Gregory "GB" Ballantyne, "Pan Rising" and "One Love." As Plummer recalled for me in our interview: "Boogsie asked me to sing his calypso and everyone thought it was a joke including me. I had never sung calypso before and it took a lot of discussing over with family and friends. So we talked it over and they said go for it. If the hundred members of Phase II and Boogsie are behind you, you go ahead and do it."[40]

"Pan Rising" is part of a large body of calypsos that celebrate the steel pan and the musicians who play it: "So we come to jam the pan / Make the whole world understand / Seasons come and seasons gone, We will still be carrying on / Steel band rising with every song."[41] Based on the recording, Plummer was asked by Austin "Blue Boy" Lyons (now known as Super Blue) to perform in his calypso tent for the season. "I couldn't believe I had the phone in my hand. . . . People were just trusting me. They were sure I could do it and the nation thought everybody else was going crazy" (Ottley, 1991: 87).

Singing in a tent allowed Plummer to be considered for the Calypso Monarch competition, and in her first year singing, she advanced to the semifinal round of the competition, which is held at Skinner Park in San Fernando. To say that Plummer had a poor showing at Skinner Park would be an understatement. This round of the competition is known as the "acid test," because a contingent of the audience takes great pleasure in making things miserable for newcomers and even veterans of whom they disapprove. Despite the fact that there had been fair-skinned calypsonians throughout Trinidad's history (examples include Atilla the Hun, Chinee Patrick, and Lord Executor) for the most part Plummer was viewed as a white interloper in an Afro-Trinidadian musical form, and the audience came to humiliate her publicly. When she took the stage, some members of the audience held signs with the slogans "Denyse Plummer go back to South Africa" and "White people don't sing calypso."[42] "It was a little disturbing how I was received the first year—not that I wasn't expecting it beforehand but it was nerve wracking nevertheless. They stoned me with everything possible: toilet paper, sucked up oranges, potties, umbrellas, whatever."[43] As an act of defiance and self-defense, Plummer decided to incorporate the audience's disapproval into her performance. "What I did was that I sort of picked up the toilet paper and the missiles and turned them in as part of the act and made it into a choreography and the people couldn't believe what I was doing. By the end of the performance, they were applauding" (Guilbault, 2007: 113).

Like Rose and Sandra, Plummer received mentorship and guidance from several male contemporaries. In addition to Boogsie Sharpe and Austin Lyons, Lord Kitchener and Black Stalin (Leroy Calliste) were major influences on her performance style. Stalin taught her the correct method of calypso phrasing and how to produce a powerful rhythmic delivery (Guilbault, 2007: 114). Lord Kitchener took Plummer on as a cast member of his Calypso Revue tent, and mentored her career in various ways, and in response she has sung several tributes to Kitchener over the years. As with many women in the music business, Plummer has also faced rumors regarding her reputation. At various times she has been accused of having affairs with her mentors. When she went on tour in Europe opening for Black Stalin, another female calypsonian wrote a song called "Denyse" suggesting that Stalin and Plummer were romantically involved. While she has of course denied the rumors, they persisted at the time, probably because Plummer's star rose so quickly. "I guess they felt I came from out of nowhere and did so well, so fast. They were there so long and they were the real thing."[44]

> In 1988 Plummer won the NWAC Calypso Queen competition with a song she co-wrote with Len "Boogsie" Sharpe and Reynold Howard, "Woman Is Boss." Like "Pan Rising" and "This Feeling Nice" the previous two years, this was also the tune of choice for the steelband Phase II Pan Groove. "Woman Is Boss" is a tribute to the achievements of the women's movement in Trinidad:

> A woman's place was always in the home,
> While her husband went outside and roam.
> Since the beginning of time we standing in line,
> Taking we grind, following behind.
>
> Now we women, have changed we course
> Without remorse, woman is boss ...

The content of "Woman Is Boss," combined with the fact that the song, with its catchy chorus and upbeat tempo, was very popular with female audiences at Calypso Revue, was probably what enabled her to win her first victory in this arena. Still, Plummer was amazed that she won that title, because of NWAC's association with the Black Power movement. It caused a temporary falling out with other female calypsonians, such as the members of United Sisters, who again felt she was an interloper. "That animosity lasted for a short period, now we have a really beautiful relationship."[45]

When I interviewed Plummer in 1998, she had won the NWAC Calypso Queen competition eight times, finally retiring from that competition. She was among the few female calypsonians who regular advanced to the Calypso Monarch finals, and was the only female contestant in the competition in 1998. That season Denyse had made her debut in the Chutney Soca Monarch competition with the song "Carnival Queen," co-written with Calypso Rose. As she said in a newspaper interview, she had no intention of winning, but as a child she had watched Indian films and always wanted to dress up and sing like a Bollywood star.[46] Plummer also qualified for the Soca Monarch finals, though as she commented to me, she knew that she was not going to place high in that competition either. Although the props for these competitions were on view in the family's garage, Denyse looked very different from how she had onstage, having removed the elaborate hair extensions she had worn throughout the season, and seemed relieved to have some time to cool down after all those competitions.

During our interview, it became clear that Plummer's career is much like any other family business. At that time, her mother Joan Plummer lived with her daughter and saw to the tending of the household.[47] Denyse Plummer's husband, Patrick Boocock, had his own business pursuits but also played a large role in raising the couple's two sons.[48] Denyse's sister Arlene also lived with the family and handles all aspects of the business side of Denyse's career, such as scheduling interviews and rehearsals, booking travel arrangements, and negotiating entertainment contracts. This left Denyse Plummer free to concentrate on the artistic aspects of her career. Thus, like the other two women who have won Calypso Monarch, Plummer has been the chief breadwinner for her family, yet the support of "team Denyse" was crucial to the maintenance of her career.

Plummer stressed in her interview a keen sense of responsibility as a role model, particularly for young people. Historically, she knew how hard women have had to fight against degrading images portrayed by male calypsonians, and how female calypsonians had to struggle to be taken seriously in the music business.

Although she had just competed in Soca Monarch, Plummer emphasized that even in her party songs she was not the sort of person to wine and gyrate like some of the younger female artists. She does realize that "if you are to get work 12 months of the year, then you must have a party song" (Mason, 1998: 141). For Plummer, this means upbeat numbers such as "Misbehave" and "Carnival Queen"—songs that in general celebrate Carnival bacchanal and dancing to Carnival music without addressing some of its more sensual aspects. However, she realized that soca was an important part of youth culture, and that if women wanted to succeed in that arena they had to be as forceful as men in terms of their performance style:

> Today, look at us, we have 250 female calypsonians, highly respected by male calypsonians and the general public. Women in calypso are seen as teachers, mothers, prophets, and a lot of is expected of them. Schoolchildren take what comes out of the mouth of female calypsonians as the gospel truth. That's why it upsets me when some of them decide to take a different route and not looking for but looking at. Women in calypso have come a long way, and we address every issue there is. When it come to wine and jam in the party with the men we have to be just as forceful otherwise you get smothered! And pushed by the wayside.[49]

In 2000 Plummer began to work with songwriter Christophe Grant; this collaboration produced the song "Tabanca." In 2001 Plummer won the Calypso Monarch competition with a composition co-authored with Grant called "Nah Leaving." This song is what calypso scholars like to call a nation-building calypso, and found Plummer addressing serious social concerns: "They say meh country so stressful, so tense / With race hate, young jail bait, too much violence / Girl pack up and go, this sweet Trinbago, I tell dem no way / Nah leaving, is here where conceive me, is here ah go dead." Plummer's production for the Calypso Monarch finals was the most lavish she had ever mounted—by this point in the competition's history, finalists were granted TT$10,000 to mount a spectacle that would attract a diverse audience. With costumes and staging designed by Peter Minshall, "a whole Carnival band of moko jumbies and angelic dancers helped Denyse Plummer snatch the Calypso Monarch's crown from Shadow."[50]

Plummer has attained a level of vocal conviction and musicianship that inspires many of her contemporaries. This, I feel, explains her enduring popularity, as does the extravagance and energy of her stage presentation, for which she has become famous:

> A lot of people look at me saying what she going to wear, how's she going to wear her hair, what's she going to do, and it costs me a lot of money. It's the show that people are looking for. I couldn't be like other calypsonians and stand up and sing in a T-shirt and jeans: it just wouldn't work. The whole package is what I sell. I don't think I'm that great a calypsonian or as a songwriter or performer. But the whole package together—that's the magic. That's where my magic comes out: the little mad white woman up there. The package is what sells me.[51]

Denyse Plummer has invested in some of the most elaborate stage attire in the business. Like the salsa singer Celia Cruz, she has an extensive collection of wigs and headpieces she has purchased over the years to create the visual spectacle her audiences have come to expect from her. Much like Calypso Rose, Plummer has gradually moved away from Carnival competitions after winning the Monarch title in 2001. In 2007 Plummer decided to "go natural" for the 2007 Carnival season, taking a more relaxed approach to her musical performances, with minimal costuming and staging.[52] She primarily focused on recording her music (she has made an album every year for eighteen years), including working with younger artists such as Synergy Soca Star contestant Justin Cross, and local hip hop team Spotrushaz. During Carnival 2008, Plummer announced that she was going to take a break during to spend more time with her family.[53] For the 2009 season, Plummer decided not to sing in Calypso Revue or any of the other tents, and restricted her appearances to Ladies Night Out 6 and her usual solo show at Normandie Under the Trees. Plummer registered for only one competition, the Chutney Soca Monarch, and performed in the finals with another collaborative tune called "Masala," which she co-wrote with Christophe Grant and performed in duet with chutney artist Sally Sagram.[54] It is likely that Plummer made these choices so that she could enjoy a more relaxed Carnival season, as well as prepare to perform at Summit Village, created to entertain delegates to the Fifth Summit of the Americas when it was held in Port-of-Spain in April 2009.[55]

From 2010–15 Plummer maintained a fairly heavy schedule of foreign engagements, and had the luxury of being selective about where she performed while at home in Trinidad. During Carnival, this typically included Ladies

Night Out, Under the Trees at the Hotel Normandie, and other performances. This has allowed her to move away from the confines of calypso competitions, and to record and perform in a style that is more to her preference at this period in her life. With a dozen wins in competitions in Trinidad and abroad, Plummer has nothing left to prove by competing, and like many of her male contemporaries, such as Black Stalin and David Rudder, can now focus on recording or pursuing performance contexts that are relevant to her interests, while reinforcing her status as an internationally renowned musician. In 2011 she was awarded the Hummingbird Medal, one of her country's highest honors, and in 2015 received a special award from NWAC at the Calypso Queen competition.[56] Prior to the 2015 Carnival, Plummer announced that she had become a born-again Christian, and would now be focusing on "singing gospelypso and groovy soca about God and His Kingdom."[57] While it remains to be seen if this a permanent change in her musical career, it is apparent that Denyse Plummer is still highly regarded for her contributions to the musical culture of Trinidad and Tobago.

The Next Generation

In contemporary Trinidad there are now competitions for calypsonians of all ages. The cultural arm of the National Joint Action Committee sponsors many of these, including the Calypso Queen competition. There are workplace competitions open to employees of various public services such as the police force, and local businesses such as Guardian Life, British West Indies Airlines, and Telecommunications Services of Trinidad and Tobago. Some of these employee competitions have been a springboard for artists to pursue calypso as a full-time career. The most famous example is Marcia Miranda, who went from being a flight attendant at BWIA to appearing professionally in various calypso tents (Ottley, 1991: 95). Over the years, she has made the finals of Calypso Queen, Calypso Monarch, and Soca Monarch several times, and is currently known as the "Parang Soca Queen."[58]

Currently, there are school-based calypso and soca competitions assisted by donations from corporate sponsors such as Sunshine Snacks and Flavorite Ice Cream. School-age singers typically are not allowed to work in the calypso tents, so the school setting allows them to perform music from an early age. The surprising fact is that girls far outnumber boys in the youth competitions, but the reverse is true in the professional calypso tents. Moreover, their first encouragement to go into these calypso competitions comes from their schoolteachers, a majority of whom are young women. Many of my classmates at the University of the West Indies were such teachers getting their degrees, with assistance from the Ministry of Education, to broaden their knowledge of local art forms and teach them to their students. Several of these young women commented that their female students took music much more seriously than their male counterparts and, hence, could pass the elimination rounds at their individual schools with relative ease. In general, girls are much more willing to do well in academics, while boys are more interested in cricket, football, and other athletic pursuits. The singers who were winning the children's competitions either seemed to come from a musical family or had attracted the attention of older calypsonians, who will write songs for them and coach their performances so that they can win competitive titles.

With women mentoring girls, and so many girls entering the school competitions, it was difficult for me to understand why there are not more adult women in the calypso tents. Denyse Plummer had the following thoughts on the matter:

> HMS: Do you think that in the junior competitions there's a dropout rate as you go along or do you think there will be more of a balance in the future?
> Denyse: No, I think there will always be less females than males, though there are a lot more now than in days gone by. So that's a good sign. You have to have plenty belly to be in this. Your shoulders have to broad and your skin have to be thick. Plenty belly—because everywhere you go it have someone bringing you down or talking you bad. Most of them smile and grin in your face and behind your back.... If you don't really love it you should get out.[59]

This is certainly a valid reason why all those promising schoolgirls lose interest in calypso as they get older. Pursuing music as a profession is not the same as excelling at music in school anywhere in the world. Finances are also a consideration; unless they have family resources, or a mentor or impresario who can support them financially as they launch a professional career, it is difficult to enter the more lucrative levels of competition or to successfully audition for a calypso tent.

However, things have definitely changed for the better. During the two decades I have been following the Trinidadian music scene, there has been a significant increase in venues for female calypsonians in Trinidad, including the junior calypso competitions. This has resulted in a dramatic increase in female representation in the Calypso Monarch competition. In 1998 Denyse Plummer was the only female participant in the Calypso Monarch finals; within several years, those numbers grew, with more representation from each year's Calypso Queen winners such as Maria Bhola and Monique Hector, and various young women who have come up through the junior calypso competitions, such as Heather McIntosh, Karene Asche, and Kizzie Ruiz. The 2009 Calypso Monarch finals included five women, more than any time in its history. Each year since then, there have typically been four or five women in the list of finalists for the competition.

In 2011 Karene Asche became the fourth woman to win the Calypso Monarch title. I first saw Asche perform in 1998; as that year's Junior Calypso Monarch she was invited to perform at the Calypso Queen competition. Her calypso was a strong commentary on absentee fathers entitled "Since You've Been Gone": "Since you've been gone, life's no longer the same / Since you've been gone, Mom hardly ever call your name / She losing weight, she hardly sleep . . . / Please tell me Dad when you coming back?" Asche won in 2011 with her entries "Be Careful What You Ask For" and "Uncle Jack." Like the women who had won the competition before her, Asche addressed topics that appealed to a large segment of Trinidad society. "Be Careful What You Ask For," composed by Errol Skeete, addressed several different topics, from domestic violence to critiques of racial tensions caused by the People's Partnership, the party that had won the previous year's general elections. The song compares choosing a new partner in love who turns out to be a monster, to choosing a new party in politics only to be greatly disappointed.[60] "Uncle Jack," composed by Christophe Grant, was an extended picong on Minister of Works and Transport, and former FIFA Vice President, Jack Warner. As Andrew Jennings observed, the calypso satirized Warner's "crimes against Trinidad's footballers, his racism, and the foolishness of giving him a government post where he can award public contracts."[61] During the FIFA scandal of 2015, Asche was planning to record a new version of the song that addressed Warner's involvement in that affair.[62]

Despite the cash prizes and recognition locally, calypso competitions are not especially lucrative financially. They do enable winners to gain local recognition for their work and provide a good chance that they will find ways to tour abroad. However, some could argue that the conservative context of calypso competitions makes it difficult to express the full range of experiences that might be pertinent to women performers and audiences. The next chapter explores the agency of women in soca and related genres, including various controversies they confront in this performance context. This will further demonstrate how musical change and innovation continue to expand the possibilities within expressive culture in Trinidad and Tobago.

4

Carnival Is Woman: Party Music and the Soca Diva

As I have demonstrated in previous chapters, changing musical styles in the context of Trinidad and Tobago's music scene accommodated greater diversity in musical practice and supported the efforts of new generations of musicians. This paralleled shifting attitudes and norms regarding gender roles, which allowed for gender diversity in various performance contexts. The purpose of this chapter is to examine how these changes have played out in soca music. As Denyse Plummer and other calypsonians have noted, party music is much more lucrative both during the Trinidad Carnival season and for obtaining work at other Carnival celebrations around the world. Soca music, as it has developed over time, created a new opening for women to participate in a style that is less conservative than other forms of calypso, and so allowed them to shape the music in ways that were meaningful to women both as performers and audiences. Although there are moral debates surrounding soca, which will be discussed below, in general soca and its offshoots have created platforms for expression by women performers that both are beneficial to them as artists and have fostered innovative change in the direction that the music has taken in recent decades. As I have noted in earlier chapters, Trinidad's musicians voice what audiences want to hear (or what they think audiences want to hear). In the case of soca, these topics include the joy found in dancing, sensuality, self-expression, self-enjoyment—topics that on the surface may not seem politically engaged, but carry great importance to both performers and audiences in a variety of contexts.

Due to the large populations of West Indians in North American cities, such as Toronto and New York, and in the British Isles, soca garners considerable international attention. Outside of Trinidad's Carnival, soca artistes are in demand at home and abroad in large-scale concert settings. Some of the more popular artists include Machel Montano, the Asylum Family led by Bunji Garlin and Fay-Ann Lyons, Destra Garcia, Denise Belfon, and Kes the Band. The Caribbean diaspora in North America and the UK tends to embrace soca as a key symbol of their homeland and its annual Carnival celebrations. In addition to Trinidad and Tobago, soca is also found in Barbados, Grenada, St. Vincent and the Grenadines, St. Lucia, Antigua, the French Antilles, particularly Martinique and Guadeloupe, and to a smaller extent, Jamaica. Since the eighties, soca has found success outside the West Indian market. Hit songs include "Hot Hot Hot," recorded by the singer Arrow (who was born in Montserrat), "Tiney Winey" by Byron Lee and the Dragonaires (who are from Jamaica), "Dollar Wine" by Colin Lucas, "Follow the Leader" by Soca Boys (originally recorded by Nigel and Marvin Lewis), and "Who Let the Dogs Out" by Baha Men (originally sung by Anselm Douglas). Some of the most successful soca artists in the Caribbean are from Barbados, including Alison Hinds, Rupee (Rupert Clark), and Biggie Irie (Carlton Cordle), all of whom are in demand in Trinidad as guest artists or competitors in the International Soca Monarch competition held every year on the "fantastic Friday" before Carnival. Despite its critics, soca has come to dominate the dance and party music of Carnival in the West Indies and its diaspora and has reached worldwide audiences wherever West Indians have settled.

As women have created a space for themselves in Carnival mas and at the fetes, a number of "soca divas" have emerged to give voice to female revelers. This and other historical trends in soca underscore the rapidly changing nature of the popular music scene in Trinidad. Particularly during the past two decades, these shifts have opened up spaces for female artists more plentiful than those discussed in previous chapters. They are also deeply controversial for a number of reasons, including the sexual nature of soca songs and performances, and the sheer commercial success of soca worldwide.

Like its parent genre calypso, soca is flexible in instrumentation, rhythmic framework, and musical form. The main feature that distinguishes soca from other styles of calypso is that it is intended to be an upbeat dance music that encourages audience participation and enjoyment. As a result, there tend to be far fewer verses than in other forms of calypso, and these verses tend to be shorter in length, usually four to eight lines. There is far more emphasis on call and response in chorus structures, to encourage audience participation when the songs are performed live. Generally speaking, the vocal line works as another instrument to enhance the polyrhythmic texture and groove of the musical arrangement (Dudley, 1996: 294).

Soca instrumentation for live performances feature the typical calypso brass band, which usually includes one or two saxophones, trumpets, and trombones. Over time, keyboard instruments have come to replace the horn lines, and some brass bands have no brass at all or band members regularly switch between brass and electronic instruments. The rhythm section of a soca band includes electric guitar, keyboards, drum set, and bass. As in reggae, the bass player plays a very active role in the ensemble. In general, there are a great number of rhythmic patterns being played by the same instrument (such as the drum set) or a group of instruments (the horn section, the rhythm section). In addition to the drum set player, soca bands tend to have at least one percussionist playing congas or other types of hand percussion. One or two keyboard players and the guitarist take up other percussive patterns, depending on the arrangement and/or the strengths of the musicians in the band. This produces an overall feel that is more rhythmically diverse than earlier incarnations of calypso. Of course, individual arrangers and bandleaders, who today include Roy Cape, Kernal Roberts (son of the late Lord Kitchener), Leston Paul, Errol Ince, Frankie McIntosh, Wayne Bruno, and Pelham Goddard, take different approaches to writing musical arrangements. Hence, there has typically been much diversity in the sound of soca music, as well as much musical change over time.

As one would expect, the music of today sounds quite different from the soca of the seventies. In the past forty years, there have been many stylistic changes, and older songs, such as "Endless Vibrations" and "Sugar Bum Bum" are regarded as "back in times music" (oldies). A turning point in soca's history came in the early nineties, by which time soca had become the most common form of music in Carnival fetes and the preferred form of music to accompany mas bands on Carnival Monday and Tuesday. The calypsonian Super Blue (Austin Lyons) won the Road March three years in a row with an energized form of soca that featured faster tempos, many instructions to dancers, and shorter call-and-response vocal phrases and melodic hooks. This "jump and wave" music came to dominate Carnival dance music in the nineties and beyond. Naturally, this led to critiques among fans of previous generations, who preferred the slower tempos of the older songs, and (somewhat ironically) felt that the jump and wave songs had lost their creativity in terms of lyrics.[1]

Today,[2] the musicians in soca bands are usually conversant in a wide range of popular dance music, from Caribbean styles such as reggae, dancehall, and reggaeton to North American genres such as rap and R&B. Soca singers either write songs themselves or in collaboration with the musical director of their bands. A typical soca song has a series of memorable choruses or choric lines that the audience can sing in response at appropriate times. Sometimes these hooks are local expressions (and this may be the actual title of the song): "Like Ah Boss," "Get On," "Ent," "Yeah Right," "Dust Dem," "Get to Hell Outa Here," "Palance," etc. In the more fast-paced songs, artists often seek to add a musical surprise in the arrangement. There might be a new musical bridge unrelated to previous material. In addition to original verses and choruses, it has become common to use quotations from preexisting musical sources. Material might be drawn from another popular song ("can you feel it, can you feel it, can you feel it," "every step you take, every move you make") or a children's game song ("there's a brown girl in the ring, tra la la la la"), and even old-time calypsos ("old lady walk a mile and half and she tailaylay"). Hooks and melodies from different types of popular songs are common, and help draw the audience further into the musical performance. Examples of this type of sampling or interpolation include two songs performed by Destra Garcia, and composed by Kernal Roberts: "It's Carnival" (interpolated from "Time After Time" by Cyndi Lauper) and "Bonnie and Clyde" (which uses the melody of the chorus from "Take On Me" by A-Ha). This practice of musical quotation is controversial, but seems to add to the success of particular soca songs, and is a type of homage common in many forms of music in the African diaspora.[3]

Throughout the nineties, further experimentation created new variations of soca music. Among these was chutney soca, which reformulated Shorty's vision of blending East Indian music and instruments such as the dholak and tassa with Afro-Creole musical expressions. Most of these artists are Indo-Trinidadians, and hence more accepted by the Indo-Trinidadian community. These performers include Rikki Jai, Sonny Mann, and Drupatee Ramgoonai. However, several Afro-Trinidadian singers have experimented with chutney soca, most notably Denyse Plummer, Black Stalin, Machel Montano, and Denise Belfon (Ramnarine, 2001; Manuel, 2006; Guilbault, 2007; Niranjana, 2008). By 1991 Jamaican dancehall had gained enormous popularity among Trinidadian youth, who called it "dub." As in its Jamaican counterpart, Trinidadian "dub" or "ragga" began with DJs such as Dr. Hyde and Chinese Laundry (Tony Chow Lin On), who played Jamaican dancehall at fetes and block parties in Trinidad in the early nineties. They also created mix cassettes that were distributed among fans or via pirate cassette vendors. Dr. Hyde Sounds produced Trinidad's first dancehall star, Curtis "General" Grant, who along with other artists participated in the widely successful Kisskidee Caravan concert series. By the end of the nineties, artists moved toward a sound that incorporated more aspects of Trinidadian soca, while still maintaining the Jamaican sound that audiences enjoyed. The term "ragga soca" is attributed to bandleader Byron Lee, who released a song by that name in 1996. Machel Montano and his band Xtatik featured a contrasting ragga section in their 1997 song "Big Truck," and it is thought they won the Road March that season because of this musical feature (Guilbault, 2007: 176). In 1998 Montano recorded "Toro Toro" with dancehall artist Shaggy, the first ragga soca hit featuring both Trinidadian and Jamaican artists. However, Byron Lee and Machel Montano were just dabbling in the style. Among the primary proponents of ragga soca during the past few decades have been Ghetto Flex (Hilton Dalzell), Maximus Dan (Edghill Thomas), Bunji Garlin (Ian Alvarez), and KMC (Ken Marlon Charles). Swagger, bravado, and aggressiveness of delivery are all hallmarks of the genre, and perhaps this is the reason that ragga soca is dominated by male performers. Among the few women creating ragga soca songs are Denise Belfon and Fay-Ann Lyons, whose careers will be discussed in detail below.

By 2007 several other styles of soca were recognized by performers and as categories in song competitions. Power soca refers to a style that has a very fast tempo (125 beats per minute or higher) with "command" lyrics that engage dancers with different dance instructions. This descendant of Super Blue's "jump and wave music" is what accompanies mas makers on the road march Carnival Monday and Tuesday. In this setting, music trucks follow alongside the mas bands with DJs or a soca band, along with soca singers sitting or standing on top, encouraging the revelers to wine, jump and wave, and show their enthusiasm, thus winning points with the judges. A contrasting style, called groovy soca, has a moderate tempo (80–120 beats per minute) with lyrics that address a variety of topics, from Carnival itself to romance and sexual interplay. Groovy soca has the ideal tempo for dancing with a partner at a fete, and this seems to be its intent; as one fan described it to me, groovy soca is for "love-making on the dance floor."

Soca lyrics tend to be as diverse as the musical arrangements that accompany them. The purpose of songs tends to be to create excitement in audiences through word and sound. Social commentary is not typically part of soca, though it is not unknown.[4] Some songs are about how to enjoy oneself at Carnival, focusing on the celebration, its various fetes and parties, and the freedom from ordinary, day-to-day life that the season affords. Some songs teach revelers a specific dance or give them a set of dance instructions.[5] Some are boasts about the singer's dancing ability.[6] Some compare dancing to sex, or express sexual desire for another person as he or she dances.[7] As with the parent genre calypso, there are numerous songs about women and descriptions of their bodies, particularly the waist and bottom.[8]

Critiques of soca lyrics take several forms. The first type questions the morality of the lyrics, saying there is far too much emphasis on "smut" and "filth." A second type of debate focuses on what critics regard as insufficient or uninteresting lyrical content. The lyrics are too scanty to be called "true kaiso"—what few lyrics there are amount to little more than dance instructions such as jump and wave, wine and jam, hold on to the bumper: "there is no lyrical quality and deep insight."[9] Soca artists are thus accused of diminishing the narrative power and storytelling skills of the calypso art form, and of creating a mass-produced product designed to last no longer than the current Carnival season (Guilbault, 2007: 190–91).

A third type of debate centers on the changing form of the music, the seemingly disposable nature of each season's songs, and how audiences will settle for "fast food" when artists could be producing more substantial and creatively interesting music. This is often related to the way soca music sounds on studio recordings. Because songs have to be produced quickly and inexpensively to ensure radio airplay by the start of the Carnival season,[10] many arrangers use electronic keyboards, drum machines, and other digital technology in place of brass players and drummers. Recently, certain producers have moved toward creating riddims, as in the Jamaican dancehall scene, to which a number of vocalists will record their songs for the season.[11] However, in live performance, soca is quite different. In the fetes, soca singers are backed by a full band, and can freely alter the structure of their musical performances as they desire. The frenzy of the crowd inspires the singers to improvise new choruses and to command new dance moves to match the energy of the crowd. The result is an intense call-and-response musical arrangement that helps people do and feel the same thing at the same time: to have the same experience and sense of community through a continually unfolding musical structure. Thus, one could say that soca music really exists in performance, and that sound recordings are merely a way for audiences to become familiar with the songs before they experience them in a live performance setting.

Most who view Carnival from abroad see it represented in formal events such as calypso tents and the main competitions that are staged in the Grand Savannah at the climax of the season. For many Trinidadians, however, the real heart of Carnival are the many fetes that begin on Boxing Day and run right up through Carnival weekend. Throughout the history of Carnival, there have been balls, dances, and parties during the season that represented different segments of society, with distinctions based primarily on class and social rank. Likewise in contemporary Trinidad, there are different kinds of fetes for different kinds of people; along with class and social rank, fetes are distinguished by community ties, age, location, price, amenities, and so forth. For younger people with fewer responsibilities, Carnival fetes are a way of life and they will attend as many fetes as possible during the Carnival season (Balliger, 2001: 152–53). A number of fetes cater to this population, the most popular being "cooler fetes" that allow attendees to bring their own coolers packed with ice and drinks and pay a relatively low admission fee.[12] Some fetes are sponsored by businesses to show appreciation for their employees and support for local arts and culture; these too are on the affordable side. On the other end of the spectrum are "all-inclusive" parties where the admission price includes all food and drinks for the evening. These are held at nightclubs and restaurants that cater to a more mature, middle- to upper-class clientele that can afford a higher admission price. All-inclusive Carnival fetes are organized by educational institutions such as Queen's Royal College and Bishop Anstey High School, and there is usually a large all-inclusive fete at the University of the West Indies early in the Carnival season that benefits the university's endowment fund.[13] At the high end are very posh VIP parties that cater to the upper classes and tourists with plenty of money to spend.[14] There are even fetes for children, such as Nikkiland, the all-inclusive hosted by comedienne Nikki Crosby.[15]

Interestingly, the most popular soca artists appear at every sort of fete, moving from one to the next in the same day or evening to appear before varying types of audiences. While the attendees are often divided by various distinctions, the artists generally do not turn down appearing at any event at which they are requested to perform, unless time restrictions would make things unfeasible. At fetes both at home and abroad, it is quite common for a number of soca singers and their bands to be featured, and there are usually a number of fetes each day leading up to Carnival Monday and Tuesday. With the rising popularity of daytime fetes and boat cruises, it is not unusual for soca artists to perform five or six shows per day during the season. The success of soca singers depends on both their vocal talents and their physical stamina, as keeping up such a performing schedule is very demanding. Soca artists contribute a great deal to the success of these fetes, and must have an excellent rapport with audiences, because revelers follow the energy of the singers and their bands, and vice versa. As I soon learned, the experience of soca music at a Carnival fete is quite different from that in a calypso tent. Today's calypso tents require attendees to stay in their assigned seats unless they are going to the bar or heading outside to lime with friends or to make a phone call. While party songs are part of the bill of fare, one must sit through other performances that are more didactic. As I indicated in chapter 2, the tents have the feel of a variety show, and thus there are lulls in energy and excitement, especially on an off night.[16] For most participants, fetes are more enjoyable because audience participation is built into these events. While the lyrics often are not profound, musical arrangements are usually tight and energetic, because revelers do not tolerate disruptions in the flow of sound. For this reason, fetes typically include DJs playing prerecorded music before the live performances begin.

At my first fete in Trinidad, which took place just after All-Years Night 1998, I was a bit confused because the bands seemed to be playing a small percentage of tunes written by the musicians in the band. Instead, they alternated between their own songs and the big hits of the season, whatever they happened to be. From my own experience, I knew that radio airplay is what brings these songs to the minds and bodies of Carnival revelers, but I soon learned that the fetes also drive the songs to success. Over the course of the season, soca bands and their singers seek to discover what music will drive audiences wild. By the middle of the season, musicians will have a good idea of which songs will bring out ecstatic crowd response, and the musicians situate these songs strategically throughout their sets. For example, the main band at my first Carnival fete was Blue Ventures, led by Ronnie McIntosh. The band warmed up the crowd by playing half a set of the season's hits. Then the individual front-line singers performed the solo songs they had recorded for the Carnival season that they would carry to the Soca Monarch and Road March competitions. Ronnie McIntosh's main song for the season was "How It Go Look," but he also sang some of his previous hits, including "Ent?!"—a song that had won him the Soca Monarch competition the previous year. He shared the stage with other singers such as Sanelle Dempster, who went on to win the Road March competition in 1999 with "The River." Blue Ventures continued with songs they had written for the season, along with the repertoire of other bands getting major airplay that Carnival, such as "Who Let the Dogs Out" by Anselm Douglas[17] " and "Footsteps," by Wayne Rodriguez, which became the 1998 Road March winner. As I went on to attend larger fetes, I noticed that there might be more than one band, for example Roy Cape All Stars and Atlantik, but the singers seemed to be relatively interchangeable, and again each band performed the popular songs of the season along with their original material. At the time, this seemed to be the normative state not only for soca music in Trinidad, but throughout the Caribbean music scene. In many cases, it was the hit songs rather than particular musicians that audiences wanted to hear. I have followed the scene for many years now, and it has become much more driven by front-line singers than in the past. This has allowed successful soca singers to move more freely from one band to another; in a number of cases they have gone on to form their own bands centered around their particular personalities and performance styles.[18]

Most fetes take several hours to really get going, and once they do one gets caught up in the volume and intensity of the music, the pushing of limits to keep up with the driving beat of the band's rhythm section, and the relentless encouragement by soca singers to express oneself in "jumping," "waving," and "wining." Wining was one of the first things I had to learn about enjoying a

Carnival fete. Familiar to anyone who has visited the Caribbean or a West Indian nightclub in North America or the UK, this is a rather sensual style of dancing that emphasizes gyrations of the hips and waist. Although I never became very good at it, the highest compliment was when my Trinidadian friends said, "You got the flavor now." At fetes, one typically sees many different kinds of wining, the most erotic of which is men wining on women from the back. This type of wining, like many dances in the Caribbean and Latin America, is clearly "the vertical expression of a horizontal desire."[19] Whether or not that desire is consummated depends on the individuals in question; allegedly, many "Carnival babies" are born every year. However, platonic friends or relatives might do a more chaste type of wining while facing each other. Women wine on other women, or wine on their own on stationary objects or open air. Thus, wining does not necessarily mean the beginnings of a sexual encounter, despite the erotic aspects of the dance. For women in particular, "the object in wining is in most cases really themselves. It is an expression of a free sexuality which has no object but itself, and most especially it is a sexuality not dependent on men" (Miller, 1991: 333).

Wining has met with a great deal of ambivalence in the press and by the public, particularly as certain people seem to be determined to go over the limit at Carnival time and in full view of television and newspaper cameras: "I don't know which aspect of a fete causes people to do strange, crazy things. Not quite sure if it is the music (Last week Friday in Brass Festival, Knycky Cordner was quoted as saying 'We on TV6. Let we show them how nasty we could get on'). Is it the alcohol? The same that was sold at the Youth Fest! What about the environment? We may never actually know what is the real cause. It could even be a breakdown of values in the family."[20]

When I first started going to nightclubs and fetes in Trinidad, I was somewhat conflicted about how to feel and react. However, as I became more comfortable and enthusiastic as a participant-observer at these events, I realized that fetes were an important release for participants, particularly Trinidadian women. These events acted in much the same way as in dancehall culture in Jamaica. As Carolyn Cooper asserts:

> Jamaican dancehall culture at home and in the diaspora is best understood as a potentially liberating space in which working-class women and their more timid middle-class sisters assert the freedom to play out eroticized roles that may not ordinarily be available to them in the rigid confines of the everyday. The dancehall, thus conceived, is an erogenous zone in which the celebration of female sexuality and fertility is ritualized. In less subtle readings of the gender politics of the dancehall, this self-conscious female assertion of control over the representation

of the body (and identity) is misunderstood and the therapeutic potential of the dancing body is repressed. Indeed, the joyous display of the female body in the dance is misperceived as a pornographic devaluation of woman. (Cooper, 2004: 17)

Today, wining meets with less ambivalence than it did in earlier time periods. As journalist Lisa Allen-Agostini observes, "wining, which was once jamette behaviour, is not only acceptable now, it's celebrated."[21] Calypsonian the Mighty Chalkdust (Dr. Hollis Liverpool), who once sang about how soca had put "Kaiso Sick in Hospital," recently explained how wining is part of the nation's African heritage: "the basics that give rise to wining were brought here by our enslaved African brothers and sisters and developed as an art, as it were, on our plantations and early carnivals.... Wining is in reality a dance movement that Trinidadians have fine-tuned and given to the rest of the countries that have adopted our style of carnival. It is a trait that many would describe as sensual and erotic. At the same time, it is filled with many historical meanings that essay our people's aspirations, desires, and sufferings."[22] Despite the party atmosphere of soca songs, I have heard a number of fans and newspaper columnists comment on how they find soca to be more "wholesome" than the music coming from North America and Jamaica.[23] In most cases, wining is somewhat tame compared to certain performances of Jamaican dancehall queens or North American singers who "twerk" or imitate strip teases or lap dancing in their musical performances. That does not mean that there are not critiques regarding revelers who go too far, but there is considerably more acceptance regarding wining today, with most people agreeing that it is an inevitable and enjoyable part of the dance culture of the Caribbean.

Soca artists have a different job to do compared to other types of calypsonians. They are essentially the choreographers of the fete, and they are expected to inspire their audiences to enjoy themselves to the utmost. The music is meant to bring people to the climax of "free up" and "breakaway," and this affects the musical structure and lyrics of the songs they perform. As noted above, the tempo in soca music tends to be moderate to fast, the rhythms energetic, and the melodies catchy and memorable. Lyrics tend to focus on the liberation revelers experience through various aspects of Carnival, including finding a nice-looking person to wine on. In many songs, the passion achieved through dancing is a metaphor for sex, usually expressed through double entendres such as "wet me down" and "rock your body." Both female and male soca singers are expected to be flashy and energetic onstage. Female singers such as Destra Garcia and Denise Belfon dress provocatively and "wine down to the ground" onstage, and their male counterparts are "winer boys" like Machel Montano,

Kees Dieffenthaller, and Shurwayne Winchester. Similar performance standards apply to both female and male soca artists.

It was obvious that the women in the audience identify with female soca artists, and see them as setting an example of how to interact with men in the fete and everyday life. Despite critiques (mostly from members of the clergy) in the newspapers about how some of the more saucy "winer women" displayed themselves onstage, the comments of my friends on their enjoyment of these performances made me realize that they were getting something powerful out of them. Perhaps it was the example of a woman expressing her desire in public forum, and how they could do the same if they chose. Or perhaps it was how the sensual atmosphere of the Carnival fete was enhanced by seeing a powerful woman onstage, issuing a challenge to a man in the audience by bringing him onstage to attempt to "wine down" with her, a standard feature of soca fetes both in Trinidad and in the Caribbean diaspora. Soca divas represent strong and independent women, in control of the microphone, the stage, and their self-representation. Dance competitions between singers and men (or women) brought on stage are sensuous/sexual. But they are also humorous, playful, and for the female as much about self-pleasuring as letting a man get a thrill by taking a wine on them.

Soca Monarch is one of the main competitions for soca artists during Carnival. There has been a separate Soca Monarch competition since 1993, and unlike the state-run Calypso Monarch competitions, Soca Monarch has always been privately sponsored (Guilbault, 2007: 175). Currently it is an international competition, open to soca artists from any country, and is hosted by the Caribbean Prestige Foundation with financial support from various corporate enterprises. Since 2005 the competition has been divided into two categories, Power Soca and Groovy Soca. Recently, the competition has taken on the flavor of television show *American Idol*, and fans both at the event and at home are able to vote for their favorite competitors via mobile phone and social media. Whereas judges make the final decision regarding the competition's winners, the winner of the audience voting earns the title of Breakout Artiste of the Year.[24] While the main purpose of the Soca Monarch finals, which usually occur on Fantastic Friday of the weekend before Carnival, is to choose the top soca artists of the season, many invited guests add to the variety of the event. There is always a "back in time" element created by appearances by older artists such as the Mighty Sparrow, Calypso Rose, and other calypsonians who were pioneers in the early days of soca. Some soca artists are so popular that even if they are not among that year's competitors, they are typically invited to perform as guests. Such artists include Destra Garcia, Denise Belfon, and Alison Hinds. The winners of the National Schools

Soca Monarch, which has categories for primary and secondary school competitors, usually appear as guest artists as well.[25]

For the audience, the experience is designed to be a cross between a fete and a sporting competition, with sections of the audience waving their flags for their favorite competitors. Crowd response is counted as 10 percent of the final score for competitors, so it is important for soca artists to create audience enthusiasm. As the years have gone by, the musical aspects of the performances have been enhanced—some say overshadowed—by various elements designed to create excitement and visual impact, such as dance choreography, stage antics, costumes, sets, and various special effects such as fireworks and explosions. Several performers have spent as much as TT$300,000 (US$50,000) for their stage presentations for Soca Monarch finals.[26] Since audiences have come to expect a large spectacle, finalists are allocated funds to help assist them in their stage presentations, and the promoters fill the venue with video display screens, light shows, and live sound equipment run by a large crew of technicians. As noted above, soca artists improvise freely on their musical arrangements, adding new verses and choruses to encourage massive audience participation and enthusiasm.

The last two days of the season, Carnival Monday and Tuesday, is when the Parade of Bands is held, and mas makers and other revelers take to the street. The atmosphere of the fete is mobilized, as mas bands hire music trucks to accompany their parade and entertain spectators. Until recently, live bands accompanied mas bands, and lead singers would ride on the top of the music trucks, commanding revelers to "jump up," "take a wine," "free up," "breakaway," "charge," "get on bad," and "make bacchanal." These artists are analogous to the old-time chantwells who led their Carnival bands through the streets in call and response lavways. Recently, DJs have almost entirely replaced live bands on the road, although some soca singers still perform to prerecorded accompaniment at various stages along the Parade of Bands. This is largely to encourage the display of the mas makers, but it also creates a fete atmosphere for those enjoying the spectacle from the sidelines. The most popular songs are played incessantly on the road to accompany the various mas bands, and a clear winner emerges for the Road March title, the people's choice award given to the song played most frequently at the judging stands along the Carnival parade route. Today women play mas in far greater numbers than men and have considerable influence on what their music trucks are playing, and thus an impact on each year's Road March title. Pertinent to this study is the fact that these women masqueraders have chosen a female artist as their Road March champion four times in the time span 1999–2015: Sanelle Dempster in 1999 (the first time a woman had won since Calypso Rose in 1978) and Fay-Ann Lyons in 2003, 2008, and 2009. Like her father Super Blue, Fay-Ann Lyons continues to dominate the local music scene, and she and her husband Bunji Garlin are among the most successful soca artists internationally.

The female calypsonians discussed in earlier chapters are the direct ancestors of today's "soca divas," who include Fay-Ann Lyons, Destra Garcia, Denise Belfon, Alison Hinds, Sanelle Dempster, Patrice Roberts, Nadia Batson, and a number of emerging artists now coming through the ranks of the National Schools Soca Monarch competitions. In the interviews I have read or conducted with female soca artists, Calypso Rose is the woman most frequently cited as an important influence.[27] It would not be a stretch to say that Rose was the first soca diva, a fact she herself emphasized with her CD of the same name in 1994. Soca tunes were, after all, were what helped her win her Road March titles in 1977 and 1978. "Give Me More Tempo" and "Come Leh We Jam," both written in collaboration with Pelham Goddard, are infectious soca tunes that express the joy of Carnival revelry and dancing to the special Trinidadian beat and tempo, and clearly influenced the direction dance music took during the late seventies and early eighties. Denyse Plummer has competed in Soca Monarch a number of times, and many of her entries in Calypso Monarch entries are uptempo songs that encourage audience participation ("Woman Is Boss," "Carnival Queen"). Her stage presence and delivery have also been influential on the direction that female artists took in later generations. As she expressed in an interview with Peter Mason, "if you are to get work twelve months of the year, then you must have a party song" (Mason, 1998: 141). This diversity can facilitate radio airplay, getting work during Carnival season, and possibilities to get work at the other carnivals and West Indian celebrations after Trinidad Carnival concludes.

Until the nineties most soca artists were men, and thus expressed things from a male point of view. Many songs of the time period express sexual desire for women, and praise the beauty of their bodies, particularly their backsides. Yet even in songs that are somewhat explicit sexually, such as Lord Shorty's "The Art of Making Love," the woman's role is equally important in the equation and the man must see to her pleasure. Kitchener's "Sugar Bum Bum" and the Mighty Duke's "This Bumsie is Mine" are classic examples of "bottom" songs, but in both cases, one gets the sense that the woman is being praised and valued rather than denigrated.[28] These songs are decidedly different from Sparrow's "Village Ram" or Duke's "Woop-Wap Man." In certain soca songs, the object of desire is not necessarily specified, and the singer is happy to just be in the company of other revelers, such as in "Somebody" recorded by Baron (Timothy Watkins).

As noted in chapter 2, female backup singers and dancers were increasingly part of calypso performance in the seventies and eighties. As soca became popular, these female artists were situated to move to the front of the band in the nineties. As Jocelyne Guilbault notes, this was influenced by the growing prominence of women in reggae, dancehall, zouk, and rap (Guilbault, 2007: 175). This went hand in hand with increased female presence in Carnival in general, and it became apparent that revelers wanted a female voice to represent their experience. For many years the main force behind music for the fetes was the musical directors of various bands, which at the time I was doing my fieldwork included Blue Ventures, Roy Cape All-Stars, Imij & Co., Invazion, Xtatik, Atlantik, Rukshun, Square One, and Charlie's Roots. While most front-line singers had been men, by the nineties band leaders were realizing that audiences at the fetes were dominated by women, and they needed to include at least one woman in their group of singers in order to ensure their economic survival. Typically, singers had to conform to a certain standard, particularly in terms of physical attractiveness and stamina: as one former soca artist commented to me, "the image was to be extremely sexy and extremely fit."[29] If a singer had a breakout hit during a particular season, better offers from other bands might come along and that singer might be performing with another band the following Carnival season. However, singers could also be let go, and I noticed that some bands would change their front-line singers each season, especially if they wanted to introduce younger, more physically attractive talent. This was particularly difficult for female artists, who as they aged or started a family became less physically fit and hence less employable. While many bands continue to emphasize youth and sexuality in their singers, both male and female, they have also served as starting points for artists to establish their careers and then move on to solo work, as the examples later in this chapter illustrate.

By the time I conducted my initial research in 1998–99, there were a number of female participants in Soca Monarch, and the same is true in 2015. However, the soca scene changes very quickly; of the five women who competed at the International Soca Monarch in 1998, only one competed in 2015: Nikki Crosby, primarily known as a comedienne, who performed a power soca tune called "Go Granny" in the comedic persona of Hott Mouth Granny. Denyse Plummer now performs a more relaxed version of her party tunes, and Marcia Miranda has helped develop a party-oriented Christmas music called parang soca. Melanie Hudson now lives in London and has a successful career in musical theatre under her married name Melanie La Barrie. Rachel "Shanaqua" Fortune, who earlier in her career sang with Machel Montano, now concentrates on more conscious forms of local music, including the

Emancipation Day calypso competition, and on recording pan tunes. Likewise, the only man from the 1998 Soca Monarch competition who competed in 2015 was Neil "Iwer" George, who along with Super Blue is considered one of the elder statesmen of the soca scene.

When I was doing my initial fieldwork, the most successful, and controversial, female soca artist in Trinidad was Denise Belfon, whose nickname "Saucy Wow" referred to the sensuality of her stage presentations. Belfon was performing in the Spektakula Forum calypso tent and as a guest artist at various fetes, in duet with ragga soca artist Ghetto Flex (Hilton Dalzell). The previous year, Belfon had taken the legal advice to refrain from explicit onstage wining to her song "Hard Wuk" so as not to be charged with a lewd public performance (Mason, 1998: 144). However, in many ways, Belfon's career, and resulting controversy, closely parallel those of the women profiled in the previous chapter, particularly Calypso Rose. She was discovered in 1990 when she appeared in La Reine Rive, the finals of the Best Village Competition. Roy Cape, who was directing the band that night, brought her to the attention of Tony Estrada, and she became the new female vocalist for Sound Revolution.[30] Just like Rose, Belfon says she had to live up to the image set by the other front-line singers in her band, including Colin Lucas, who developed the erotic "Dollar Wine" dance: "I just look at what Colin Lucas and Derek Seales were doing and say this is what I have to do." Thus were the origins of Belfon's now infamous bicycle wine, tremble "juk," and other ribald behavior such as whip licks and spanking.[31] Belfon's first big hit was a song called "Kakalaylay," in which she instructs women in the art of wining: "When de horn men blow / We going down low, low, low, low / Kaka laylay yuh bam bam / Kaka laylay, kaka laylay."

After giving birth to her children, Belfon decided to go back to performing, despite being thirty pounds heavier than when she started her career with Sound Revolution. Her decision to continue to wine despite being a heavy woman increased her appeal among female fans. When I first saw Belfon perform at Spektakula Forum, she was performing a passionate duet with ragga soca artist Ghetto Flex called "Rock Yuh Body," which like many songs throughout Trinidad's history compared dancing to lovemaking all night long. During the song, Belfon demonstrated some of her more infamous dance moves, including one called "the bicycle," which some conservative critics felt went over the line in terms of bodily display. One of the most frequent questions I asked of various music fans and musical artists was their reaction to Denise Belfon's stage choreography. Denyse Plummer had the following thoughts: "Well, they always ask me about Denise Belfon's behavior onstage. I say, if that's how she gets the money to feed her children and pay her bills, she gotta do it! Because while all us quarreling she laughing all the way to the bank. I cannot condemn her, though I don't do that myself."[32] Belfon often comments that her songs are sung for the women in the audience: "People are always amazed at how a woman my size could move so I think a lot of women respect me for that."[33] I found this was the case with the young people who enjoyed her performances; young woman commented to me, "she shows a big woman could wine and bubble."

I still have some of the videos from the Spektakula Forum, as well as other performances by Denise Belfon that other fans have shared with me on the Internet. Looking back at Belfon's dances, they are far more playful and humorous than I remembered. As Maude Dikobe notes in her own analysis of Belfon's performances, "Denise differentiates between offering herself to a male audience as a sexual object, and celebrating her own sexual power" (Dikobe, 2004: 9). Moreover, despite the criticism, Belfon gives voice to sexual desire that had previously been the domain of male singers; and like Calypso Rose, Belfon has presented various gender themes in calypso from the woman's point of view. For example, Belfon wrote and performed "Looking for an Indian Man" during the 2004 season at both the Soca Monarch and Chutney Soca Monarch competitions. The song is clearly an answer to the many calypsos by male singers who sing about their desire for an Indian woman (Niranjana, 2006: 212): "Tonight I looking for an Indian man / Yes, I calling for an Indian man / I want you hold on me and jam / Inside the session."

Like many of her contemporaries, Denise Belfon always emphasizes in her newspaper interviews that she is a responsible wife and mother, and that she prays before every performance.[34] Her Carnival act is just that: an act that is a means of providing for her family the rest of the year. Thus, journalists and feminist scholars tend to be sympathetic and even enthusiastic about singers like Belfon who display themselves as strong female presences on stage.[35] There is a double standard in the soca business; one does not see the same sort of articles about male artists regarding responsible parenting. As in previous generations, female artists must be above reproach when offstage, whereas male artists typically are not subject to the same sort of scrutiny.

When I had the opportunity to interview Denise Belfon in 2011, she emphasized some of these issues herself.[36] She said that when she began her career, it was very difficult because she was one of the few females in the business, and people were not ready for the kind of entertainment that she was doing at the time. "I received ridicule and disrespect for the way that I gyrated. Also, women especially felt very insecure: they thought that their men were watching and think that I go take their man. Now women understand that I am not a family disrupter. They ask if know where I could open a school to learn to dance like me. . . . because I bring out a side of them they wish they could express in public. But they could take that to the bedroom and experiment with their husband." She also emphasized how her fans are the most exciting aspect of her career as an entertainer: "The feeling of creating songs and delivering them and being able to entertain gives me an adrenaline rush that is more rewarding than the nice house and car that comes from being a successful entertainer."

Belfon acknowledged to me, as well as in interviews with journalists, that she was gradually changing how she presented her songs, and redirecting some of her energies toward mentoring her own children, all of whom showed interest in music and dance, and other young people from her neighborhood who looked to her for guidance. Her daughters Shaquilla and Cassandra were assisting Belfon with designing a children's carnival band, called Poise: "Poise is about everything that is beautiful and graceful. And that is what children are."[37] Thus, even as we discussed some of the more controversial aspects of her performance career, Belfon returned to her values as a strong mother figure, and a positive role model for people of all ages. As an early soca diva, Belfon clearly continues to inspire the latest generation of female artists.

At the Soca Monarch finals, in any given year at least half the finalists are women. The introduction of the groovy soca category in the competition has also facilitated the participation of female artists, since many of them prefer to sing slower tempo songs. In fact, the first groovy soca monarch competition in 2005 was won by Michelle Sylvester, whose winning tune "Sleeping in Your Bed" continued the theme of songs such as "What She Go Do": "Somebody sleeping in your bed . . . / You want to know when? / You want to know how? / Well this is a taste of your own medicine and I sure that you go catch yourself now."

Other developments in the soca music business have also benefited female artists. Over the past decade, there has been a general trend toward popular soca singers taking control of their own careers by forming their own bands, an example first set by Machel Montano and Xtatik and adopted by a number of other singers, both male and female, since that time. In terms of female artists, as of 2015 the two top female soca artists were Destra Garcia and Fay-Ann Lyons, both of whom had established enormously successful solo careers both in Trinidad and Tobago and abroad. Both were the lead singers of their own bands (Lyons in partnership with her husband Bunji Garlin), with whom they tour the Caribbean and North America after Carnival is over.

Destra Garcia: Queen of Bacchanal

Destra Garcia's career trajectory is typical of the current generation of calypso and soca artists. Destra[38] comes from a musical family; both her grandfather Frankie Garcia and her father Lloyd Garcia were accomplished musicians who played with various dance bands. Destra Garcia started singing at the age of ten, and like many musical artists her age she is a product of the Junior Calypso Monarch competitions. She won her school's calypso monarch competition five times with songs of her own composition, and was a finalist in both the NCC Junior Monarch competition and several NJAC junior calypso competitions. By the time she was fifteen Destra was working as a vocalist for the recording studio Caribbean Sound Basin, recording her first album of R&B standards at age seventeen. In 1999 she recorded the lead vocal for "Ah Have Ah Man Already" for soca artist Third Bass. This recording brought her to the attention of bandleader Roy Cape, who asked her to audition to be one of his band's front-line singers. In 2000, at age twenty-two, she became the first female lead vocalist for Roy Cape All Stars, replacing departing lead singer Kurt Allen.[39] Destra quickly became a hit with audiences, as Roy Cape is one of the most influential bandleaders in contemporary Trinidad and Tobago; in 2001 she placed fourth in the Soca Monarch competition with the song she was performing that season with Roy Cape, "Tremble It." This song is a typical "rag tune," in which the singer encourages audience participation by waving the hand towels nearly all fete goers carry to wipe off the sweat from dancing as well to express their energy and joy when they are enjoying a good soca performance: "Yes, we come out to fete / Tremble up your rag until you work up a sweat / We waving until we mad, mad, mad / We behaving bad."

In 2002 Destra left Roy Cape All Stars, and joined the band Atlantik, then led by Ronnie McIntosh and Cliff Harris. She also released her first solo album *Red, White, and Black*, an unusually bold move for a female soca artist at the time. On this CD, Destra began a long-lasting collaboration with Kernal Roberts, the son of Lord Kitchener. This CD featured a duet with Machel Montano called "It's Carnival," which has remained one of her most enduringly popular songs.[40] On her 2005 release *Laventille*, Destra collaborated with David Rudder on a remake of "The Hammer," with which Rudder had won Calypso Monarch in 1986:

> "The song is almost 20 years old, and would have debuted when I was a little girl," she recalls. "Rudolph Charles was considered a role model in the community of Laventille, and the work he did with the band always filled everyone with a sense of unity and pride. When he died, the entire community was grieving, and the song

was very uplifting. I just thought, with all the crime and everything that has been going on in Laventille, I could revisit something that filled them with a sense of joy, and prove to the youth that there is still something in Laventille to be proud of."[41]

Destra's energetic performance style is often compared with that of Denise Belfon's saucy stage presence. Maude Dikobe goes so far as to call Destra a "sophisticated jammette" because she emphasizes her slim body and designer outfits in her interviews. Yet "in spite of her sexy outfits, seductive wining, and suggestive lyrics, she has (unlike Belfon) managed to remain within the limits of 'respectable' female performance in Trinidad" (Dikobe, 2004: 12). Destra herself has not ignored the inevitable comparisons with Belfon. She agrees that her own abilities are quite different than those of Belfon: "It's so easy for somebody like Saucy to control a wining tune," Destra says. "For me it's much easier to do a rag tune.[42] That's like second nature. But with a wining tune ... I mean, I pull it off ... but it's not easy to do." In the same interview, Destra notes that female soca artists may be interpreted in opposing ways by male and female fans: "Carnival is fun and the music lets you have a good time. All year round you're under stress, you're working eight-to-four. Carnival is about freeing your mind. This is our culture. I did not create this. So I am not ashamed of what it says ... wining, waving, whatever. But it all goes back to order. Yes the music might send a message to men but I also send a message that as women we have to be positive, strong, focused."[43]

As with other artists discussed earlier in this book, Destra also stresses her deep and abiding faith in God and family. Like Calypso Rose, she has recorded inspirational music in addition to the Carnival songs for which she is best known. "Yes you see me wining on stage, but I am nothing without God. God is very much a part of everything I do. You have to believe in something. For me, that is Jesus Christ."[44]

Several fans I have talked with compare Destra to R&B artist Beyoncé, probably because both performers are among the most visible and outspoken women in their respective genres, and place strong emphasis on fashion and glamour both onstage and off. During the 2009 season the comparison was inevitable due to Destra's decision to perform Beyoncé's "Single Ladies" in the fetes that year. However, Destra has also noted that Beyoncé is not able to wine like a Caribbean woman: "It's in our blood. Nobody can take that from us."[45] Thus, rather than seeing Destra capitulating to the whims of the music industry, I feel that she simply hears in the message "all the single ladies, put your hands up" the same kind of command lyrics that are a standard feature of the soca songs she writes herself, and knows it is a message with which Trinidadian women easily relate.

One achievement that has eluded Destra so far is winning either the Soca Monarch competition or the Road March. She took a hiatus from the Soca Monarch competition from 2005 to 2009, though she was frequently an invited guest. Destra gave birth to her daughter Xaiya in 2010, which kept her from performing during Carnival that year. She returned to the stage in 2011; at this point she had taken over the leadership of Atlantik and was now in a position to have full creative control over her career.[46] In late 2013, Destra renamed the band Bakanal, sharing front-line vocals with Olatunji Yearwood and Stuart Silva. In 2015 Destra was one of four artists who gave solo concerts during the season.[47] Entitled House of Bakanal, the concert was held on Carnival Wednesday, and featured guest appearances by various artists with whom Destra has collaborated, including Denise Belfon and Bajan soca artist Alison Hinds.

These and other achievements have made Destra one of the biggest soca stars in Trinidad and Tobago. Like most popular soca artists, Destra was a strong presence at the Carnivals and fetes that take place during the spring and summer months following Carnival in Trinidad, including Carifesta in Toronto and Crop Over in Barbados.

Soca Runs in the Family: Fay-Ann Lyons

In terms of awards and similar recognition, the most successful and celebrated female soca artist is Fay-Ann[48] Lyons, three-time winner of the Road March competition[49] and the first woman to win the power soca division of the International Soca Monarch competition.[50] It was probably inevitable that the daughter of two famous calypsonians, who was born in 1980, would enter the profession herself. Fay-Ann's mother is Lady Gypsy (Lynette Steele), who herself is from a musical family and is the sister of the calypsonian Gypsy (Winston Peters). Fay-Ann's father is Super Blue (Austin Lyons, formerly known as Blue Boy), the most celebrated soca artist of all time. Fay-Ann's younger sister, Terri Lyons, is also a soca singer. As with many young singers, Fay-Ann got her start in the Junior Monarch circuit; her main advantage was that her parents were able to provide expert assistance as she found her voice as a singer and songwriter. As her father recalled in an interview for Trinidad Express writer Nazma Muller:

> She came to me with a book. I ent know she writing all dem songs—a setta songs. So she wrote the songs and I put the melody to it. I say, I don't want to rush you into it. So we start and I showing her what to do. She start to say, My dream is to

be Junior Road March (Monarch). I say [laughing], It have Trinidad and Tobago to beat—not me! I say, I will write your first song. Then try to teach allyuh the best way I could. The way to show allyuh the assets are. I will get the first fish and then teach you how to fish—how to bait your hook. How to fish for life. Where to fish. You can't go in a swimming pool to fish. You have to follow your instinct because you trying thing that was never done before just to get ahead.[51]

By her early twenties, Fay-Ann had forged a career for herself as a soca artist, performing as one of the front-line singers for the band Invazion. In 2003 she became the youngest person to win the Road March competition with her song "Display." Like her father's road march "Get Something and Wave," Fay-Ann commands her audience to show their flags and colors: "I want to see everyone put up something to beautify."

In 2006 Fay-Ann married Bunji Garlin (Ian Alvarez), one of the originators of the ragga soca style and who, along with Super Blue, Iwer George, and Machel Montano has dominated the International Soca Monarch competition. Fay-Ann chose to join her husband's group, renamed the Asylum Family Band, thus reinstituting the custom of husband-and-wife teams in calypso music.

Unlike Destra or Denise, I have hardly ever heard the words "sexy" or "saucy" applied to Fay-Ann. In her own words, "I am a tomboy and will be a little rougher than some females. I am addicted to jeans and must own more than 50 different pairs." For this reason, she has been complimented by older calypsonians for her performance style and lack of vulgarity.[52] Fay-Ann's style of singing often reflects an influence from ragga soca, including chanting and rapping that is quite different from most other female soca artists. "Yes, Bunji influences me artistically, but that is very limited. I believe that the Lord give you a talent and you're supposed to explore it to the fullest; not just limit yourself to doing one thing."[53] Her ability to easily assimilate new innovations in soca is probably the key to Fay-Ann's success in various music competitions. However, like her predecessors and her contemporaries, she has also run into the sexism inherent in the business. For example, in 2008 Fay-Ann found herself in the unusual position of competing against both her husband and her father in the International Soca Monarch competition. After seeing her performance, however, both Bunji and Super Blue felt that she had won, or at the very least had come in just behind her husband. Instead, Fay-Ann placed third, behind Iwer George, with another woman, Nadia Baston, placing fourth in the competition. Coverage of the event emphasized the unfairness of the judging, and aroused suspicions that the results had been rigged to favor male artists:

The results, announced at 5.30 am, were not welcomed by the audience, who were rooting for Fay-Ann for the Power Soca Monarch. Screams of "They just don't want a woman to win" were heard everywhere, and disappointed patrons pelted plastic bottles at the stage.

Meanwhile, Lyons-Alvarez is vowing that she will not enter next year's competition.

"No matter if my song is as high as the Berlin Wall I am not going to enter, as I felt I was cheated by the judges, who obviously view women as second best to men."[54]

Apparently, the people had a different opinion of Fay-Ann's song "Get On," because they awarded her another Road March title, again proving that female masqueraders have considerable influence on the songs that are played by their mas band's sound system at the judging points during Carnival.

The summer before Carnival 2009, Fay-Ann found that she and her husband were expecting their first child. Normally, female artists would use the opportunity to take a one-year hiatus, as the typical schedule for Carnival fetes is exhausting for anyone, let alone a woman who is seven or eight months pregnant. Instead, the Alvarez family decided they would pour considerable effort into Fay-Ann's tunes for the season, and work on a strategy that would allow her to give a satisfying performance at the fetes and song competitions despite her physical condition. Naturally, she received considerable criticism for this decision, and found herself explaining her choice in the local news:

> Fay-Ann herself has made it clear over and over again that she is pregnant— not sick, but various people have suggested that a pregnant woman has no right performing on stage and there has been some suggestion that she could be endangering her child. Fay-Ann begs to disagree and in this stance she has the support of both doctors and the local feminist organization.
> "Other people are making a number of stupid comments but the reality is there are a lot of women who, during their pregnancy, go on about their daily activities as normal," she said.
> Fay-Ann maintains that she has always been a fit and healthy person and she does not understand why some people are interpreting pregnancy as unhealthy.
> "Especially at a time where obesity is rampant especially in the youth, they should be promoting the opposite," she explained. The Road March queen thinks it is amusing that some people actually think she would perform without consulting a physician.
> "I am responsible for another life inside me of course I would consult a doctor," she said.[55]

One of the choices Fay-Ann made that was an emotional one for everyone involved was to write a song about her detractors from the previous year, entitled "Meet Superblue": "Tell them I am not my father, bad like him but de truth be told / Like me there will be no other, who God bless don't put asunder / If you don't believe that this is true / Meet Super Blue." The song was also a tribute to her father, who himself had battled a number of obstacles over the years, including drug addiction, and the career and financial problems that result from substance abuse. Many had not seen him in public since the previous year's Carnival season, and wondered if he would come out in support of his daughter's tribute to him. Onstage at the Army Fete, one of the largest fetes of the 2009 season, Fay-Ann presented her father with a lifetime achievement award. "Bringing tears to the eyes of older partygoers, who could easily recall the wild jubilation of his golden years with hits like Flag Party, Super Blue climbed onto a speaker box and hyped the crowd on behalf of his pregnant daughter."[56]

In a similar manner, the International Soca Monarch finals of 2009 became Fay-Ann's event as well: in fact, it was truly a women's festival in many ways.[57] In addition to Fay-Ann's performances, many of the other finalists were talented female artists such as Nadia Batson and Patrice Roberts. Destra Garcia, as a guest artist, performed at the interval between the Groovy and Power Soca Monarch segments of the program. Alison Hinds and Denise Belfon joined Destra Garcia for their collaborative tune "Obsessive Winers (They Can't Wine Like We)," demonstrating the vocal and dance skills of the Caribbean's most successful soca divas. Although an odd choice for the Soca Monarch finals, NWAC Calypso Queen Twiggy performed "Sing One for Obama," her tribute to both the American president and the late Miriam Makeba. Calypso Rose was also on hand as a special guest performer.

Fay-Ann competed in both the Groovy Soca and Power Soca divisions. Her groovy soca tune was "Heavy T Bumper," a song that paid tribute to the "heavy structure girls" who enjoy Carnival alongside their slimmer sisters. She humorously called attention to her own "heavy structure" by dancing onstage in a Dame Lorraine costume along with a troupe of dancers portraying the same traditional Carnival character. Contestants from the Miss Big and Beautiful Competition joined Fay-Ann onstage, but the real crowd pleaser was when Calypso Rose came up to wine her own "bumper" and thus demonstrate the connection between the two generations of female soca artists. For the Power Soca competition, Fay-Ann used another humorous strategy:

> ... dressed in black and blue, she belted out her song "Meet Superblue" as she paid tribute to her father, Austin "Superblue" Lyons who danced around on the stage next to his daughter, hugging and kissing her as she performed.

She then sent the crowd into a frenzy when she introduced them to her baby by putting the microphone to her belly and a child-like voice singing a verse to her song was heard.[58]

By the end of the competition, Fay-Ann had walked away with three awards: first place in both the Groovy Soca and Power Soca Monarch competitions, and the People's Choice award. Carnival Tuesday she won her third Road March title for "Meet Superblue," and seemed well on her way to continuing to be a dominant force in the soca music business.

By 2012, Fay-Ann and her husband Bunji Garlin had decided to retire from competing in the Soca Monarch competition—a choice many artists have made over the years in both the calypso and soca realms. Instead, they focused their efforts on full-length concerts with their band the Asylum Family, and recording music that can appeal to both local and global audiences. In songs such as "Differentology," recorded by Bunji Garlin in 2014, and "Raze," Fay-Ann's single for Carnival 2015, there is considerable influence from global electronic dance music (EDM) in terms of tempo, vocal style, audio production, and overall musical form. The Asylum Family have taken their music beyond the usual West Indian diaspora concert circuit to venues that can showcase soca music for a more diverse audience, such as the South by Southwest Festival in Austin, Texas, and the Glastonbury Festival in the UK. Although they have faced some criticism for blurring the conventions of soca music, the efforts of Fay-Ann Lyons and Bunji Garlin have also been seen as positive contributions to making Trinidad and Tobago's music known and appreciated by a global audience.

There are a number of women performing soca today, and having a female voice is crucial to the success of any soca band. As in other forms of calypso, it is as vocalists that female soca artists have approached equality with men. Few women have been performing as instrumentalists in soca bands; one exception was Juliet Robin, who played keyboards with Roy Cape All Stars and later Shandileer, led by Eman Hector (Guilbault, 2014: 108–9). As of 2015, several women instrumentalists are accompanying calypsonians and soca artists, including Chantal Esdelle, who leads her own band Moyenne. During Carnival, this band accompanies calypso artists; the rest of the year it is more focused on island jazz. The all-female soca band Sass, led by Nadia Batson, also has been part of the soca scene for several years.[59]

As with older forms of calypso, the presence of women in soca and other forms of party music means that songs will present life experience, including gender relations, from a female point of view. Soca offers female singers a context to present performance skill and talent, and to express female identity in various ways, some sensual, others celebratory. Each generation reinvents soca according to its own needs, just as other forms of calypso are reinvented from era to era. As in previous time periods, new music creates a generational rift, with much debate as to what kinds of music are taking the nation's culture forward and for what purpose. Artists meet critiques that resemble those of earlier time periods. While soca artists put Trinidadian culture on the world stage and allow an international audience to recognize the unique beauty and expressiveness of this region's music, there are also some critiques of how these artists must bend to the trends of international musical demands. The EDM influence in songs by Fay-Ann Lyons and her husband Bunji Garlin is just one of many examples of artists continuing to transform local music to make it congruent with a global contemporary music scene. As women soca artists break the barriers of earlier times and win accolades and awards for their contributions, they are also becoming primary agents of musical and artistic change in this expressive realm.

5

Pan Rising: Women and the Steelband Movement

This final chapter explores how women have contributed to the steelband movement over the course of its history, and how women are now playing key roles as pannists, arrangers, and educators today. On the surface, steel pan music is a different realm of performativity from calypso or soca: as instrumental music, it follows different conventions and practices from the genres of vocal music. However, the participation of women in the world of pan closely parallels their changing roles in various forms of expressive culture discussed earlier in this book. Changing attitudes toward local expressive culture that allowed it to be viewed as "respectable" rather than merely "reputation based" have facilitated women's participation in the steelband movement. As in the realms of calypso and soca, musical innovation has accommodated greater diversity in musical practice and supported the efforts of new generations of musicians. The parallel shift in attitudes and norms regarding gender roles has allowed for gender diversity in various performance contexts, as well as professional advancement for women in both artistic and social realms. Performers who learned music in other contexts are finding opportunities to transfer those skills to the musical realm of the steel pan and further enhance their involvement with local culture. Women have both maintained tradition and have been key musical innovators in steelband music, and have assisted in promoting the nation's music as a form of cultural capital[1] that benefits both themselves and the culture at large.

Like many of my Trinidadian friends, a much anticipated aspect of Carnival for me was Panorama, Trinidad's annual steelband competition. During my first Panorama I discovered that it is both a serious musical competition and a full-out fete. Judges and fans intent on hearing all the nuances of the musical arrangements pay for expensive tickets in the Grand Stand, which also restricts them to a very controlled, respectable environment. In contrast is the bacchanal of the North Stand, where people settle in for the day by bringing their own coolers and food, and liming the whole afternoon. The fans in the North Stand put on a show that rivals what the pannists are producing onstage, with rhythm sections and other fans beating time along with the music on the PA system and frequently neglecting to quiet down even when the next steelband comes onstage.[2]

As the day and night wears on, the serious action is on "the track," the paths leading up to the Savannah stage where the steelbands continue to rehearse their musical arrangements in preparation to going onstage. This is where you find the strong supporters of the steelband movement. There is no admission charge, everyone is free to lime on the track, and purchase food and beverages from the dozens of vendors that ring the Savannah and surrounding streets. Because it is possible to walk from band to band and hear their selections for the competition, many prefer to spend all of Panorama on the track rather than waiting in the stands for the bands to take their turn in front of the judges. This also allows the grassroots class to support their bands without a large financial outlay. These are the same supporters who help push the racks of pans onstage, and who dance with abandon while the pannists set up for the performance. Although security moves them offstage while the band plays, these fans crowd all four sides of the Savannah stage, continuing to dance and jump up with joy and abandon as their steelband plays through their ten minutes in the spotlight. While they dance, they are also waiting to assist their musicians offstage and congratulate them for a masterful performance.

In 2015 it is difficult to imagine that the steel pan and its players were once widely disdained in their country of origin. Today, pan is an international instrument, with steelbands in places quite remote from Trinidad, such as Sweden and Japan. Yet when they first started in the thirties and forties, panmen and their music were perceived as marginal both by the British government of Trinidad and by upwardly mobile Afro-Trinidadians who viewed the musical practice as the latest manifestation of the jamette tendencies they sought to cleanse from the grassroots class. The story of the steelband movement typically stresses how the "panmen" who developed the instrument overcame the adversity of colonialism and gradually won the support for the steel pan with the middle and upper classes and elevated it to the position of national instrument.

However, women were involved with the culture of the steelband from the very beginning, and even today the steelband movement could not survive without the many supporters who provide various kinds of support to the bands even if the do not "beat pan." Today there are many "panwomen," from young schoolchildren to arrangers and adjudicators. Along with the musical practices discussed in earlier chapters, the steelband movement has become a type of cultural capital for women. Its roots in the lower classes of Trinidad make it a particularly viable arena for those who do not have the financial resources or industry connections required for other types of artistic expression in Trinidad—an activity that allows them, to paraphrase the national motto, to "aspire and achieve" within the context of communal cooperation.

As discussed in earlier chapters, Trinidad's best-known expressive traditions emerged from the world of the urban grassroots class of nineteenth-century Port-of-Spain. The authorities of the British colonial government had always viewed with suspicion the drum dances of their slaves, fearing that they carried the potential of turning into outright insurrection, as in the Haitian revolution. As former slaves settled in hillside communities such as Laventille and Morvant, they brought with them their village dances, canboulay processions, and developed masquerades for the urban celebration of Carnival. For the first time, the island's most African expressions were visible, and more importantly, audible to the upper and middle classes who lived in the valleys of St. Clair and Belmont. The sound and volume of the drums that accompanied Carnival and other cultural events assaulted the sense and sensibility of the privileged classes. In 1884 a musical ordinance outlawed the use of drums to accompany public celebrations and seriously curtailed their use in other types of gatherings, including drum dances and Orisha worship. This ordinance applied equally to Afro- and Indo-Trinidadians. The ban was specifically on skin drums, and included the tassa drums used to accompany Hosay, a Muslim street procession that commemorates the martyrdom of Imam Hussein. In fact, an attack by police on the Hosay procession of 1884 in St. James resulted in thirteen deaths and over one hundred wounded (Hill, 1972: 44).

It is possible that an instrument as unique as the steel pan might not have been invented if Trinidad's if laws had not prohibited grassroots musicians from playing African-style skin drums. However, the subsequent musical innovations that they developed were not merely rebellious responses to British noise abatement legislation. The immense creativity and musical experimentation that brought about the contemporary steel orchestra is also an artistic answer the grassroots class gave to a society that saw them as incorrigible and worthless. Out of censure and adversity, this class created new musical instruments to accompany stickfighting sessions and dances, both during Carnival and throughout the year.

The first such innovation was the tamboo bamboo bands, which are similar to other types of stamped or struck bamboo percussion found in Africa and in other parts of the Caribbean. Made from bamboo stems, these instruments took over the function of the African drumming ensemble. The "boom" bamboo, which is stamped on the ground, took over the basic rhythm and bass function. The fuller or tenor bamboo, which consists of two pieces of bamboo struck together, provided various ostinato patterns. The cutter or soprano bamboo, which is struck with sticks, took over the lead part. Since the bamboo can be cut to various lengths, it is possible to create melodies through the use of hocket within the tamboo bamboo bands. Other instruments might include shac-shac, scrapers, rum bottles struck with spoons, and other types of ad hoc percussion. Eventually, bamboo bands had as many as twelve cutters, twelve fullers, six bass, five bottle and spoons, and two scrapers (Stuempfle, 1995: 26).

Competition between the various bands created further musical innovation during the twenties and thirties. The poverty of these musicians caused them to turn to resources readily available in an urban environment: empty paint cans, butter tins, garbage can covers, brake drums, tempered pieces of steel, and a particular favorite, a Bermudez biscuit container. Metal instruments were brighter, louder, and more durable than bamboo, which had a tendency to split apart during several days of Carnival revelry. Before long, the bamboo instruments became less common as band members searched for ways to use metal instruments in new ways. No one person invented the steel pan, an instrument that for obvious reasons is never called a steel drum within Trinidad and Tobago. Various people and ensembles all lay claim to introducing the pan era of Carnival music, yet it is impossible to prove any of these assertions (Dudley, 2008: 31). Although there was some collaboration, the steel pan largely developed through intense rivalry and competition between bands. By the mid-forties, bands were arranging pans by the quality of notes each produced: cuff booms, tenor kettles, bass kettles as well as a rhythm section made up of irons, chac-chac, and scrapers. In terms of musical development, this was all directed toward the ability to play recognizable tunes when the bands performed (Dudley, 2008: 43).

The socioeconomic climate of Trinidad also had an effect on the trajectory of the development of this musical instrument. The Great Depression was a time of social upheaval in Trinidad, with numerous strikes, riots, and other forms of social unrest. Unemployment was high and poverty reigned in the working-class neighborhoods of Port-of-Spain. For the working classes at this time, steelbands were the preferred type of musical accompaniment for masquerade bands, for the most part replacing the tamboo bamboo bands by the forties. As noted in earlier chapters, middle-class Afro-Trinidadians had been working since the 1890s to improve Carnival. As with calypso, the presentations of mas bands became more organized, with each band choosing particular themes. Some of these presentations, such as fancy sailors or soldier mas, were clearly military in nature and primarily served as a way to reinforce male camaraderie during Carnival. However, there were also "fancy bands," who adopted as their themes various events in history, fantasy, or mythology and competed for prizes including king and queen of the bands. It is here in this "improved" Carnival where women of the working classes found a space to jump up in the street festival, although as I indicated in earlier chapters, the majority of Carnival revelers in this period in history were men.

During World War II, when British and American armed forces were stationed on the island, the street processions associated with Carnival revelry were banned as a security measure. Calypso tents continued to provide entertainment for both locals and military personnel. However, musicians could no longer take to the road, nor could the mas makers they accompanied. Thus the innovation that had gone into creating a Carnival presentation was diverted to improving these new instruments, again in competition with other bands and often in intense secrecy. In essence, the war gave panmen the relative luxury of time that was necessary to create and continually develop the steel pan in order to improve its capabilities as a musical instrument and to expand the steelband ensemble. While it was clearly young, Afro-Trinidadian men who developed these early instruments, their panyards were not cut off from contact with the rest of the urban proletariat, including women. Certainly there were mothers, sisters, wives, girlfriends, and daughters who provided material and emotional support for panmen. The open yards in which the bands rehearsed were common areas through which all members of specific neighborhoods would pass on their way to other parts of the urban environment.

For the most part, the panyard of the war years was largely a man's place, and was structured around the interests of a young urban proletariat, including sports, card playing, and other recreation that took place alongside musical activities. (Even today, the atmosphere of the panyard has aspects that are an extension of the male rum-shop lime.) There was drinking and various hustles, including illegal gambling and drug dealing. Musical rehearsal was a chance to "gallery" (show off) alongside one's peers. In many ways, this is how the panmen took the "man of words" competition prevalent throughout the West Indies into the realm of instrumental music. Based on existing neighborhood rivalries, these bands of young men developed clear identities based on a number of symbolic features of the urban landscape. Images from the cinema, particularly Westerns and war movies, and the presence of military personnel during the war years influenced steelband identity, such as the names of bands: Desperadoes, Tokyo, Renegades, Casablanca. The internal structure of the bands reflected a military orientation, such as calling leaders "captains" and other ranks within the band "lieutenants" and "soldiers." In those days, panmen favored the wearing of hats and pieces of uniforms that they had received from American soldiers and sailors as gifts. Moreover, the bands identified themselves as symbolically at war with other bands in a war of both musical talent and defense of territory. This rivalry often broke out into actual physical violence when bands met on the road, or when Carnival was suspended, at fetes and other celebrations. As with the calinda bands of the nineteenth century, the panyards developed as arenas to enhance male reputation in relation to men of their own steelband and challengers from outside their band (Lee, 1997: 71).

Associated with this subculture was the dramatic rise in prostitution during the American military occupation. The women who were "working for the Yankee dollar" typically had a male protector, who received cash from her and perhaps several other women as well. Many young men liked to emulate these "saga boys"—particularly their sharp sense of dress and personal style. In the case of young men associated with the steelbands, this contributed to their poor reputation among the more respectable elements of their world. Although the war effort created jobs and a certain amount of economic prosperity for some segments of the population, for young men in their teens and twenties there were no real career opportunities, just hard labor on the military bases. Many young men opted out of full-time work and chose instead to live with parents or other family, working the odd job here and there to pay for flashy clothing, and using their ample leisure time as they pleased. Young women who consorted with the members of steelbands did include prostitutes. A notorious example was Yvonne Smith, known as "Bubulups," who plied her trade on George Street in Port-of-Spain. "By the early 1940s she was wining and waving flag for Bar 20 steelband, leading them into battle like an enormous, brown Joan of Arc" (Johnson, 2002: 411). This tainted the reputation of women who merely wanted to support the men of their bands, usually by jumping up with the band during Carnival, waving flags, and providing material support for the musicians. In general, a woman who associated with one band would cause trouble if she decided to change her alliance to another band, as fights would break out between men over their "property" (Stuempfle, 1995: 47–49).

Due to this violence and association with illicit elements of society, the attitude of the general public toward the steelbands was often quite negative. Despite changing attitudes toward Carnival expressions such as mas and calypso, panmen represented to the culture at large the very worst traits of the urban working classes. Since the steelbands were made primarily of unemployed youth, the middle and upper classes saw them as little more than street gangs. The police treated panmen quite brutally, even invading the panyard to harass and arrest players. These musicians did not receive widespread acceptance within the grassroots class either. Told again and again by the upper levels of society that nothing good came from "behind the bridge," the Afro-Trinidadian working class internalized this mentality and viewed panmen as a subculture within their already underprivileged group. Although many of their neighbors enjoyed jumping up to their music during Carnival, they viewed the panyard as a den of iniquity. Children were warned not to go in the panyard or they would face "licks" when they reached home, and it was disgraceful for a young women to be seen even talking to a panman. The women I knew who grew up during this time say they still cannot go to a panyard without a twinge of guilt about "how it go look" with their family and peers.

During the forties and fifties, the steelband movement went through dramatic transformations analogous to those of calypso and Carnival noted in earlier chapters. The maturing nationalist movement of the post–World War II era generally embraced indigenous expressions as a way to connect with the grassroots class and elicit their support of emerging political parties. Leaders in the nationalist movement saw the steelband as part of a distinctly Trinidadian cultural identity that needed to be reinforced alongside the political identity that they and other politicians were forging for the new nation. At the same time, several special committees were created to study the problem of steelband violence, which eventually led to the creation of the Trinidad and Tobago Steel Band Association in 1950. Officers came from the leaders of the various steelbands themselves, rather than the middle class. Thus the steelband movement created internal controls on violence within its ranks, and redirected their bands' energies toward musical creativity. Several prominent citizens, such as Trinidad *Guardian* editor C. S. Espinet, helped create competitions for the steelbands in order to rechannel their clashes to musical forums (Lee, 1997: 73). More importantly, panmen were adapting various types of musical repertoire, both Afro-Trinidadian and European, in various innovative and imaginative ways (Dudley, 2008: 56).

Support from the nation's intellectuals also assisted in enlightening the general public as to the legitimacy of pan. One of the key figures in this endeavor was Beryl McBurnie, who lived just a few blocks from the Invaders panyard. In 1946 she invited members of the band to participate in one of her dance programs, presented at the Prince's Building, which was among the first staged presentations of the steelband.[3] By now, the technical innovations of Ellie Mannette and his contemporaries had resulted in instruments capable of rendering a wide range of musical styles, from the latest calypsos to Chopin etudes. In 1947 dramatist Errol Hill and lawyer Lennox Pierre arranged for the broadcast of steelband music on the *Voice of Youth* radio program (Dudley, 2008: 89). As McBurnie's Little Carib Theatre, founded in 1948, became fashionable among the Afro-Trinidadian middle class, the more progressive among them saw the potential for further elevating the steelband's musical possibilities. McBurnie provided an environment in which formally trained musicians could teach classical pieces to the panmen. The panmen in turn appreciated the chance to enhance their musical skills as well as to engage in a forum that counteracted the harassment they received from the police. Thus, the middle class championed the cause of the steelbands, proving its worth by placing it in the "formal settings of genteel cultural institutions" (Stuempfle, 1995: 86).

Another major project that enhanced the profile of the steelband movement was the Trinidad All-Steel Percussion Orchestra (TASPO), a group that the Trinidad and Tobago Steelband Association formed specifically to perform at the Festival of Britain in 1951. The impresario for this event was Edric Connor, the "local Paul Robeson," who had migrated to England in 1944. He had gained acclaim for his recitals of Trinidadian folk songs on which the calypso was based, and later published collections of folk songs and customs in which he discussed their African origins (Connor, 1958). Pan pioneers Winston "Spree" Simon, Ellie Mannette, and Tony Williams were all members of the organization, but because they had no formal musical training, Sergeant Joseph Griffith of the Trinidad Police Band directed rehearsals. Preparations for this event involved a number of design changes to the pans. Mannette and Williams created melody pans capable of playing twenty-three notes, including a complete chromatic scale. The range of the double second was expanded to fourteen notes to enhance its harmonic capabilities. New styles of bass pans were developed, again to expand the range of the ensemble. Bands now fashioned all of their instruments from the large oil drums, which created a uniform quality of sound. Griffith, who wanted to have the ensemble visually resemble a classical orchestra, arranged rudimentary orchestral scores that he taught the panmen to read by identifying each note with an Arabic number. He arranged a variety of tunes, from foxtrots to calypsos to light classical pieces, to demonstrate the versatility of the new steelband (Hill, 1972; Stuempfle, 1995; Dudley, 2008).

"Operation Britain" began with a series of concerts staged for the Trinidadian public, which also were intended to help raise funds for TASPO's trip overseas. Contributions to the band's travel expenses also came through private donations, from prominent citizens but also through grassroots fundraising efforts by shopkeepers and band members soliciting by playing on the streets. By the time they left for the festival, the members of TASPO were local heroes, supported by many different groups within Trinidadian society. TASPO was an immediate success in Britain, and the orchestra was invited to give a number of engagements there following their appearance at the festival. This positive response in Britain greatly enhanced the reputation of the steelband back home, and gradually led to further acceptance of the musicians and their endeavors (Stuempfle, 1995: 99–100).

Although TASPO disbanded shortly after returning to Trinidad, the band members returned to their respective steelbands with new musical knowledge and a standardization of instrumentation that could enable further innovations. The Trinidad Music Festival, a biennial competition established in 1948 to showcase the rendering of European classics by local musicians, added a steelband class in 1952. The festival provided a platform for steelbands to receive feedback from formally trained musicians. Because steelbands collectively own the pans, and the instruments are maintained by the band through its fund-raising efforts and sponsors, participation allowed these musicians a creative outlet and chances for musical achievement (particularly in performance of the classics) that would have been difficult or impossible for them to do otherwise. Experience with the classics spurred the development of new types of pans to expand the range of the steel orchestra, as well as refinement of instrument building, tuning, orchestration and arrangement (Dudley, 2008: 98).

As they received more encouragement and support from the Afro-Trinidadian middle class and the emerging leaders of what would be the PNM, panmen aspired to move further toward respectability. The Carnival Development Committee started Panorama in 1963 to further "big up" the bands and give them their own arena for musical performance during the Carnival season. To reinforce the image of the steelband as a post-independence and hence postcolonial expression, the committee mandated that the bands must play local music, that is, calypso. Pan and calypso thus became intimately connected, with the needs of the steelband influencing the direction of musical change in the calypso. Certain calypsonians, most notably Lord Kitchener, developed reputations for writing songs particularly suited for pan. Experience with the classics influenced the way arrangers developed their arrangements of Panorama tunes, and over time created standard conventions for Panorama arranging and performance. As musicians were showcased to the public in performance contexts such as Music Festival and Panorama, their designation shifted from "panmen" to "pannists," signifying that they were now regarded as legitimate musicians pursuing respectable artistic goals.

According to many older Trinidadians I spoke with, the first panwomen were the girlfriends or sisters of men in the various bands. A good example was Daisy James McLean, whose older brother was a member of Casablanca. In 1944, at age six, Daisy James began playing her brother's pan, which he had brought home from the Casablanca yard. Several years later, her brother brought her to play for tourists at the panyard, but it was some time before her parents recognized that she had talent and should be allowed to play. While she would sometimes sneak away to play with Casablanca, she and her brother founded a family steelband called City Syncopators, which rehearsed on the James family's property. Playing under the watchful eye of her parents was a more comfortable arrangement. However, as steelbands became more established through events such as Panorama, McLean was able to join Casablanca as a regular player, and she played with them for more than twenty years (Dudley, 2008: 104–5). A few other bands in the forties had young women as players, though typically these panyards were on their family property and the young women played on stage rather than accompanying revelers during Carnival (Johnson, 2011: 237–38).

Another development in the postwar years was that the middle class began to move beyond their role as supporters to actual participation in the steelbands. Students from Queen's Royal College and St. Mary's College began to express an interest in playing pan, and cultivated relationships with experienced panmen to expand their musical knowledge. A number of these "college boys" played with Invaders in Woodbrook, a middle-class neighborhood located near Queen's Royal College and St. Mary's College. By playing with Invaders, the middle-class youths of this generation, such as Ray Holman, learned arranging skills and went on to form their own steelbands, such as Silver Stars, Starlift, Dixieland, Nightingale, and Dem Boys (Stuempfle, 1995: 100–101). Silver Stars in particular tapped into the middle-class following of pan begun by Invaders, and helped increase respect for panmen and the music that they made (Dudley, 2008: 99–102).

Middle-class involvement with the steelband movement facilitated women's participation as pannists in steelbands, which included the formation of all-woman bands under the tutelage of established steelbands and their leadership. Interestingly, the very first all-woman band was formed as part of the curriculum of a correctional institute run by Carmelite nuns. According to Kim Johnson, the inmates of the Girls Industrial School in Belmont heard a recital by the steelband Casablanca on the radio, and asked if they could play pan (Johnson, 2011: 239). In 1950 the White Stars Steel Orchestra was formed. The nuns had asked the members of Casablanca to teach the girls' band, and using the instruments owned by that band, the girls rehearsed under the tutelage of the band's captain Oscar Pyle (Gonzales, 1978: 27).

In 1951 schoolteacher Hazel Henley formed the Girl Pat Orchestra with her closest female friends, who were mainly middle-class teachers, civil servants, and shop clerks. Henley and her contemporaries benefited from the folklore revival begun by Beryl McBurnie; Henley had studied folk dance at Tranquility Girls School with Umilta McShine, and also performed at McBurnie's Little Carib Theatre (Dudley, 2008: 106). The women who formed the Girl Pat Orchestra rehearsed in the Invaders panyard and received instruction from its captain Ellie Mannette. However, they did not play for Carnival; instead, they found a niche playing in Beryl McBurnie's shows at the Little Carib Theatre, and performances by La Petite Musicale, led by Olive Walke. They also played at fundraisers for organizations such as the Red Cross, and gave concerts at the Roxy Theatre (Dudley, 2008: 106). The band became quite popular during its short existence, and mainly disbanded because the job commitments of its members made it difficult to accept foreign engagements (Blake, 1995: 263). The band did tour Guyana in 1951, and performed with Beryl McBurnie's dance company on a tour of Jamaica in 1952 (Dudley, 2008: 106).

Other all-woman steelbands emerged at this time, though like Girl Pat they did not last for more than a few years. These included Laventille All Girls steelband, which formed in Success Village, Laventille, shortly after Girl Pat became successful. Dem Girls was comprised of the sisters of the boys in Dem Boys steelband of Belmont. In similar fashion, Krazy Rhythm grew from the efforts of the sisters of the boys in Silver Stars in Newtown (Johnson, 2011: 241–42). Eventually, the novelty of all-girl bands wore off. By the sixties, a few women were braving the rough masculine culture of the panyard and joining bands such as Desperadoes and Casablanca. Gradually, women became a more notable presence in the steelbands, made possible by changing expectations regarding women in society in general. Women were now postponing having children, pursuing careers, and enjoying aspects of public life that men had always enjoyed. "In playing pan many women, particularly those with middle class backgrounds, found a new avenue for utilizing skills acquired through music lessons and membership in choirs" (Stuempfle, 1995: 179).

The musical expertise of middle-class women, gained through formal music instruction and participation in choirs, made them an asset to the male steelbands as adjudicators, arrangers, and coaches. When a steelband class was added to Trinidad and Tobago's biannual Music Festival in 1952, several women were influential in the development of this event.[4] Umilta McShine composed test pieces for the festival from 1960–62, including "People of the Islands," the test piece for 1962. Girl Pat alum Jocelyne Pierre arranged "In a Monastery Garden" by English composer Albert Ketèlbey, the tune of choice for Invaders for the 1960 Music Festival. Pierre also served as an adjudicator in the 1962 festival (Johnson, 2011: 245; Dudley, 2008: 106). In 1968 pianist Winifred Atwell became interested in collaborating with the Pan Am North Stars steelband to explore the possibilities of combining the piano with the steel pan, thus bringing together her classical training and the national instrument of Trinidad and Tobago. Atwell scored arrangements of standard repertoire such as George Gershwin's *Rhapsody in Blue* and Claude Debussy's *Clair de Lune*, and wrote an original work for the band called *The Devil's Daughter*. The result was a series of concerts in Trinidad and New York titled *Ivory and Steel*; these arrangements were captured in 1969 on a recording of the same name on the RCA label. For this achievement and her support of music scholarships in the West Indies, Atwell was awarded the Gold Hummingbird Medal.[5]

In addition to these concert settings, steelband music continued to be vital to the celebration of Carnival. Before the advent of DJ trucks and soca, steelbands were the preferred type of musical accompaniment for masquerade bands and were in big demand at Carnival fetes. The Carnival Development Committee started Panorama in 1963, providing yet another respectable performance context for steelband music. As they did for Music Festival, women trained in the classics assisted in the direction that competition took. Umilta McShine was one of the adjudicators of the first Panorama competition (Johnson, 2011: 245). Merle Albino de Coteau, who grew up in Laventille, was another asset to steelband arranging and adjudication. While her brother Martin gave up formal music instruction to play pan with Savoys steelband, Merle, who would not have been allowed to play pan in the panyard, continued with piano studies and eventually began playing the organ in church. However, the popular music of the steelbands fascinated her, and she gradually was able to share her musical expertise with Savoys, particularly in arranging classical material for the band. When she took over for her brother arranging for the Savoys of Laventille, Merle recalls that she initially was met with a great deal of discrimination despite the fact that she had a Bachelors of Music from McGill University. "Yes, they saw me as the pan lady, but they still would want to know what the harmony was doing. The captain would say, oh, 'but Martin would do that, Martin would do this.' They were glad to know a woman was there, but still there was that discrimination."[6] In 1972 Merle Albino de Coteau became the first woman to arrange for a steelband in the Panorama competition, and for many years has adjudicated for that competition (Dudley, 2008: 106).

As in the performative realm of calypso, the Black Power movement of the seventies facilitated women's participation in pan, as one of the main goals of this movement was inculcating pride in black music and culture.

Grassroots women joined steelbands in significant numbers; in bands such as Desperadoes, women were accepted with and pride and ensured that they could feel comfortable playing in the panyards (Johnson, 2011: 254). As in earlier years, many came in because they had brothers or boyfriends already in the band. Ursula Tudor, recognized by Pan Trinbago as the longest-playing female pannist in the world, describes those days as follows:

> Well, I started with Despers when I was 19 years old. I had a friend, he used to play pan, and he teach me to play pan and he bring me in the band. But when I started it hadn't any women at the time. The band had women long before but they never stayed. They'd just pass through and learn to play there. You see in my time when I was 19, my parents wouldn't approve of my playing pan. But now, the parents are coming with their children and allowing their children to play pan, because you see how pan reach now. It now reached a long way. But in those times I like to say people used to fight in the panyard and thing, and they didn't like their children to play pan. And my parents used to make noise about this, until I make my first trip and I start traveling they ain't making noise again. But they used to quarrel and thing and tell me I mustn't go to the panyard.[7]

Like many women of her generation, Tudor had to go against her family's wishes to pursue her interest in pan. As she observes, it was men in her own peer group who mentored her as she went through the learning process on the instrument.

Another important development that expanded women's participation in steelbands during the seventies was the introduction of steel pan instruction in schools. Some of the earliest programs were facilitated by Umilta McShine, who promoted steel pan instruction at Tranquility Girls School, as well as Ester Batson, who provided steel pan instruction at Arima Government Secondary and other schools in the sixties. Under the auspices of the Ministry of Education and Culture, Merle Albino de Coteau was hired to teach a musical literacy course for pannists, which helped benefit schoolchildren as well (Dudley, 2008: 249). One of the earliest school steelbands was established at St. Francois Girls College in Belmont, when in 1972 a group of students chose music as their project in the competition for the Duke of Edinburgh Award (Johnson, 2011: 233). The school organized a formal steelband in 1974, and set the precedent of forging ties with neighborhood steelbands to provide instruction to students and to share instruments. The school shared instruments with the steelband Power Stars and brought in the band's director McDonald Redhead to provide instruction (Stuempfle, 1995: 180).

Since school is an extension of the "inside" world of the home, it is logical that in the school setting, there would be greater opportunities for young women to participate in steelband music. School offered an environment where proceedings were supervised by teachers, and focused on the discipline of learning musicianship and theoretical aspects of music. For parents, school was a socially acceptable and physically safe place for their children, both girls and boys, to learn pan. There were enough school bands by 1976 to hold the first Junior Panorama competition. There has been such a competition at Carnival nearly every year since then, as well as a separate music festival for the performance of classical repertoire on the instruments of the steelband. Steel pan training in schools and ties between school and community bands has greatly changed how musical knowledge is transmitted in this musical context. Whereas in earlier generations pannists learned by rote from more experienced players, it is more likely that young people will first learn how to play pan in school and then make the transition to a community band. As Michelle Huggins-Watts, a graduate of Francois Valley Girls' School (whose career as an arranger is discussed in detail below), observed when I interviewed her in 1998:

> Because of the pan in schools project that was started in the late 1970s and more the introduction of the school pan festival in 1980, we've seen a lot more youth come into the pan arena. So you find that the young people will learn in their school bands and graduate to the adult bands even while in school. It's more accessible to them. And the stigmas that were attached are no longer there. So we have people from all over getting attached and getting involved now.
>
> Because women have gotten involved it has opened a lot of acceptance. But also a lot of pannists have been excelling academically. So you have more educated people getting involved. Because pan came from a sector where people were not perceived as well educated. So now you have a nice mix and as you mentioned before the doors are now open and embraces any and everyone.[8]

In the junior bands, girls outnumber boys. The oil boom years allowed for the development of youth sports programs, and it is possible that sports are offering a greater attraction for boys who would otherwise play pan. Several friends who are music teachers suggested that "maybe the boys' head is more hard" and girls are more willing to accept the discipline required for the school steelbands. In general, more young people are joining community steel bands, and there is more gender balance between young women and men within this age group (Dudley, 2008: 250). In Trinidad there are a significant number of women with advanced degrees in music. Perhaps this is because men have better opportunities to receive music training in the police or military bands, while women are better able to receive their training in academic settings. Dr. Anne Marion Osborne, coordinator of the music program at the St. Augustine campus of the University of the West Indies, feels that female students are more likely to take advantage of creative arts courses in general. Many of her students at the University of the West Indies are women schoolteachers who have received grants from the Ministry of Education to further their knowledge of music and Carnival arts. Part of their education includes proficiency in pan, analogous to the piano proficiency required in American musical academies. As a result, there tends to be more women than men in music education in Trinidad today, and increasingly women may be more familiar with pan than some of their male contemporaries.[9]

When middle-class women, as well as Indo-Trinidadians and various ethnic minorities such as Chinese and Syrians, started getting involved with the steelband movement, the bands began to belong less to one particular neighborhood and more to a self-identified community called "we band." Thus, bands associated with grassroots areas, such as Desperadoes located in Laventille, has a number of supporters from the middle and upper classes because of the musicianship of its players and arrangers. However, middle-class involvement with the steelband has not usurped the place of the working class as the movement's primary leaders, participants, and supporters, and the majority of pannists today still come from working-class families (Stuempfle, 1995: 177). While some may lament that neighborhoods cannot stake the same claim to steelbands that they did in the past, others also argue that recent trends enhance the role of the panyard as a community center for the neighborhoods and villages that support them (Dudley, 2008: 174).

The current governing body of the steelbands is Pan Trinbago, who fund each ensemble based on size and type of band. Today these are divided into small, medium, and large conventional orchestras and single-pan bands, so called because they only use the tenor pan section. Although the top posts of Pan Trinbago are still occupied by men, much of the day-to-day operations of the organization are in the domain of women officers, particularly those in charge of pan in schools and other educational programs. Most bands find it impossible to exist without some form of corporate sponsorship in addition to the funds they receive from Pan Trinbago. This financial support has assisted the musical advancement of steelbands, allowing them to hire expert arrangers for Panorama, purchase new instruments, and hire tuners to maintain them. Today, sponsors also provide the steelbands with costumes, flags, pan racks, and other items necessary for staging their Panorama presentation. Of course, this provides advertising and public relations to businesses that support the steelbands, such as Amoco, Petrotrin, Carib Brewery, BWIA, West Indian Tobacco Company (WITCO), and the many other sponsors of the steelbands. Today there are approximately 135 conventional steel orchestras and 58 single-pan bands recognized by Pan Trinbago. When in 2004 the conventional orchestras were broken down into the three size categories, this created a more level competitive structure, as bands with smaller memberships had never been able to compete seriously against powerhouses like Trinidad All Stars or Phase II in the Panorama festival. It has also allowed for the emergence of talented new arrangers, which include a number of women. While there are bands distributed throughout Trinidad and Tobago, the heaviest concentration is in Port-of-Spain and the East-West corridor leading to outlying areas. With ranks swelling to a hundred or more during Panorama, this means that 15 percent of the population of the nation has hands-on experience with the steel pan. If one includes Junior Panorama and various school programs, that number climbs to more than 20 percent, even if one accounts for the participation of schoolchildren in the senior bands. Thus, the considerable opportunities for playing pan in Trinidad and Tobago have continued to add to the diversity of the people who are involved with the steelband movement today.

My own experience as a pannist is that women can usually feel safe and comfortable in a contemporary panyard, since the longtime members of the band are conscious of protecting their bandmates from harm. Since rehearsals are at night, and go quite late, personal safety is an important consideration. For this reason, bands often arrange transport for their members who do not have their own vehicles and would otherwise have to rely on finding public transportation at a very late hour. Conflict within the band, or between members of other bands based on individual personalities or perceived slights, is nearly always a verbal contest of insult and abuse. I only witnessed one instance of physical violence, when some bottles were thrown in an argument over who would play iron in our band's engine room. However, players face certain dangers when going to rehearsal. The increase in drug- and gang-related violence in Trinidad has led to violence in the panyards, including drive-by shootings that have led to injuries and deaths of players and supporters in recent years. Women in the steelband tend to be treated with respect, particularly if they are experienced musicians. They are expected to set examples of good behavior, especially for the schoolchildren in the band. The more mature women in the band are expected to help the captain and other leaders get things back on track when an argument or other "foolishness" erupts in the panyard.

As a foreigner, I was initially worried that I would not be accepted as taking the instrument or the band seriously. When I found that I was well received, and shared my surprise with an American woman playing with another steelband, she said it was because we did not offer the same kind of competition to the men of the band that male foreigners do. Male pannists, especially the older generation, are still very competitive toward each other, and a male outsider enhances that spirit of contest and challenge. It also helped that I was still learning the basics of playing pan when I joined Courts Laventille Sound Specialists, so experienced players did not feel I was challenging their rank within the band. Instead, they could bring me along and teach me the way of doing things in their panyard. As a foreigner, I had a more ambiguous status than other band members. Most players tended to lime in single-sex groups before rehearsal and during breaks, unless of course they were interested in getting to know someone better. Understandably, there is a considerable amount of flirting between young men and women in the panyard: most secondary schools are single-sex and the panyard is one of the few places that young women and men can converse with less censure than they would in other contexts. Since I was older than that age group, and married at the time, I tended to lime with the more mature members of band, and used breaks to catch up parts of the arrangements that I had missed earlier in rehearsal.

Even the smaller panyards have become comfortable places for people to lime during Carnival. For women especially, it is an opportunity to join in activities that men have always enjoyed. I asked Michelle Huggins-Watts about this trend:

HMS: I noticed that women really like to go to listen to pan. I have neighbors who just can't wait to get all dressed up and go out to the panyard. And I'm wondering if you think there's the reason for that. Half the women I know would rather hear pan than calypso in the tent.

MHW: Half of it might be that it's the thing to do at Carnival. It's a nice lime and a nice social experience. People just like to hang out. So half of it is definitely that. The other half could be comprised of a number of things. The comfort of being in a panyard is something that a woman can now feel. In the past it might be a scary event, but they have no qualms. Of course they might have brothers and husbands in the bands. Or wives of workers or sponsor the bands and listen to the bands they sponsor. But I think that most of it is it's a nice lime, it's the fat for carnival.[10]

For a pannist participating in a steelband for Panorama, the process is a long and time-consuming one: at least five or six hours per night for six to eight weeks. An arrangement is usually ten to twelve minutes in length. More than half the points awarded to a band depend on its execution, including interpretation of the arrangement, dynamics, balance, holding the tempo, and application of the rhythm section. Pan rehearsals are where the arranger makes decisions regarding dynamics and other aspects of interpretation. Of course, the arranger is not alone in this endeavor. There is a whole hierarchy within the steelband, which is headed by a captain, under whom are section leaders for each type of pan. In my band, many of the section leaders were women who had played with the band for a number of years. There was also one or more drillmasters who would "run the tune" and keep the pannists disciplined while the arranger listens for things that need revision within the arrangement. Drillmasters also assess which players are best able to play the arrangements, and if necessary, will drop players from the band if they are not making adequate progress. The more experienced players are expected to help maintain control and discipline in each section, and again this is an area where the experienced female pannists have a large role to play.

The choosing of calypso for Panorama often depends on their complexity, and it is a choice made collectively by the band and its officers. It is typical for an arranger to come to a band with one or more potential Panorama tunes. After rehearsing some test pieces, the band's leadership and arranger decide on which tune to use. Although steelband arrangers each have their own particular style, Panorama arrangements must meet certain expectations in order to win points in the judging for the various rounds of competition. The calypso of choice must be one sung or published for the first time after Ash Wednesday of the previous year—with some exceptions, old music cannot be used for Panorama.[11] David Rudder's "High Mas" was a popular choice in 1998 because of its chanting element, based on the monophonic chants used the Roman Catholic Mass, unusual phrase structure, and modulations. This allowed pan arrangers to do complex improvisations on one chord, yet also do harmonic extensions that might not have been possible with a more conventional song structure. Some arrangers write their own tune for Panorama competition: for example, Ray Holman, Len "Boogsie" Sharpe, and Andy Narell wrote original calypsos for Starlift, Phase II, and Skiffle Bunch, respectively, during my fieldwork in Trinidad.

Although pannists start converging in the panyards around New Year's Day, their arrangers probably will not have a full arrangement the first night of rehearsal. In fact, it is often the case that the first arrangement that he or she brings to the band is discarded and replaced with a better version. The band might decide it does not like the calypso of choice and may request another one. Each night, the arranger will try out new material and most likely will keep changing it as rehearsals go on night after night. Although more and more pannists can read music notation, Panorama arrangements are usually not learned from a musical score. Instead, the arranger teaches the drillmaster(s), the band's captain, usually a tenor pannist, and each section leader their parts, a few bars at a time, which they commit to memory. As the other pannists come to the yard, they will join their sections and "take down" the parts with the help of their section leaders. Officially, rehearsals start at 7:00 p.m., but I quickly found that the greener players like myself were the ones who show up at that time, since we need that extra rehearsal simply to memorize the arrangement. Some of these players include women in their thirties and forties, who are returning to playing pan after having raised their children. The skilled players usually filter into the yard an hour or more later, by which time the captain, section leaders, and arranger have also arrived and are checking on the progress of the different sections. Eventually, the captain calls us to order and the drillmaster or arranger rehearses the whole orchestra on what we have just learned, while the late arrivals take down the music from their neighbors. Once the arrangers and various assistants help the band take down all the music, they attempt to run the tune several times a night. Initially, there are frequent interruptions to correct notes and phrasing, or even make improvements to the arrangement. Once they are confident that the band has the arrangement down, the drillmaster and arranger rehearse the band at ever-increasing speeds to work up to the allegro tempo necessary for Panorama competition. This rehearsal practice continues throughout the evening, with one or two breaks, usually ending between midnight and 2:00 a.m.

As the preliminary rounds of Panorama approach, there is often a process of elimination within the band. The more successful bands always have more pannists come out to rehearse for Panorama than they are allowed to bring onstage. Thus the section leaders are carefully monitoring the progress of their musicians, instructing those who are just "skating" to work harder or risk being sidelined for the competition. Ideally, by the time they reach the stage to be judged, each band member will have the tune down and can play each note perfectly. In practice, the size of the different sections allow for a player to "bust" a note every now and then because there are many pannists covering the same part. The judges too know that there will be much improvement between preliminary rounds and finals, and when the race is close they appear to add points when a band comes out stronger than the previous round of competition.

The introductory section of a Panorama arrangement can take a variety of forms. The arranger may simply use the calypso verse or chorus for this section, or take a melodic motif from inside the song and develop it through melodic extension, or create entirely new material. Melodic development usually begins after the first statement of the calypso's verse and chorus by the front-line pans. The most common method of development is through theme and variations. The front-line pans typically introduce these variations while the background pans take over portions of the main melody, although countermelodies specific to different mid-range pans are not uncommon. To add drama to the melody of the arrangement, the arranger will usually do revoicings to disguise the tune, or use new melodic motifs "quoted" from other musical works. In the arrangement I played with Courts Sound Specialists, arranger Seon Gomez introduced motifs from Panazz Players' version of the calypso "Portrait of Trinidad and Tobago." The selection of this kind of material is one of the freedoms the arranger has, and he or she will draw upon their own musical experience for inspiration.

Reharmonizations are introduced alongside the melodic variation on the original calypso's verse and chorus: this involves one or more key changes as well. Among the typical modulations are to the dominant or relative minor but often there will be more distant modulations, requiring additional transition material to return to the original key. Even in the first statements of the calypso verse and chorus chord changes, there is considerable variation on the harmony of the sung version of the calypso. Here the arranger will change the voicings of chords in different sections of the pan orchestra, use substitute chords or extended chords, blues progressions (I V7 IV vi I vi ii V) or other creative harmonizations that are not typically found in the sung form of calypso or soca. An arranger will usually write one or more "jams" or "break down" sections that create the impression of improvisation over jazz or montuno-style chord changes, even though everything has been composed and rehearsed ahead of time. The fastest and most intricate improvisations fall to the tenor pan section. As in "packing" the sung version of calypso, this is what creates drama when the arrangement is performed in front of the Panorama judges and audience (Dudley, 2008: 195).

As in the singing of calypso, steelband in the Panorama context is far more than the careful rendering of musical sound. Each steelband creates a visual spectacle, reflected in the colorful logos painted on the pans themselves, the decoration and design of pan racks and trailers, the elaborate flags of the flagwoman and other banner carriers, and the costuming of all pannists and other band personnel. Within limits, each player can add their own flair to their costume and other aspects of their physical appearance: hair color, nail polish, glitter, face paint, fancy shoes, scarves, face masks, wigs, etc. The music is well rehearsed by now, so everyone adds physical display, flash, and "antics" to the presentation (Dudley, 2008: 182). Enthusiasm is an unofficial part of judging the steelband's interpretation, and each band member enacts the excitement of participating in the event, playing it up for the crowd and TV cameras. Certain bands make a point of making a grand entrance, as Exodus did in 1999 with a team of moko jumbies leading the way. Arrangers also act up onstage, conducting the band, dancing, and making antics as the arrangement unfolds. All of this takes the spectacle of Panorama way beyond the musical arrangement to critical interactions between musicians, their supporters, and the overall audience at this event.

As noted above, girls far outnumber boys in the junior steelbands, while in the adult bands less than half the membership is women. The amount of time necessary to learn Panorama arrangements may account for the large attrition rate of women between the junior and senior level bands. Since Trinidadian women assume a larger responsibility for the home in comparison to their male contemporaries, there is less time for outside pursuits such as pan. However, women may drop out for a time and return to the panyard once they have fewer responsibilities or feel they can manage their time to allow for rehearsals. Ursula Tudor had the following thoughts:

> Maybe you really have to have it as a commitment. Because if you marry and have children maybe that's why most of the women don't really stay in the pan. I don't know, with me, I don't know how I managed to stay in the pan. I work, and I still go in the panyard. And we rehearse late, and we still get up to go to work. And I go home and I still have to cook. But you see, not everybody would do that. Maybe that's why we don't really have a lot of women in Despers—they play it for fun and they just leave. Though a lot of women play until they reach a certain age, like me, when it don't have that, so you have more mature women in some of the bands.[12]

In general, the largest group of women in the senior steelbands tend to be in their late teens or early twenties, an age when Trinidadian women either have not begun to raise children or can count on mothers or grandmothers to watch their children while they go out to rehearse. Returning to pan after having a child was especially important for women who had excelled in pan in previous years. One of my bandmates in Courts had just given birth in December, having participated during her pregnancy in the Steelband Music Festival in November while eight months pregnant. She returned to the panyard for Panorama, as did her mother, who also played with Courts. Thus traditional roles are not necessarily barriers to participation in a steelband.

One area where women participate quite significantly is in the steelband's engine room. This is the steelband's rhythm section that consists of drum set, "iron" (converted brake drums), congas and bongos, shac-shac, tambourines, scrapers, and various other percussion instruments. Although it may look to a casual observer as though a crowd of supporters spontaneously jumped on stage to join in, the members in the engine room rehearse as many hours as the rest of the steelband and will be replaced if they are not carrying their part adequately. There is a certain amount of variation in the types of instruments and rhythms they can play, and in the case of bands such as Phase II Pan Groove and Invaders, the influence of Brazilian and Afro-Cuban percussion is evident. However, the rhythm section, particularly the drum set and iron players, are responsible for keeping time for the pannists for a ten-minute tune, during which their may be a great deal of syncopation in the melodic and harmonic aspects of the arrangement. Hence, "a steelband is only as good as its engine room" (Blake, 1995: 123). Overall, women as members of a band's engine room make a significant contribution to the overall sound of the steelband arrangement.

Women's roles as "mere" supporters of pan should not be underplayed. Their support goes back to the days of jamette Carnival, and the steelband movement is as much about the community of fans as its musical personnel. From the beginning, women of the community showed their support for their steelband in many different ways even if they did not "beat pan." This included raising money for the band, cooking food for the panmen, and playing mas as the band rolled through the streets during Carnival. Today, even as the fulfill their roles as musicians in the steelband, many women and men help out with the non-musical aspects of keeping the band together, such as selling food and souvenirs to visitors in the panyard, and holding fetes to raise money for maintenance of the band and its instruments. The steelbands could not have the necessary impact at Panorama without their non-musical personnel, such as the flag women (or in some cases, flag men) who add color and movement to the band's stage presentation (Dudley, 2008: 185). Thus, a band's supporters and its community are vital to its existence. These people assist with everything from assembling costumes, flags, and canopies to fixing racks and trailers that carry pans along the track to the Savannah stage for Panorama. During the band's performance at Panorama, it is the collective energy of the players and their supporters that creates the visual and audio spectacle necessary for a successful performance (Dudley, 2008: 181).

As noted above, the musical expertise of middle-class women, gained through formal music instruction and participation in choirs, made them an asset to the male steelbands as adjudicators, arrangers, and coaches.

Women are clearly prominent as players in the steelbands of contemporary Trinidad, from the junior to senior level, from the small single-pan bands to the large conventional orchestras. They are pannists, section leaders, captains, band officers, and arrangers. They direct steelbands in schools and are prominent in bringing up the younger generation in the art of pan. As noted above, women have arranged for steelbands since the fifties, and they have also served as adjudicators, drill masters, and coaches in the steelbands. Still, women arrangers are relatively few, particularly for the conventional orchestras that compete in Panorama. There are several reasons that might explain this situation. First, the rise of the arranger to a status analogous to an orchestral conductor, came about during the sixties and seventies, before women were present in any significant numbers in steelbands. Many of these star arrangers, such as Ray Holman, Len "Boogsie" Sharpe, Pelham Goddard, and Leon "Smooth" Edwards, are still working today. Often, these arrangers are hired by several bands during Panorama, thus reducing the opportunities for up and coming arrangers. There may be reluctance to hire unproven talent when the goal is to earn prize money in the competition. Star arrangers are typically in Trinidad and Tobago for Carnival, and then spend the rest of year doing workshops and clinics, touring as soloists, and arranging for competitions in other countries. The few women who arrange for Panorama do so alongside careers in other professions, usually education at various levels. They tend to live in Trinidad and Tobago year round, though some do go abroad for pan competitions and performances in other countries. Arranging demands a large investment of time and energy, as with senior levels of competition in the calypso arena, sheer economics and the burden of commitments to family and employers may keep many talented women away from arranging.

In the steelband world, women arrangers are caught in a conundrum. An established arranger gives great prestige to a band at Panorama, but to become an established arranger one must gain experience arranging. However, as I noted above the restructuring of band organization in 2004 has created more room for newcomers to arrange, particularly for the medium and small orchestras. This has become an important platform for arrangers to prove their talents, and provides them with a chance of advancing to more lucrative work once the old guard retires. Due to the increasing importance of Junior Panorama, and the prizes and money at stake in this competition, arrangers find this another good way to establish themselves in order to get more lucrative work in the future. This has opened space for a number of young women to be hired as arrangers, thought typically for a far smaller arranger's fee than some of their male counterparts.

Currently, the most respected woman arranger in Trinidad and Tobago is Michelle Huggins-Watts. When I interviewed her in 1998, she had become the first woman to hold the role of captain in a large conventional steelband, Phase II Pan Groove. Since then, Huggins-Watts has gone on to accomplish many things, including becoming the first, and thus far only, woman to win a first place Panorama title in the senior band division, which she accomplished in 2011. As mentioned above, she first played pan as a student at Francois Valley Girl's School, in the first generation of students to benefit from the establishment of pan instruction at that institution: "I started playing pan at the age of fourteen, and I really got involved through my school band, though it was an all-girls college. We got started through the Duke of Edinburgh awards scheme. Ever since, I have been involved in pan. I never stopped playing except when I needed to embark on some serious studies—I needed to stop for a while and make time for study and writing of exams. Apart from that I've always been there rehearsing."[13]

After graduating from St. Francois Girls School, Huggins-Watts moved on to tertiary education at Trinity College and the University of the West Indies. At the same time, she continued to play pan, first with Power Stars, and then Casablanca, with whom she toured London and New York.[14] She finally joined Phase II in 1988. In 1987, she was asked to prepare the St. Francois school band for Junior Panorama, which she continued to do for several years. Under her leadership, the band did respectably, placing fourth in 1987 and fifth in 1989.[15]

In 1994 Huggins-Watts was asked to arrange for Power Stars. She explained that this opportunity to arrange for this senior band came about because of the mentorship that the band gave to her school band: "I got my break now [with Phase II] because I arranged for Power Stars for Panorama in 1994 and 1995. And I got my break there because of my relationship with them in the past. My school band used their instruments and they saw fit to call me in to do some work with them. You know the pan is really a male oriented arena so it created waves! You know a lot of interviews were done about this bold female arranger. And things just started to happen for me because of that."[16] It would seem that at the time, the judges were not ready for a female arranger. In 1994 Power Stars did not make it past preliminaries, and in 1995 the band missed the semifinals by a point (Johnson, 2001: 259). However, as Huggins-Watts finished her education and became a music teacher at Trinity College, she took on the role of arranger for the school's band, which was fairly successful in the Junior Panorama competitions of 1996–98. Meanwhile, as a musician and later captain of Phase II, Huggins-Watts benefited from the mentorship of one of country's most talented arrangers, Len "Boogsie"

Sharpe. In 1998 she won her first title in Junior Panorama, arranging "Clear De Way" for WoodTrin Steel Orchestra.[17]

In 2002 Huggins-Watts began her fruitful tenure as the arranger for Valley Harps, a senior steel orchestra located in Petit Valley. In 2003 the band placed in the Panorama semifinals for first time in twenty-eight years. In 2004 Valley Harps benefited from being reclassified in the new medium band category. That year, the band placed third, and in 2005 placed fifth.[18] In 2011 Huggins-Watts came to the band with an arrangement of Len "Boogsie" Sharpe's "Do Something for Pan." This tune had all the features she looks for in a Panorama tune: rhythm, interesting chord progressions, and a good theme that offers room for ideas for interpretation and melody.[19] Her resulting arrangement contained much of the rhythmic and melodic excitement that demonstrates the influence of her mentor, as well as her own development as an arranger in that style. The result was that Valley Harps tied for first place, making Huggins-Watts the first woman to win a Panorama title in the senior band division. Although Valley Harps has not placed quite so high since 2011, this achievement raised Huggins-Watts's profile considerably: she is now referred to as Trinidad's "First Lady of Pan." When interviewed in 2012, when she was a defending Panorama champion, she said that "I think that more doors will begin to open for women arrangers as a result of this victory."[20]

In 2012 Huggins-Watts was invited by the BBC to partner with conceptual artist Jeremy Deller for the series Collaboration Culture. The result was a one-off public performance in the Valley Harps panyard of Huggins-Watts's arrangement of a British dance anthem "Pacific State" by 808 State. In describing the song, Huggins-Watts said: "It's really different, not something you'd readily hear on the pan—but there are some interesting parts. My main thing is to get the song down on steel pan, but have room to add my own stuff into it."[21] The performance included all the Carnivalesque aspects of a Panorama performance, including flag wavers and supporters, as well as traditional Carnival characters such as Wild Indians and moko jumbies.[22] Such projects have further raised both the profile of Michelle Huggins-Watts and that of her band. In 2015 they were invited to France to collaborate with Pan'n'Co Steelband on a concert series and a double CD entitled *Twinning Souls*.[23] In all her accomplishments, Michelle Huggins-Watts serves as a role model and inspiration for young women who wish to pursue a similar career path.

Another well-known and well-respected woman who has achieved a great deal in the steel pan world is Natasha Joseph. Like Michelle Huggins-Watts, she started playing pan while a student, at Malick Secondary Comprehensive School under the tutelage of Richard Gaskin. Within three months of learning the instrument, she was arranging for her school band. Joseph joined Potential Steel Orchestra for the 1992 Panorama season, and became their drillmaster from 1994–97.[24] When I interviewed her in 1998, Joseph was playing as a seasonal member of Phase II, and for Panorama had been arranging for a single-pan band in Tobago. However, she was best known for being the only woman performing in the group Panazz, made up of members of Potential Symphony who wanted to explore improvisational possibilities in a small combo format. As she explained to me, she was very persistent in her efforts to join the group when the first started practicing at the Potential panyard:

> So after Panorama, I still used to go up in the panyard and there was this group of guys practicing. It was the same guys who are in Panazz now, they played for Potential too. . . . And I used to go and just play drums for them, keep a rhythm. They were looking for an extra player. So I asked them if I could play. And they wound up saying no. So I come back the next night and I asked them again. They said "no." And I came AGAIN, and they said no! After that it was explained to me they wanted someone who could solo or improvise with the band. . . . And so I went home that night. Next day I spent the whole day making up a solo. And I came back that night and played for them—and I got to play. But that was the one time that I really had to prove myself. Like show them that I could do this to get to play with a group.[25]

Panazz Players became quite popular with audiences within a year or so of its debut in 1993, and regularly won the annual Pan Ramajay competition. They played for a number of years at events and festivals, and traveled to perform at jazz festivals in St. Lucia, Grenada, the United States, and Japan. They released a number of recordings before disbanding in 2002, but reformed briefly to celebrate the release of a twentieth anniversary CD and DVD set.[26] This was a significant launching point for Natasha Joseph's career as a soloist, and a testing ground for her own arrangements and compositions. The experience afforded her a number of opportunities to perform as a soloist in other contexts, and led to other opportunities both in Trinidad and abroad.

When I interviewed her in 1998, Joseph was expressing her discouragement regarding her first experiences as an arranger, including obvious biases and gender discrimination. Like Michelle Huggins-Watts, over the years Joseph has benefited from the mentorship of Len "Boogsie" Sharpe. In addition to arranging for Phase II, Sharpe typically arranges for several other bands during Panorama. In 2007 he recruited Joseph to be drillmaster for Carib Dixieland, who won the Tobago Panorama that year with Sharpe's arrangement. Joseph's role as drillmaster in conducting rehearsal sessions is thought to have played a large role in the band's success. In 2013 and 2014, Sharpe hired Joseph to be drillmaster for Phase II Pan Groove, his large conventional orchestra that had won Panorama five times. Musician and commentator Chantal Esdelle describes the scope of this undertaking:

> In the three to five weeks preceding the first Panorama performance there could be as many as one hundred and fifty people flocking to Phase II's panyard to play. In this number, some people play well but only play at Carnival, some play all year, some are just beginning, some have been playing for years, some have come to lime 'cause that is what they do at carnival, some might be passing through for a smoke, others may have a romantic interest, some players from outside of Trinidad and Tobago who have come for the experience of playing.... Of this number only one hundred and twenty are chosen to play. Natasha's job is to get all of these people to execute the funky, well orchestrated, technically challenging, oral historical sonic story of Len Boogsie Sharpe's arrangement and, perhaps even the more socially challenging task, be one of the lead people in deciding which players are most capable of delivering this performance.[27]

Joseph's coaching was considered to have played a large part in Phase II winning Panorama in 2013 and 2014. If her skill as drillmaster is a good indication, she will likely be arranging for medium or large orchestras herself in the near future.

Another area that assists up-and-coming arrangers is the fact that most steel orchestras continue to perform once Carnival is over. Nearly every steelband these days has a "stage side" made up of twenty to thirty of the band's best players. This is the core of the band that rehearses throughout the year and performs at events outside Carnival and the biannual World Steelband Festival (occasions for which the full orchestra is required). In part, this is a response to increased tourism, but it benefits the bands in terms of both public relations and musical development and innovation. As a result of these trends, panyards have evolved into outdoor theatres, with bleachers for fans and establishment of cultural complexes, along with other renovations. For certain bands, whatever benefits the steelband also helps the surrounding neighborhood because it spurs urban renewal and public works projects. The 2001 Carnival was the first year that bands held concert nights, where fans had the opportunity to go from yard to yard and hear a full rendition of each band's Panorama tune. After Carnival, most bands today are keeping the yards open for stage sides to rehearse and give public concerts. This arrangement also allows for the panyards to be used for other calypso and arts presentations, concerts by the youth steelbands, fetes, and concerts. "In this way, the panyards are engineering a partial return to the barrack yard days, when the old calypso tents would be a magnet for all sorts of activities" (Mason, 1998: 74–75). When I made return visits to Trinidad in 2001 and 2011, there were many more venues for pan, including shows at local bars and restaurants, and at newly built outdoor amphitheatres on the Western Main Road in St. James. These performances tend to have more of a cabaret feel to them, with repertoire to suit: bossa nova, R&B, and pop music favorites. One performance by Skiffle Bunch that I attended included two young women from the band singing the theme song from the movie *Titanic* and other pop favorites when not playing tenor pan on other arrangements.

As I have demonstrated throughout this chapter, women have participated in the steelband movement in various ways since its beginnings. Their expanded roles as pannists, educators, and arrangers came about as the pan gradually came a source of national pride—in fact, it is now the national instrument, and its music is one of the national art forms. Since the base of support for the steelband movement remains among the working classes of Trinidad, this makes pan a particularly viable arena for those who do not have the resources for other types of musical expression. In some senior steelbands, there are as many women as there are men (Dudley, 2008: 108). Historically, very few women have arranged for Panorama, though this is changing as discussed above. As the career trajectory of Michelle Huggins-Watts demonstrates, the leadership role of women schoolteachers for the junior bands has had a significant impact. The junior steelbands are where women continue to play a significant role, and while the arrangements for the junior ensembles are usually less complex than they are for the senior ensembles, the process is still time consuming. Due to the increasing importance of the junior panorama, and the prizes and money at stake in this competition, arrangers find this a good way to establish themselves in order to get more lucrative work in the future. Currrently, women's prime leadership role in pan is in mentoring young pannists and writing arrangements for school bands: that is, as music educators, which are typically female and underpaid roles within this and other music cultures. However, pan has become an international instrument, and has created opportunities for Trinidadians to go abroad to teach and perform. As the above examples demonstrate, women pannists, arrangers and composers, as well as their strong roles educators, are helping their male counterparts chart the new directions for pan as they create new types of musical expressions and foster new arenas for the performance of steelband music. It is likely that there will be more gender equality in future generations, as women continue to strengthen their presence in the steel pan art form.

Conclusions

Whenever I engage in fieldwork in Trinidad, or encounter Trinidadians in North America, I am continually reminded of the importance they place upon self-expression, the opening of space to display one's self, whether verbally, musically, or kinesthetically. In terms of interpersonal communication, Trinidadians are passionate about speaking up in the presence of an audience who can appreciate, and participating by adding their voices. Verbal skill and sociability makes up the fabric of life in Trinidad, as it does in much of the Caribbean. "Trinis are very passionate people: if we are excited about something and trying to tell you a story you'd better stand back if you doh want to get 'lick way' because you know, the words are not enough, you have to have the antics too."[1] Performance of self, whether through music, language, or visual display, is a critical way to share experience and observations that empowers the performer and engages his or her audience. Just as in everyday life, great value is placed on verbal performances, gossip and "picong," folk and popular music in Trinidad uses social commentary, derision, and inventive wordplay to great advantage. Yet these performances must also spur the audience toward active engagement: "indeed a performance that does not inspire enthusiastic collective participation—and thus does not become 'hot'—is a failed performance" (Bilby, 1985: 201). In Trinidad, a failed performance might find the performer showered with toilet paper or orange rinds, and the audience heaping verbal abuse upon a performer who displeases them. These contexts have a competitive aspect, and Trinidad is filled with formalized competitions for many of the expressive forms practiced in that country, the ultimate goal being communal participation and renewal of social bonds (Burton, 1997: 170–71).

As I have emphasized several times in this book, it is impossible to discuss the Caribbean in any meaningful way without addressing its music. Music, and expressive forms that depend on music such as dance and festivals like Carnival, play a pivotal role in the lives of Caribbean people, and are often central to their discussions about what makes them distinct from other peoples of the world. Regardless of their class or ethnicity, I found that Trinidadians are keenly interested in music and culture and are proud of the local music that has emerged from their nation and the Caribbean as a region. With very few exceptions, most Trinidadians I have spoken with are proud of what makes Trinidad unique culturally, and express detailed opinions about what matters most to them: Carnival mas, calypso tents, soca or chutney fetes, steel band and Panorama, and so forth. While each person has individual preferences and does not enjoy every cultural expression Trinidad has to offer, each voices strong opinions about the quality of the things that matters most to them, and is quick to critique bad music or performances.

It is clear that women have been instrumental in the maintenance, transmission and innovation of musical practices in Trinidad and Tobago. In their roles as performers, arrangers, composers, and music educators, they are like their sisters in other Westernized countries who have "worked hard to erase the boundaries between public and private during the last few generations" (Post, 1994: 47). Changing attitudes regarding Trinidad's indigenous expressive forms—calypso, the steelband, the Carnival arts, Caribbean literature and fine art—came hand in hand with other freedoms, and it is clear the nationalistic project assisted in making women more visible contributors to Trinidad's music and expressive arts. Musical change and innovation also accommodated greater diversity in musical practice, and supported the efforts of new generations of musicians. This has naturally led to a greater appreciation of the value of women's contributions to various expressive forms. Shifting attitudes and norms regarding gender roles in Trinidad also facilitated gender diversity in various performance contexts, as well as professional advancement for women in both artistic and social realms.

There are questions regarding the limitations of certain performance contexts. It could be argued that the competitive nature of cultural performances, such as the Calypso Monarch competition, restricts the discursive freedom of its participants. In fact, the more cynical of my informants during my fieldwork commented that innovation can be quite difficult, particularly if that innovator is a female musician and songwriter. Yet competition has long been part of West Indian expressive culture. The man or woman of words exhibits his or her talents best in contest with other performers, and so it may not be competition in and of itself that constricts creativity and freedom of expression, but rather the conservative nature of the institutions that claim ownership of national culture. Over time, various forms of patronage facilitate cultural creativity and exchange and continue to do so to the present day. However, as Jocelyne Guilbault notes and my examples of various soca divas demonstrate, musical competitions set up by private entrepreneurs during the nineties have often created more diversity and musical innovation than those sponsored by the state or political parties, and these new competitions have particularly benefited women as new voices in the creation of Trinidadian popular music (Guilbault, 2005: 57–58). However, it may be in the freer context of noncompetitive performances such as Carnival parades, fetes, and private concerts, both at home and abroad, that one experiences the true potential of musical expression in the context of Trinidad and Tobago's music scene, as well as a more organic interaction between performers and their intended audiences.

As the examples I have given in this book demonstrate, the quality of life of women and their ability to earn a living has improved dramatically from the independence period to the present. During the past two decades, girls have exceeded boys in academic performance at nearly every level of the academic system in the West Indies. As a result, women are now the majority at all three campuses of the University of the West Indies, and in recent years the graduating class has been as much as 70 percent women (Lindsay, 2002: 61). One common theory for this is the overall process of gender socialization in the Caribbean, summarized under the slogan "tie the heifer and loose the bull." This ideology allows boys to exercise their freedom in the public sphere and ties girls to the domestic sphere, which creates an environment for male academic underperformance (Figueroa, 2004: 147–48). Additionally, higher education no longer results in the same kinds of rewards it did in the past. As certain professions become more feminized—particularly education—women find it necessary to go to college or graduate school to get ahead economically. Education, the health professions, and the law are other examples of professions that are coming to be female-dominated yet economically less lucrative in recent years. Meanwhile, some of the most well-paid jobs in contemporary Trinidad are in the construction trades. This is an area in which men can obtain jobs without much education, and which women are typically discouraged from pursuing (Lindsay, 2002; Figueroa, 2004). For the most part, however, male marginalization did seem to be a reality in the lower strata of society, with young men increasingly dropping out of school to become involved in the drug trade and violent crime.[2]

Despite the many advances that the women's movement has accomplished in the region, there are still lingering problems. Since the early nineties there had been a steady increase in the reported incidences of domestic violence and rape, including instances of the abduction and murder of women. Furthermore, it was evident that the contemporary economic trends centered on the exploitation of female workers and the curtailing of workers rights in general, as it did in the rest of the developing world (Mohammed, 1991 and

1998; Safa, 1995; Reddock, 1998 and 2004). Issues such as domestic violence, rape, sexual abuse of minors, and human trafficking are taken extremely seriously in the contemporary Caribbean, and considerable space in the local press and more informal discussions among West Indians is devoted to these issues and how they might be addressed and resolved. As women become more prominent as lawyers and judges, their female clientele receives a more sympathetic ear toward their concerns than they did in previous generations. As I was finishing this manuscript, Prime Minister Kamla Persad-Bissessar was making it a priority to strengthen laws regarding domestic violence and rape.[3] Issues such as abortion and LGBT rights were also under discussion, but were difficult to address due to the current political climate and protests from conservative religious groups.[4]

Expressive culture has assisted in this project of creating better social conditions for women. Women calypsonians use their music as a platform for wider social concerns, imploring their audiences to take action against various forms of gender inequality and also addressing issues that involve the nation as a whole, such as political corruption, gang-related crime and violence, kidnapping and extortion, drug trafficking, and HIV/AIDS. The intersection of music and feminism in the Caribbean is and has always been ultimately a human rights project. In Trinidad and Tobago, women and men successfully use the same genres rather than creating gender-specific expressive forms and performative contexts. It is possible that this use of common genres produces utopian longing for both genders, and creates a vision upon which they both can act. The ability to share common identities and concerns is crucial to the survival of a feminist project, and this includes culture in common as well as politics in common. Colonial and postcolonial material relations are humankind problems: "we cannot liberate women without liberating men, nor can we liberate men without liberating women" (Mark, 1991: 251).

For the musicians who participated in my study, musical performance is a venue for empowerment, commentary, and critique. Women popular musicians participate in a vernacular feminist project that resists domination while at the same time inspiring audiences to question the relations that cause domination in their own lives. Hence, through various Trinidadian musical forms and performance contexts, a space is opened to suggest new ways of organizing social relations. This can happen even when music is not acting in social commentary mode, such as in Carnival fetes and masquerade. As in earlier generations when Carnival acted as a form of political emancipation, for the past three decades it has also acted as a form of gender emancipation (Miller, 1994: 124). Likewise, the rehearsal space of the panyard is one of the few coed environments in Trinidad, allowing young women and men to engage in gender relations that, on the musical/artistic level at least, are equal in terms of contribution and appreciation. Thus, music in the Trinidadian context takes an important place alongside larger political projects and concerns in creating dramatic social change. In various performance contexts, musicians attempt to negotiate and solve the problems that women, and men, face in their everyday lives. It does seem that the old dichotomies of reputation/respectability are breaking down, combining the best of both "to move beyond opposition, which so paradoxically reinforces the structures it contests, into a world in which power, wealth, opportunity, and self-value would be far more equally distributed" (Burton, 1997: 267).

Most of the expressive forms discussed in this book take place in the context of Trinidad and Tobago's annual Carnival. As Mikhail Bakhtin observed, "carnival becomes the place for the working out of a new mode of interrelationship between individuals, brought to life in concretely sensuous, half-real and half play-acted form that permits the latent sides of human nature to reveal and express themselves" (Bakhtin, 1984: 122–24). According to Victor Turner, Carnival is "the subjunctive mood of society" (Turner, 1987: 25). The undisciplined quality of certain Carnival behaviors offers an alternate subjectivity and platform for resistance. Yet there is also insecurity in this resistance, and pleasures of the body might be co-opted to channel resistance into more socially acceptable Carnival pleasures (Averill, 1994: 224). Breakaway, leggo, get on bad, play yourself, misbehave—these are all West Indian terms for the enjoyment one experiences during Carnival and similar times of festive engagement. "Play yourself" in particular is an interesting Trini expression; it literally means to enjoy oneself to the utmost degree, to show off, to parade oneself around in enjoyment. Yet this local term is illuminating because it suggests that the enjoyment and abandon expressed during Carnival and other festive occasions represent the real self. While Carnival is called a mas/mask, it truth it may be that the everyday self is itself a mask behind which one's real self and real concerns are hiding. Thus Carnival allows you to play yourself—enjoy yourself thoroughly—by playing yourself, that is, being the person you really feel yourself to be outside of various colonial/normalizing institutions. As Pamela Franco notes, women use Carnival mas to voice their concerns, symbolically inverting the social order and "articulating their desire to be unfettered from the societal laws that serve to oppress and suppress them" (Franco, 2001: 191).

Within Trinidad, expressive culture, including popular music, is clearly a strong forum for communicating possible interpersonal and inter-gender relations. Thus, Carnival pleasures, such as soca music and fetes, pretty mas, and so forth, take an important place alongside the more direct examples of social commentary and critique showcased in calypso competitions. The experience of "free-up" and "breakaway" are a welcome relief from the many hardships and anxieties that face the residents of contemporary Trinidad. At the same time, these expressive forms can be read as creative and beautiful venues for self-expression that convey local and regional identities that are continually reshaped with each generation. Carnival, of course, is a temporary space in which certain license is given to express things one normally would not. However, more and more, the musicians of Trinidad and Tobago break outside of these boundaries to occupy space and times outside of the official Carnival season: in festivals throughout the Caribbean, in celebrations created by West Indians in the diaspora, as well as performances that attract international audiences of various nationalities and ethnicities. This of course "requires an openness to the horizon of possibilities" Trinidadian musical performers convey through their various art forms (Guilbault, 2007: 276). These possibilities include the role of musicians as cultural ambassadors to the rest of the world; and as this book has demonstrated, women musicians in Trinidad and Tobago are deeply invested in bringing their musical expressions to a variety of audiences. Ultimately they are transmitting not only various forms of music, dance, and communal celebration, but also the potentially transformative effects of these expressive forms on various issues and concerns that are shared by people the world over.

Notes

Introduction

1. "De River" lyrics by Sanelle Dempster, music by Blue Ventures.

2. I am not the first researcher to explore women's role in Trinidad's music and Carnival, nor am I the last. For more studies on this topic see Ottley, 1992; Gottreich, 1993; Maison-Bishop, 1994; Franco, 2001; Cynthia Mahabir, 2001; Dikobe, 2003 and 2004; Shaw, 2005; Niranjana, 2006; Noel, 2009; Sierra, 2009.

3. Again, this study builds on earlier ones that address this same topic. For works by Trinidadian scholars in particular, see Warner, 1985; Rohlehr, 1990; Mohammed 1991 and 1998; Ottley, 1992.

4. In this study I tend to focus almost exclusively on Trinidad, hence my usage of "Trinidad" and "Trinidadians" rather than the more colloquial "Trinbago" and "Trinbagonians."

5. *The World Handbook 2013-2014*. Washington: Central Intelligence Agency, 2013, available at www.cia.gov/library/publications/the-world-factbook/geos/td.html (accessed July 27, 2015).

6. In June 2015, Prime Minister Kamla Persad-Bissessar announced that general elections were scheduled for September 7, 2015.

7. Words and music by McArtha Lewis (Calypso Rose). This is taken from the version available on the two-CD collection *The Best of Calypso Rose*, Rituals CMG1305.

8. Earl Manmohan, "Women blamed for men's failures." *Trinidad Express*, April 14, 1997.

9. For an in-depth study of the relationship of calypso and literary works of the Caribbean, see Sierra, 2009, as well as Sandra Pouchet Paquet, Patricia J. Saunders, Stephen Stuempfle, eds., *Calypso and the Caribbean Literary Imagination*. Kingston/Miami: Ian Randle Publishers, 2007.

10. Lomax's Trinidad recordings have been rereleased as *Caribbean Voyage: Carnival Roots: The 1962 Field Recordings*. Rounder 1166117252 (2000).

11. Fulbright Alumni Association of Trinidad and Tobago Distinguished Lecture and Book Launching by Dr. J. D. Elder, City Hall, Knox Street, Port-of-Spain, Tuesday March 31, 1998.

Chapter 1

1. As Jocelyne Guilbault notes, music bands within the Caribbean have typically been associated with excessive drinking, the use of drugs, and illicit activities such as gambling

and prostitution (Guilbault, 2007: 142–43). Although this is changing due to greater opportunities to receive musical training at UWI and UTT, there are relatively few women contributing to calypso arranging or accompanying.

2. See Bourdieu, 1986: 245; DeWitt, 2008: 39 and 251 n44.

3. Amerindian is the preferred term of Caribbean scholars, who obviously must make a distinction between "Indians" of local origin, and Indians from South Asia. Therefore, I also use this term to refer to the indigenous peoples of Trinidad and Tobago.

4. Within the Anglophone Caribbean region today, in fact, the estimate is only slightly higher, with 25 percent of Afro-Caribbean families living in what conforms to the definition of a nuclear family (Senior, 1991: 8).

5. For details of these commentaries, see Brereton, 1979; Cowley, 1996.

6. In this book I use the spelling *calinda*, which is used by Gordon Rohlehr and Errol Hill. J. D. Elder uses the spelling *kalinda*, as do John Cowley, Stephen Steumpfle, and Shannon Dudley.

7. The arena for calinda matches.

8. Bacchanal has a number of meanings in the Caribbean, including, in this case, scandal and the resulting loud protest.

9. It is Cowley who concludes that Sophie Mattaloney was a "matador" based on her frequent court cases for assault and criminal mischief (see Cowley, 1996: 170). Raymond Quevedo refers to her as "that rare species of artiste, the female kaisonian" (Quevedo, 1983: 15). Donald Hill, who spells her name Mataloney, calls her "the brawling, quarrelsome jamet who was one of the few female calypsonians of the era" (Donald Hill, 1993: 151).

10. Ordinance 11 of 1883 required the owner or occupier of a property to obtain a license for the playing of drums between 10:00 p.m. and 6:00 a.m., and restricted the ability of "rogues and vagabonds" to assemble for the purposes of holding drumming sessions and drum dances (Trotman, 1986: 265).

11. This ordinance was repealed in 1951. Today, followers of the Spiritual Baptist faith are allowed to practice their beliefs openly, and marriages performed by their religious leaders are legally recognized.

12. Attilah Springer, "Carnival Was Woman." *Trinidad Guardian,* February 8, 2001.

13. Sheldon Osborne, "Remembering Audrey Jeffers." *Sunday Mirror,* February 12, 2006.

14. Horace Harragin, "Legacy of Perfection from May Johnstone." *Sunday Guardian,* November 16, 1997.

15. This practice continues today; many mas bands have security men who prevent outside revelers from entering the band, guard against molestation of band members, and prevent theft of personal items (jewelry, mobile phones, etc.) from the masqueraders.

16. This is known as the Destroyers for Bases Agreement, signed on September 2, 1940.

17. As Donald Hill notes, this ordinance was routinely flouted, particularly by young working-class men associated with the emerging steel band movement (Donald Hill, 1993: 206).

18. Pearl Connor, "Obituary, Beryl McBurnie." *Trinidad Guardian,* April 28, 2000.

19. Judy Raymond, "Beryl McBurnie: First Lady of Caribbean Dance." *Caribbean Beat* 20 (July/August 1996).

20. David Cuffy, "Little Carib is 50." *Trinidad Guardian*, November 20, 1998.

21. Hope Munro Smith, "Beryl McBurnie." *Dictionary of Caribbean and Afro-Latin Biography*, forthcoming from Oxford University Press.

22. "Massa Day Done," public lecture at Woodford Square, March 22, 1961.

23. Eric Williams's research in this area is included in his book *From Columbus to Castro*.

24. "NWAC, an Historical Perspective." Unpublished paper distributed by the National Joint Action Committee of Trinidad and Tobago.

25. http://stte.gov.tt/.

26. As of 2015, Patricia Mohammed had transferred to the faculty of the St. Augustine campus of UWI to become the director of the Gender and Development Studies Institute. Mohammed's role as director of the Mona Campus Institute was assumed by Leith L. Dunn. Rhoda Reddock had become the Deputy Principal at the St. Augustine campus of UWI.

27. Mission statement from the CAFRA T&T website www.facebook.com/CAFRATT/info.

28. As both Jocelyne Guilbault and Peter Manuel have noted, most Trinidadians are not in the habit of building large collections of recordings. Local music stores do not tend to have older releases in stock, and that makes it difficult to obtain historical recordings. There has not been a consistent effort to build an archive of recorded material in Trinidad. The appearance of YouTube and similar sites has led certain collectors to share their personal archives with a larger public. While these recordings are not high fidelity, they can give researchers valuable information about music from earlier time periods. Likewise, the appearance of legal downloading sites such as Trinidad Tunes has made it possible for audiences in Trinidad and abroad to have immediate access to new music, and perhaps has increased the likelihood that audiences will collect music over time.

29. The Road March title goes to the performer whose song was played the most frequently during the Parade of Bands on Carnival Monday and Tuesday.

30. Some recent examples: Dixie-Ann Dickson, "Calypso Still Alive: Experts Say." *Trinidad Guardian*, February 13, 2009; Tony Fraser, "The slow death of true calypso." *Trinidad Guardian*, February 22, 2012.

31. For a detailed analysis of the politics of gender in Carnival mas, see Franco, 2007.

32. "Play yourself" has a different meaning in Trinidad and Tobago than it does in African American culture. Here it means enjoying oneself to the utmost, and to parade oneself around in enjoyment.

Chapter 2

1. See Rohlehr, 1990: 531, on the collaborative process in calypso, as well as Dikobe, 2003: 43–44.

2. Some exceptions today include children's afternoons at the calypso tents as well as special events during Carnival that cater to families with young children.

3. Thompson is referring to the Indian girl who is the object of Iwer George's affections in his soca hit of the 1998 season, "Bottom in de Road."

4. There have been a few middle-class calypsonians. Both Philip Garcia (Lord Executor) and Raymond Quevedo (Atilla the Hun) attended St. Mary's College, a Roman Catholic secondary school, and worked at white-collar jobs after graduation.

5. "Matilda" was first recorded by King Radio in 1938. It has become a calypso standard over the years. Most North Americans are probably familiar with the version recorded by Harry Belafonte in 1953.

6. "Ugly Woman" is considered a standard, and has been covered by Sir Lancelot (Lancelot Pinard), the Duke of Iron (Cecil Anderson), MacBeth the Great (Patrick MacDonald), the Charmer (Louis Farrakhan's stage name when he was performing calypso), Hollywood actor Robert Mitchum, Bomber (Clifton Ryan), and Relator (Willard Harris). The song is also the basis for "If You Wanna Be Happy," recorded by American vocalist Jimmy Soul (James Louis McCleese) in 1963.

7. "Brown Skin Gal" is another calypso standard recorded by a number of singers, including Harry Belafonte.

8. Sexual fantasy is only one theme presented in this song. For a lengthy analysis of "Congo Man" and its historical context, see Rohlehr, 2007. Today, the meaning of "Congo Man" seems to have expanded. I have seen Sparrow perform "Congo Man" a number of times, and he typically uses the opportunity to throw picong at various men in the audience. This of course delights the women in attendance, and they gleefully join Sparrow in the chorus "never eat a white meat yet."

9. The Mighty Spoiler's version of "Bedbug" can be found on the anthology *Unspoilt* released on Ice Records in 1995.

10. "My Pussin" can be found on the anthology *Klassic Kitchener Vol. 2* released on Ice Records in 1995. "Dr. Kitch" can be found on numerous anthologies of Lord Kitchener's work.

11. This does not mean that the "smutty" calypsos pass by without critique, and every year there is talk about banning certain songs from the radio.

12. Calypsonians are primarily vocalists, though many can play guitar, cuatro, or piano to write their songs or to accompany themselves in certain performance contexts.

13. In Trinidad, these are usually called brass bands. The instrumentation typically includes clarinets and saxophones, trumpets, trombones, as well as a rhythm section consisting of piano, bass, guitar, and drum set.

14. Much of the following paragraph is based on discussions with bandleader and composer Michael Low Chew Tung. Some of this historical material is outlined in his book *Kaiso Koncepts: A Modern Approach to Playing Calypso*.

15. John Cowley states that initially the single-tone calypso referred to songs sung in French Creole and the double-tone calypso to songs sung in English, circa 1896–1900 (Cowley, 1996: 138).

16. This calypso was recorded for Decca Records in 1941. Thanks to Ryland Burhans for sharing this recording and transcription.

17. Most of the information quoted here regarding Lady Trinidad, including the song lyrics, is from the obituary "A Woman for All Calypso Seasons." *Sunday Express*, January 31, 1999.

18. When Kitchener returned in 1962 to remain in Trinidad, he created a new tent, Kitchener's Calypso Revue.

19. Despite extensive inquiries, I have been unable to uncover the given names of the last two calypsonians in this list.

20. Many of the songs discussed in this section are available on the two-CD collection *The Best of Calypso Rose*, Rituals CMG1305.

21. As Alison McLetchie notes, this was true of a number of calypsonians, including Sparrow, Kitchener, and Shorty (McLetchie, 2013).

22. Alison McLetchie, "Doh Interfere with Husband and Wife Business: Domestic Violence in Trinidad and Tobago." Paper presented at the University of South Carolina Women's and Gender Studies Conference, Columbia, SC, February 28–March 1, 2013.

23. Alison McLetchie, "Carnival Ooman: David Rudder, Women and Power." Paper presented at the Calypso and the Caribbean Literary Imagination Conference, University of Miami, FL, March 17–19, 2005.

24. Ibid.

25. Plummer interview with the author, 1998.

26. Ibid.

27. In 2005 Abbi Blackman won the Calypso Queen Competition and was included in the semifinals of the Calypso Monarch competition, but did not advance to the Calypso Monarch finals. It was later found that her score was not calculated correctly in the semifinal round, and that she should have been included in the Calypso Monarch finals.

28. That is, the fourteenth competition since it had been taken over by NWAC.

29. Shirlane Hendrickson and her sister Lady Wonder (Dianne Hendrickson-Jones) are the daughters of the calypsonian All Rounder (Anthony Hendrickson), and got their start performing as his backup singers. They were perennial favorites and winners at this competition during the nineties.

30. Author interview with Christophe Grant, April 22, 1998.

31. Pan tunes are a colloquial term for calypsos written about the steel pan art form. Typically they are adapted as the tune of choice for steel bands in Panorama.

32. "Pan for Carnival," by Raf Robertson, was performed by Renegades in the Panorama finals; "Clear de Way," by Alvin Daniel and Len "Boogsie" Sharpe, was performed by Phase II Pan Groove in the Panorama finals.

33. Ray Holman composed "Oh Trinidad" for Starlift Steel Orchestra, for which he was arranging during Carnival 1998.

34. The Mas Camp Pub is now called De New Pub. The development of Ariapita Avenue into a dining and entertaining strip occurred between 2001–11. When I was doing my fieldwork in 1998–99 it was still largely a residential area, with relatively few commercial businesses.

35. For a lengthy discussion of calypsonians who were successful in the New York nightclub scene, see Donald Hill, 1993. In earlier times, calypsonians were part of vaudeville shows and entertained patrons between features at movie theatres (Donald Hill, 1993: 1). Hill also states that calypsonians "sometimes participated in ribald shows in barrack yards and brothels" (1993: 55).

36. Late summer and Christmas are popular times for calypsonians who live abroad to return to Trinidad and Tobago, as friends and family are typically on vacation then. Performers also make appearances during public holidays that occur in August, such as Emancipation Day (August 1) and Independence Day (August 31).

37. Grant interview, 1998.

38. Donna Pierre, "Now is the time for an all-woman calypso tent." *Trinidad Guardian*, October 24, 2003.

39. Terry Joseph, "Song, dance, and fashion at Divas Cabaret." *Sunday Guardian*, January 23, 2005.

40. "Rudder joins Ladies Night Out." *Trinidad and Tobago Newsday*, December 28, 2007.

41. "Do Dem Back" is a song by Calypso Rose.

Chapter 3

1. There are limitations on expressions of gender identity within the Trinidadian context. For example, there is little room for expressing LGBT identity. Both male and female same-sex sexual activity is illegal in Trinidad and Tobago, though these laws are rarely enforced. During Carnival there is a certain amount of license for gays and lesbians to display their orientation openly, but generally they are deeply closeted at other times (Paur, 2001: 1044). Homosexual behavior is rarely depicted as acceptable in Trinidadian popular culture. Typically, it is a source of humor, as in comedic drag performances, or calypso lyrics that use double entendre to imply sexual relationships between men, who are ridiculed in the song. Examples of such songs include "Berlin" by All Rounder and "Kim" by Lord Shorty.

2. Abbi Blackman, for example, designs and sews most of her costumes and those for her collaborators onstage. The year I saw her and her singing partner Shanaqua perform, they designed outfits that portrayed Portuguese dancers, Chinese peasants, Bollywood dancers, and West African highlife singers.

3. The exceptions are the finals of the Calypso Monarch competition, where performers are typically given a cash advance to help prepare their spectacle for Dimanche Gras.

4. Joel Julien, "Talented Angel wins prison calypso titles." *Trinidad Express*, February 4, 2011; Ralph Banwarie, "Demali crowned Women's Prison Calypso Monarch." *Newsday*, January 30, 2013.

5. Of course, in the tent environment, limitations on time and physical space affect how elaborate a calypsonian's performance can be.

6. In 2014 the calypso monarch Roderick "Chucky" Gordon was awarded TT$1,000,000 (approximately US$160,000). The second and third place finishers received TT$500,000 and TT$250,000, respectively.

7. Deborah John, "The Petals Have Not Withered." *Trinidad Express*, January 23, 2003.

8. Lewis interview with the author, 2007.

9. Kavery Dutta, *One Hand Don't Clap*, 1991.

10. Lewis interview, 2007.

11. Pascale Obolo, *Calypso Rose: Lioness of the Jungle*, 2011.

12. The songs discussed here are available on *The Best of Calypso Rose: Calypso Queen of the World.*

13. Lewis interview, 2007.

14. Ibid.

15. Ibid.

16. Interview with Keith Smith, quoted in Rohlehr 2004b: 365.

17. "Calypso Rose: the Woman Behind the Music." *Caribbean Belle* online magazine, June 2013.

18. Lewis interview, 2007.

19. Ibid.

20. Ibid.

21. Patricia Meschino, "At 68, Calypso Rose still winning new fans." Reuters News Service, January 23, 2009.

22. This documentary was released in 2011 as *Calypso Rose: Lioness of the Jungle.*

23. "Calypso Rose launches new album." *Trinidad Guardian*, December 18, 2008.

24. Simon Lee, "Get Ready to BYTE—Allen Celebrates the Barrack Yard." *Trinidad Guardian*, January 26, 2015.

25. Michael Goodwin, "One Voice from the Ghetto." *Caribbean Beat* (January/February 2000).

26. Des Vignes interview with the author, 1998.

27. Ibid.

28. Ibid.

29. Ibid.

30. Ibid.

31. Ibid.

32. Ibid.

33. Ibid.

34. Ibid.

35. Verdel Bishop, "Pumping Soca at Ladies Night Out." *Newsday*, February 8, 2009.

36. Denyse Plummer is among a growing number of calypso singers who do not use a sobriquet. Plummer is Denyse's maiden name; her husband is Patrick Boocock and her married name is Denyse Plummer-Boocock.

37. Plummer interview with the author, 1998.

38. Terry Joseph, "Redemption Song." *Trinidad Express*, February 28, 2001.

39. I would like to thank Dmitri Subotsky for sharing this information at his former website www.calypsoarchives.co.uk.

40. Plummer interview, 1998.

41. Sharpe self-released "Pan Rising" as a 45; it has long been out of print. I was able to obtain a recording via YouTube.

42. Ucil Cambridge, "I thought Shadow had won." *Trinidad Express*, March 4, 2001.

43. Plummer interview, 1998.

44. Cedriann J. Martin, "The Eternal Queen." *Sunday Express*, January 29, 2006.

45. Cambridge, "I thought Shadow had won."

46. Kris Rampersad, "Plummer fulfils childhood fantasy." *Sunday Guardian*, January 11, 1998.

47. Joan Plummer passed away in 2010. Denyse's father, Dudley "Buntin" Plummer, passed away in 2011, after spending twenty-three years in long-term care following a stroke.

48. The couple's older son is Jesse Boocock; their younger son is Robert Boocock.

49. Plummer interview, 1998.

50. Judy Raymond, "Denyse Calypso Queen Heats Calypso Monarch." *Trinidad Guardian*, February 27, 2001.

51. Plummer interview, 1998.

52. Camille Bethel, "Denyse Plummer reinvents herself for 20th Anniversary." Woman-Wise supplement to *Sunday Guardian*, January 14, 2007.

53. Cedriann J. Martin, "Denyse taking a break next year." *Trinidad Express*, February 10, 2007.

54. Wayne Bowman, "The Queen is back." *Trinidad Express*, January 16, 2009.

55. Joan Rampersad, "Lots of Trini entertainment for the Summit." *Trinidad & Tobago Newsday*, April 13, 2009.

56. Sasha Harrinanan, "NWAC honours Denyse Plummer." *Trinidad and Tobago Newsday*, January 21, 2015.

57. Essiba Small, "Born-again Denyse says goodbye to calypso." *Trinidad Express*, October 15, 2014.

58. Parang is a style of Christmas music performed in Trinidad and Tobago. With origins in Venezuelan caroling traditions, the lyrics are usually in Spanish or a blend of Spanish and English. Parang soca is a party-oriented form of parang, with mainly English lyrics.

59. Plummer interview, 1998.

60. Despite the fact that the she is the first woman to hold the office of prime minister, Kamla Persad-Bissessar has received as much criticism as her predecessors in her office. Generally, these critiques break down along party lines rather than critiques based on her gender. The People's National Movement, which was voted out in the 2010 general election, tends to have more support from Afro-Trinidadians, and hence, in general, the calypso fraternity. Persad-Bissessar's party, the UNC, which formed part of the coalition government the People's Partnership, is widely perceived as representing Indo-Trinidadian interests at the expense of those supported by the PNM. Calypsonians who have supported the PP, such as Gypsy (Winston Peters), have received a great deal of criticism from their colleagues.

61. "Why we all love Karene Asche & Kizzie Ruiz: the Calypso Queens that Mock Warner." Andrew Jennings blog entry, March 18, 2011. www.transparencyinsport.org/Calypso_Queen_Mocks_Warner/calypso_queen_mocks_warner.html.

62. Wayne Bowman, "'Uncle Jack'—The Final Chapter." *Trinidad Express*, June 9, 2015.

Chapter 4

1. In one discussion group I read, several people insisted that there has not been any soca worth listening to since Super Blue's "Soca Baptist" of 1980, including everything Super Blue had recorded since that year.

2. Much of the general information on musical style is also contained in my entries on soca and ragga soca for the *Bloomsbury Encyclopedia of Popular Music of the World. Volume IX, Genres: Caribbean and Latin America.*

3. See for example, the practice of recycling earlier tunes and recordings in the creation of dancehall songs. (Manuel, 2006: 200–202).

4. Many of David Rudder's compositions, which straddle the line between calypso and soca, could be described as social commentaries masquerading as party songs. Some good examples are "One More Officer," "Madness," and "Panama."

5. Examples might include "Bacchanal Time" by Super Blue and "Whoa Donkey" by the United Sisters.

6. These include "Winer Boi" by Machel Montano, "Dollar Wine" by Colin Lucas, and "Wining Queen" by Denise Belfon.

7. These include "Do Wha Yuh Want" by Natalie Burk and "Don't Bowl Me Too Hard" by Karla Gonzales.

8. Well-known examples include "Sugar Bum Bum" by Lord Kitchener and "Bottom in de Road" by Iwer George.

9. Tony Fraser, "The Slow Death of True Calypso." *Trinidad Guardian*, February 12, 2012.

10. These recordings also circulate widely on various social media platforms, including YouTube, SoundCloud, and ReverbNation.

11. Popular riddims for the 2015 Carnival season included Day Fete, Vibezy, Bitter, Ignition, Knock Knock, and Tribe.

12. In 2015 the average price for a cooler fete was US$50.

13. Ticket prices for these events ranged from $US150–250 in 2015.

14. Tickets for these sorts of fetes can be as much as $US500.

15. This is a family-oriented event; tickets for both children and adults were approximately US$25 in 2015.

16. Jocelyne Guilbault comes to a similar conclusion regarding calypso competitions, which often feel like they are exclusively for promoting a national culture and exercising control over its social, political, and cultural contours (Guilbault, 2007: 81).

17. Most readers are probably more familiar with the version of this song that the Baha Men recorded in 2000.

18. The most successful female artists following this formula as of 2015 were Fay-Ann Lyons, who along with her husband Bunji Garlin leads the Asylum Family Band, and Destra Garcia, whose band is called Bakanal.

19. This quote is usually attributed to the Irish playwright George Bernard Shaw.

20. Candace Guppy, "What happens in de party." *Trinidad Guardian*, February 6, 2005.

21. Lisa Allen-Agostini, "Wining Words." *Caribbean Beat* (January/February 2006).

22. Hollis Liverpool, "Carnival wining came from African slaves." *Trinidad and Tobago Newsday*, February 14, 2011.

23. Randall Sumairsingh, "Hurricane dancehall storms T&T: Music not only affecting fashion but attitude." *Trinidad Guardian*, July 22, 2008.

24. Caribbean Prestige Foundation, Rules and Guidelines Governing the Play Whe International Power Soca Monarch, Digicel Groovy Soca Monarch, and Carib Breakout Artiste of the Year Competition 2014.

25. The junior competition has been held off and on since 1999. Like its senior counterpart, the National Schools Soca Monarch takes place in preliminary, semifinal, and final rounds. The final competition usually occurs a week before Fantastic Friday. This competition is sponsored by the Caribbean Prestige Foundation, as well as corporate entities such as Flavorite Ice Cream and Sunshine Snacks.

26. This figure was provided by Bunji Garlin in several interviews when he and his wife Fay-Ann Lyons decided not to compete in the Soca Monarch finals in 2013.

27. Ideally, I would have interviewed all these artists myself. However, because of extensive touring schedules, soca artists are often hard to reach either in person or by telephone, hence my dependence on newspaper interviews for the quotes from some of the soca artists in this section.

28. For a lengthier discussion of such songs, see Dikobe, 2004.

29. Participating in Carnival requires a certain amount of physical fitness, particularly if one wants to play mas. Immediately after Christmas, the newspapers are filled with articles on how to get in shape for Carnival, often discussing the fitness regimens of popular soca artists.

30. "The Ultimate Rude Gyul." *Trinidad Express*, December 17, 2002.

31. Laura Dowrich-Phillips, "Still Saucy after ten years." *Trinidad Guardian*, January 23, 2005.

32. Plummer interview, 1998.

33. Nicole Duke-Westfield, "Denise makes them panic." *Trinidad Guardian*, February 9, 2001.

34. Darcel Choy, "Denise Belfon: Soca Royalty." *Trinidad & Tobago Newsday*, January 25, 2009.

35. Lisa Allen-Agostini, "While mommy's on stage." *Trinidad Guardian*, February 24, 2001.

36. My attempts to record this phone interview were not successful, hence the lack of lengthy direct quotes.

37. Roslyn Carrington, "The softer side of Saucy." *Trinidad Guardian*, November 21, 2010.

38. Destra is usually referred to by her first name only; thus I am following convention in the discussion of her career.

39. Nicole S. Farrell, "Candidly Destra." *Trinidad Express*, February 7, 2015.

40. Tracy Assing, "Destra: Proud of her roots." *Trinidad Guardian*, January 25, 2004.

41. Tracy Assing, "The Woman with the Hammer." *Caribbean Beat* (January/February 2005).

42. As explained above, a rag tune is one that instructs the audience to jump and wave the hand towels most carry to a fete to wipe the sweat from dancing.

43. Cedriann J. Martin, "Love, life and soca: Destra Garcia." *Trinidad Express*, January 12, 2008.

44. Nathelie Taylor, "Sassy soca diva." *Jamaica Gleaner*, April 18, 2004.

45. Shaliza Hassinali, "Soca Divas Unite." *Trinidad Guardian*, January 31, 2009.

46. Farrell, "Candidly Destra."

47. The other three artists were Iwer George (Iwer Saturday concert), Machel Montano (Machel Monday), and Kes the Band (Tuesday on the Rocks).

48. The reader will note that in newspaper articles the artist's name is variously spelled as Faye-Ann, Fay-Ann, and Fay Ann. I have used the spelling used on the Asylum Family website and Facebook page, as well as the convention of referring to her by her first name.

49. Fay-Ann won in 2003 with "Display," in 2008 with "Get On," and in 2009 with "Meet Superblue."

50. As noted above, Michelle Sylvester was the first woman to win the Groovy Soca Monarch division, in 2005, the year that category was introduced.

51. Nazma Muller, "Meet Superblue." *Trinidad Express*, February 22, 2009.

52. Gizelle Morris, "Petite powerhouse." *Trinidad Guardian*, January 25, 2004.

53. Verdel Bishop, "Soca Royalty." *Trinidad and Tobago Newsday*, January 19, 2008.

54. Leah Sorias and Tabhiry Men Kau Ra, "Soca Monarch Bunji: Fay-Ann should have won." *Trinidad Guardian*, February 3, 2008.

55. Darcel Choy, "Fay-Ann: Pregnant, proud and perfectly fine." *Trinidad and Tobago Newsday*, February 8, 2009.

56. Cordielle Street, "Meet Superblue." *Trinidad Guardian*, February 22, 2009.

57. Although I was not able to attend Carnival in 2009, I watched the Soca Monarch finals live on pay-per-view, as do many people of the West Indian diaspora.

58. Darcel Choy and Joan Rampersand, "Fay-Ann triumphs at Soca Monarch." *Trinidad and Tobago Newsday*, February 22, 2009.

59. The lack of women as accompanists in calypso and soca is largely a result of historical circumstances rather than deliberate exclusion. Until the eighties, there were few opportunities for young people to pursue instrumental music instruction in Trinidad and Tobago. Those who did were boys who received instruction at institutions such as the St. Dominic's Orphanage in Belmont, or via membership in the Police Band. (For further discussion of this, see Guilbault, 2014.) Although there are numerous steelbands for elementary and secondary school students, there are few opportunities for schools to provide instruction on other types of instruments. Generally, boys and girls who play string, wind, and brass instruments learn via private lessons and after-school programs. Currently, there are adequate opportunities to study music at the university level, at both UTT and UWI, and talented musicians have gone abroad to study at universities in the United States, Canada, and the UK.

Chapter 5

1. See Bourdieu, 1986: 245; DeWitt, 2008: 39, 251 n44.

2. The setting I describe has changed in recent years. In 2007 the Savannah complex was demolished to make way for a new structure. In the place of the Grand Stand and North Stand, a temporary structure was built during Carnival for the bands to assemble and perform. The entire North Greens of the Savannah is dedicated to accommodating the

audience, and there is a separate area set aside for Panorama judges. When the Savannah complex was rebuilt, the Greens remained alongside the new Grand Stand and North Stand facilities.

3. Hope Munro Smith, "Beryl McBurnie." *Dictionary of Caribbean and Afro-Latin Biography*, forthcoming from Oxford University Press.

4. One of the founders of this event was Helen May Johnstone, who was also the founder of the Trinidad Music Association, the sponsor of Music Festival.

5. Hope Munro Smith, "Winifred Atwell." *Dictionary of Caribbean and Afro-Latin Biography*, forthcoming from Oxford University Press.

6. Albino de Coteau interview with the author, 1999.

7. Tudor interview with the author, 1998.

8. Huggins-Watts interview with the author, 1998.

9. Personal communication, 1999.

10. Huggins-Watts interview, 1998.

11. The dates of Carnival can fall as early as the first week in February. In years when the Carnival season is so short, steelbands are permitted to use older calypsos as their tune of choice.

12. Tudor interview, 2001.

13. Huggins-Watts interview, 1998.

14. Robbie James, *When Steel Talks* www.panonthenet.com/woman/2006/Michelle%20Huggins-Watts.htm.

15. Ibid.

16. Huggins-Watts interview, 1998.

17. Joseph, 2011: 259. "Clear De Way" was written by Len "Boogsie" Sharp and Alvin Daniel, and was the "own tune" for Boogsie's Phase II Pan Groove in the 1998 Panorama competition. Boogsie himself did not place first that year; that honor went to Clive Bradley, who arranged David Rudder's "High Mas" for Nutones Steel Orchestra.

18. James, *When Steel Talks*.

19. Interview with *When Steel Talks*, 2012: www.panonthenet.com/tnt/2012/interviews/michelle-huggins-watts-panorama-1-22-2012.htm.

20. Ibid.

21. "Valley Harps to Feature in 7-Part BBC Series." *Trinidad Express*, July 27, 2012.

22. The program can be viewed at the BBC's website: www.bbc.com/news/magazine-18889040.

23. Excerpts from this CD can be heard at the following website: http://panncosteelband.bandcamp.com/album/digital-double-album-twinning-souls.

24. "Meet Natasha Joseph." *When Steel Talks*; http://www.panonthenet.com/woman/2014/natasha-joseph.htm.

25. Natasha Joseph interview with the author, 1998.

26. David Cuffy, "Panazz Brings out the best." *Trinidad Guardian*, November 28, 2012.

27. Chantal Esdelle, "Behind Every Good Thing is a Good Woman." *Chantal Esdelle Caribbean Jazz Corner*, March 2, 2014. https://chantalesdelle.wordpress.com/2014/03/02/behind-every-good-thing-is-a-good-woman/.

Conclusions

1. From the Harts Carnival web site: www.hartscarnival.com.
2. Similar theories regarding academic underperformance among boys have also been applied to the United States and the UK.
3. "Domestic violence laws being beefed up." *Trinidad Express*, March 15, 2015.
4. With the 2015 general election looming, politicians were reluctant to discuss abortion, which is illegal in Trinidad and Tobago except in case of threat to the life or health of the pregnant woman. Both male and female same-sex sexual activity is illegal in Trinidad and Tobago, though these laws are rarely enforced. Prime Minister Kamla Persad-Bissessar has spoken out against discrimination based on sexual orientation, but met with resistance regarding changing legislation during her term in office, and hence no progress has been made on this issue.

Glossary

Anansi stories—trickster folktales of African origin. Named for the protagonist of the stories, who is a large black spider, the weakest yet cleverest of all the animals.

bacchanal—any situation where there is much noise, rowdy behavior, and/or scandal. Can refer to either celebration or confusion.

badjohn—literally a bad guy; hustler, street-tough. Also used to refer to someone who pushes their weight around, in politics for example.

band—a group of players. This refers to playing music (a brass band, a steel band, a soca band), and playing mas (a Jouvay band, a mud band, a pretty band).

bele, bélé, belle, belair, bel air—an Afro-Creole dance with French origins, known throughout the West Indies

big truck—a mobile sound system, amplifying either a band or DJs who ride aboard alongside the sound equipment. The many bass, mid-range, and high-end boxes encase and support two stages. The lower stage houses the band, while the singers ride on top of the truck, actually a sixteen-wheel tractor-trailer. These trucks are hired by mas bands to accompany them as they parade through the streets on Carnival Monday and Tuesday.

bois—the wooden stick used in stickfighting (calinda). Usually made from poui, gasparee, balata, or anare wood.

bongo—Afro-Creole music and dance associated with all-night wakes for the dead.

break away, breakaway—going wild, dancing with absolute joy and abandon. Also a calypso that inspires such behavior.

buss—to break up, burst, bust. To "buss a note" or "buss the tune" means to play badly. To "buss on stage" means to falter and stop completely in the middle of a performance.

calabash—the tree *crescentia cujete*, its fruit, or a vessel or musical instrument made from the tree's fruit.

calinda (also spelled kalinda, kalenda, calinda, calenda, calender, calenda, batille bois)—a term that refers to all aspects of stickfighting, including its dance and songs.

callaloo—a West Indian stew made from dasheen leaves, ochro (okra), coconut milk, and salt meat or crab. It can refer to any kind of colorful or unlikely mixture, such as the various cultural groups that make up Trinidad and Tobago.

calypso—an Afro-Creole popular music and rhythm native to Trinidad.

calypsonian—a musical artist who sings calypso.

canboulay, cannes brulees, cannes brûlées, cannes brulées—literally, "burning cane," a procedure used before harvesting to control reptiles, centipedes, scorpions, and other pests. Since emancipation, canboulay has been re-enacted as a type of parade on 1 August (Emancipation Day) and Jouvay morning.

Carnival Monday—the Monday before Ash Wednesday.

Carnival Tuesday—the last day of Carnival before Ash Wednesday.

chac-chac—a percussion instrument made from a calabash or gourd filled with seeds or small stones used for percussion, similar to maracas.

chantwell—in the nineteenth century, the lead singer of a Carnival band, a prototype of today's calypsonian.

chutney—taken from the name for an East Indian relish of green mango and spices, this music is based on songs sung by women to the bride the night before her wedding.

chutney soca, soca chutney—a style of music that blends chutney and soca. Singers may use Hindi or English lyrics, or a mixture. The arrangements tend to foreground Indian instruments such as the harmonium and hand drum, though most bands simulate these sounds using synthesizers and rhythm tracks rather than live drummers.

commesse—gossip or slander repeated in an artful way, enhancing the speaker's reputation. Also the wheeling and dealing that accompanies it and confusion that results from such activity.

cuatro—a four-stringed guitar brought to Trinidad either by Venezuelans or the Portuguese. It resembles the ukulele of Hawaii or cavaquinho of Brazil. It is primarily used to accompany Christmas parang music, though a few players accompany folk choirs or popular bands at special occasions or on recordings at other times of the year.

Dimanche Gras—the Sunday before Ash Wednesday.

dingolay—to dance with creative or unusual arm and leg movements, associated with they way Lord Kitchener danced onstage.

dudup—A portable two-note bass drum used in pan, carried by a strap around the neck.

engine room—the percussion section of a steelband, consisting of drums, tambourines, bells, brake drums, scrapers, and chac-chac. Probably named after the engine room of a ship, because it "drives" the whole steelband.

extempo—a form of calypso that features singers extemporaneously composing verses, usually ones that are humorous and clever.

flambeaux—torch made from a bottle filled with kerosene and lit with a cloth wick. It was used to accompany canne brulee processions.

horn—(as in the horns of the cuckold). To cheat on one's romantic partner.

Hosay/hosein—A Muslim holy festival that commemorates the martyrdom of Imam Hosein, the grandson of the Prophet Mohammed. The festival in Trinidad consists of models of the Taj in which Hosein was buried paraded through the streets, usually accompanied by tassa drumming.

jamette, jamet—from the French *diameter,* meaning boundary or border, it refers to the "other half" or "underworld." Eventually, the term became attached to the women of the underclass, particularly prostitutes.

Jouvay—from the French *jour ouvert*, opening day. This is the official beginning of Carnival in the early morning hours of Carnival Monday.

las lap—literally, the very last hours of Carnival Tuesday.

lavway—call-and-response singing, associated with calinda in nineteenth-century Trinidad. Today, popular calypsos and soca tunes often use lavway structures.

leh go, leggo—let go or let oneself go. Sometimes used interchangeably with lavway or breakaway to refer to an especially upbeat song or chorus, and the dance that goes with it.

liming—to spend time talking, laughing, drinking with other people.

mas, mas—masquerade.

mas camp—the location where designs of mas costumes can be viewed and ordered. The costumes are made at the mas camp or a workshop nearby. During the days before Carnival, the members of the band pick up their costumes at the mas camp and socialize with other band members.

Midnight Robber—A traditional Carnival character whose costume is based on the "black hat" of Hollywood westerns. Part of his performance is accosting spectators, who must pay him for the privilege of hearing his "robber talk."

Moko Jumbie—a traditional Carnival character, based on African stilt-walking dancers. The mas represents the spirit of Moko, the Orisha of fate and retribution.

obeah—in the positive sense, a West African–based system of healing and magic that uses potions, charms, and fetishes. In the negative sense, witchcraft, spell casting, entrapment, poisoning, etc.

ole mas, old mas, ol' mas—a satiric masquerade that usually acts out a pun or parodies a current event or public figure. Ole mas is usually portrayed and judged at a certain point during Jouvay morning.

Old talk, ole talk, ol' talk—social chit-chat or idle banter between peers. Also refers to argumentative, cheeky responses to questions.

Orisha, Orisa—the Afro-Caribbean religion of Trinidad and Tobago, analogous to Brazilian candomblé and Cuban santeria. Sometimes (and incorrectly) called Shango by anthropologists, after one of the religion's principal deities.

pan—a musical instrument invented in Trinidad, fashioned from steel oil drums.

Panorama—the primary steelband competition of Trinidad and Tobago, held during the Carnival season. The finals of Panorama, formerly held on Dimanche Gras, are now held on the Saturday before Carnival.

pan round de neck—a steelband that carries its pans suspended from a strap around the neck or over the shoulders. Also called traditional steelbands or single-pan bands.

panyard—the home turf of a steelband, where instruments are stored and rehearsals are held, as well as other events to raise money for the band.

parang—from the Spanish *parrandar*, to revel, carouse; the Christmas music of Trinidad, based on folk music from Venezuela.

pelau—a one-pot cook-up of rice, pigeon peas, and chicken or beef. Very portable, it is a dish people like to take to the beach or have on hand during Carnival to serve to people who drop by.

picong—teasing, joking, making fun of a person to their face.

play mas—to masquerade, wear a costume and play with a mas band.

play yourself—to enjoy yourself to the utmost degree; to show off, to parade oneself around in enjoyment.

ramajay—sustained whistling of a bird; improvised musical solo; to show off musically or verbally.

rapso—a "rapped" form of calypso influenced by the speech of traditional masquerade character the Midnight Robber, as well as other speech poetry from the Caribbean, such as dub poetry and toasting.

Savannah—while most communities in the islands have a clear space for public recreation that they call a savannah, *the* Savannah is the Queen's Park Savannah in Port-of-Spain. This is the site of Trinidad's Carnival competitions.

soca—a style of calypso created by various calypsonians and bandleaders in the 1970s. Lord Shorty called it sokah to emphasize that it is a fusion of African and East Indian rhythms. Once performers such as Sparrow and Kitchener began to imitate the style, they called it "soul calypso" or soca.

steel band, steelband—a musical ensemble made up of steel pans of various sizes, representing the different voices of an orchestra: tenor, double tenor, double seconds, guitar, cello, and bass.

tamboo bamboo—a musical ensemble made up of bamboo sticks of varying lengths that are beaten on the ground, struck together, or struck with wooden sticks to produce melodies and rhythmic patterns.

tassa drums—large, bowl-shaped drums of East Indian origin made from clay and covered with goat skins that are heated by a fire in order to tune the heads to the correct pitch for playing. They are carried with a shoulder strap and played with two small, flexible sticks.

wine, wining—to wind or rotate the hips provocatively, to musical accompaniment. One can wine on one's own, or "wine on" (in full contact with) the front or back of another person's hips (wining in front, wining in back).

Bibliography

Abrahams, Roger. 1967. "The Shaping of Folklore Traditions in the British West Indies." *Journal of Inter-American Studies* vol. IX, no. 3: 456–80.

———. 1972. "The Training of a Man of Words in Talking Sweet." *Language in Society* vol. 1: 15–29.

———. 1983. *The Man-of-words in the West Indies: Performance and the Emergence of Creole Culture*. Baltimore: Johns Hopkins University Press.

———. 2007. "Afterword." In Garth Green and Philip Scher, eds., *Trinidad Carnival: The Cultural Politics of a Transnational Festival*. Bloomington: Indiana University Press.

Aho, William R. 1987. "Steel Band Music in Trinidad and Tobago: The Creation of a People's Music." *Latin American Music Review* (Spring/Summer 1987).

Ahye, Molly. 1978. *Golden Heritage: The Dance in Trinidad and Tobago*. Petit Valley, Trinidad and Tobago: Heritage Cultures Limited.

———. 1991. "Carnival, the Manipulative Polymorph, and Interplay of Social Stratification." In Selwyn Ryan, ed. *Social and Occupational Stratification in Contemporary Trinidad and Tobago*. St. Augustine: Institute of Social and Economic Research, University of West Indies. 399–426.

———. 1996. "Festivals," in *Insight Guides, Trinidad and Tobago*. Boston: APA Publications Ltd.

Ahyoung, Selwyn. 1977. *The Music of Trinidad*. Bachelor's thesis, Indiana University.

———. 1981. *Soca Fever!: Change in the Calypso Music Tradition of Trinidad and Tobago, 1970–1980*. Master's thesis, Indiana University.

Aiyejina, Funso, and Rawle Gibbons. 1999. "Orisa (Orisha) Tradition in Trinidad." *Caribbean Quarterly* (December 1999).

Anthony, Michael, and Andrew Carr, eds. 1975. *David Frost Introduces Trinidad and Tobago*. London: Andre Deutsch Limited.

Aparicio, Frances. 1998. *Listening to Salsa: Gender, Latin Popular Music, and Puerto Rican Cultures*. Middletown: Wesleyan University Press.

Averill, Gage. 1994. "Anrage to Angaje: Carnival Politics and Music in Haiti." *Ethnomusicology* vol. 38, no. 2, Music and Politics issue (Spring-Summer 1994): 217–47.

Bakhtin, Mikhail. 1984. *Problems of Dostoevsky's Poetics*. Minneapolis: University of Minnesota Press.

Baksh-Soodeen, Rawwida. 1998. "Issues of Difference in Contemporary Caribbean Feminism." *Feminist Review* 59: 74–85.

Ballantyne, Gregory. 1998. "People's Perceptions and Paranoia in Calypso." *Caribbean Dialogue: A Journal of Contemporary Caribbean Policy Issues* vol. 3, no. 4 (October/November 1998): 39-42.

Balliger, Robin. 1999. "Popular Music and the Cultural Politics of Globalization among the Post-Oil Boom Generation in Trinidad." In Ralph Premdas, ed. *Identity, Ethnicity and Culture in the Caribbean*. St. Augustine: Institute of Social and Economic Research, University of West Indies. 54-79.

———. 2001. *Noisy Spaces: Popular Music Consumption, Social Fragmentation, and the Cultural Politics of Consumption in Trinidad*. Diss., Stanford University.

———. 2007. "The Politics of Cultural Value and the Value of Cultural Politics: International Intellectual Property Legislation in Trinidad." In Garth Green and Philip Scher, eds., *Trinidad Carnival: The Cultural Politics of a Transnational Festival*. Bloomington: Indiana University Press.

Barnes, Natasha. 2000. "Body Talk: Notes on Women and Spectacle in Contemporary Trinidad and Tobago." *Small Axe* 7 (March 2000): 93-105.

Barriteau, Eudine. 1998. "Theorizing Gender Systems and the Project of Modernity in the Twentieth-Century Caribbean." *Feminist Review* 59 (Summer): 186-210.

Barrow, Christine. 1998. "Caribbean Gender Ideologies" and "Caribbean Masculinity and Family: Revisiting 'Marginality' and 'Reputation.'" In *Caribbean Portraits: Essays on Gender Ideologies and Identities*. Kingston: Ian Randle Publishers.

Bauman, Richard. 1977. *Verbal Art as Performance*. Prospect Heights: Waveland Press.

Beckles, Hilary McD. 1998a. "Centring Woman: the Political Economy of Gender in West African and Caribbean Slavery." In *Caribbean Portraits: Essays on Gender Ideologies and Identities*. Kingston: Ian Randle Publishers.

———. 1998b. "Historicizing Slavery in West Indian Feminism." *Feminist Review* 59: 34-56.

Béhague, Gerard. 1984. *Performance Practice: Ethnomusicological Perspectives*. Westport: Greenwood Press.

———. 1994. *Music and Black Ethnicity: The Caribbean and South America*. Miami: North-South Center.

Bellour, Helene, and Samuel Kinser. 1998. "Amerindian Masking in Trinidad's Carnival: The House of Black Elk in San Fernando." *Drama Review* vol. 42, no. 3 (Fall 1998): 147-69.

Berry, Venise. 1994. "Feminine or Masculine: The Conflicting Nature of Female Images in Rap Music." In Susan Cook and Judy Tsou, eds. *Cecilia Reclaimed: Feminist Perspectives on Gender and Music*. Urbana and Chicago: University of Illinois Press.

Besson, Jean. 1993. "Reputation and Respectability Reconsidered: A New Perspective on Afro-Caribbean Peasant Women." In Janet H. Momsen, ed. *Women and Change in the Caribbean*. Bloomington: Indiana University Press.

Best, Curwin. 2001. "Technology Constructing Culture: Tracking Soca's First Post-." *Small Ax* 9 (March 2001).

Bilby, Kenneth. 1985. "The Caribbean as a Musical Region." In Sidney Mintz and Sally Price, eds. *Caribbean Contours*. Baltimore: Johns Hopkins University Press.

Birth, Kevin K. 1994. "Bakanal: Coup, Carnival, and Calypso in Trinidad." *Ethnology* vol. 33, no. 2 (Spring 1994).

———. 1999. *Any Time Is Trinidad Time: Social Meanings and Temporal Consciousness.* Gainesville: University Press of Florida.

———. 2008. *Bacchanalian Sentiments: Musical Experiences and Political Counterpoints in Trinidad.* Durham and London: Duke University Press.

Blake, Felix. 1995. *The Trinidad and Tobago Steel Pan: History and Evolution.* Port-of-Spain: Felix I. R. Blake.

Bolles, A. Lynn. 1998. "Working on Equality: Commonwealth Caribbean Women Trade Union Leaders." In *Caribbean Portraits: Essays on Gender Ideologies and Identities.* Kingston: Ian Randle Publishers.

Bourdieu, Pierre. 1986. "The Forms of Capital." In John G. Richardson, ed. *Handbook of Theory and Research for the Sociology of Education.* New York: Greenwood Press. 241–58.

Brereton, Bridget. 1979. *Race Relations in Colonial Trinidad 1870-1900.* Cambridge: Cambridge University Press.

———. 1981. *A History of Modern Trinidad 1783-1962.* Oxford: Heinemann Educational Books.

Brodber, Erna, 1982. *Perceptions of Caribbean Women: Towards a Documentation of Stereotypes.* Cave Hill, Barbados: Institute of Social and Economic Research, University of the West Indies.

Brown, Ernest D. 1975. "Carnival, Calypso and Steelband in Trinidad." *Black Perspective in Music* 18, no. 1-2: 81–100.

Brown, Jarret. 1999. "Masculinity and Dancehall." *Caribbean Quarterly* 45, no. 1 (March 1999).

Burton, Richard E. 1997. *Afro-Creole: Power, Opposition, and Play in the Caribbean.* Ithaca: Cornell University Press.

Chang, Carlisle. 1998. "Chinese in Trinidad Carnival." *Drama Review* vol. 42, no. 3 (Fall 1998): 213–19.

Citron, Marcia. 1993. *Gender and the Musical Canon.* Cambridge: Cambridge University Press.

Connor, Edric. 1958. *Songs from Trinidad.* London: Oxford University Press Music Department.

Cooper, Carolyn. 1993. *Noises in the Blood: Orality, Gender, and the "Vulgar" Body of Jamaican Popular Culture.* Durham: Duke University Press.

———. 2004. *Sound Clash: Jamaican Dancehall Culture at Large.* New York: Palgrave MacMillan.

Cowley, John. 1996. *Carnival, Canboulay and Calypso: Traditions in the Making.* London: Cambridge University Press.

Crowley, Daniel J. 1956. "The Traditional Masques of Carnival." *Caribbean Quarterly* iv (1956): 42–90.

Cupid, John. 1998. "We Have Been Called Carnival People." *Drama Review* vol. 42, no. 3 (Fall 1998): 96–107.

Cyrille, Dominique. 2002. "Sa Ki Ta Nou (This Belongs to Us): Creole Dances of the French Caribbean." In Susanna Sloat, ed. *Caribbean Dance from Abakuá to Zouk: How Movement Shapes Identity.* Gainesville: University Press of Florida.

Davies, Carole Boyce. 1990. "Women is a Nation . . . : Women in Caribbean Oral Literature." In Carole Boyce Davies and Elaine Savory Fido, eds. *Out of the Kumbla: Caribbean Women in Literature.* Trenton: Africa World Press.

Davis, Angela. 1998. *Blues Legacies and Black Feminism: Gertrude "Ma" Rainey, Bessie Smith, and Billie Holiday*. New York: Pantheon.

De Albuquerque, Klaus, and Sam Ruark. 1998. "Men Day Done: Are Women Really Ascendant in the Caribbean?" In *Caribbean Portraits: Essays on Gender Ideologies and Identities*. Kingston: Ian Randle Publishers.

De Leon, Rafael ("Roaring Lion"). 1978. *Calypso: From France to Trinidad, 800 Years of History*. Port-of-Spain: Trinidad Broadcasting Co.

De Ledesma, Charles, and Simon. 1994. "Out of the Orchid House: Calypso and Soca From Trinidad and Beyond." In *World Music: The Rough Guide*. London: Penguin.

DeWitt, Mark. 2008. *Cajun and Zydeco Dance Music in Northern California*. Jackson: University Press of Mississippi.

Di Leonardo, Micaela. 1991. *Gender at the Crossroads of Knowledge: Feminist Anthropology in the Postmodern Era*. Berkeley: University of California Press.

Diehl, Kiela Mackie. 1992. "Tempered Steel: The Steel Drum as a Site for Social, Political and Aesthetic Negotiation in Trinidad." M.A. thesis, University of Texas at Austin.

Dikobe, Maude Modimothebe. 2003. *Doing She Own Thing: Gender, Performance and Subversion in Trinidad Calypso*. Diss., University of California, Berkeley.

———. 2004. "Bottom in de Road: Gender and Sexuality in Calypso." *Proudflesh: New Afrikan Journal of Culture, Politics and Consciousness*. www.proudfleshjournal.com/issue3/issue3.htm.

Dudley, Shannon. 1996. "Judging 'By the Beat': Calypso versus Soca." *Ethnomusicology* 46 (1): 135–64.

———. 2001. "Ray Holman and the Changing Role of the Steelband, 1957-1972." *Latin American Music Review* (Fall/Winter 2001).

———. 2004. *Carnival Music in Trinidad*. New York: Oxford University Press.

———. 2008. *Music from Behind the Bridge*. New York: Oxford University Press.

Edmondson, Belinda. 2003. "Public Spectacles: Caribbean Women and the Politics of Public Performance." *Small Axe* 13 (March 2003): 1–16.

Elder, Jacob Delworth. 1966a. *Evolution of the Traditional Calypso of Trinidad and Tobago: A Socio-historical Analysis of Song Change*. Diss., University of Pennsylvania.

———. 1966b. "Kalinda: Song of the Battling Troubadours of Trinidad." *Journal of the Folklore Institute* iii: 192–203.

———. 1968. *From Congo Drum to Steel Band: Social Development of the Traditional Calypso of Trinidad and Tobago*. St. Augustine: University of the West Indies Press.

———. 1998. "Cannes Brûlées." *Drama Review* vol. 42, no. 3 (Fall 1998): 39–43.

Eldridge, Michael. 2002. "There Goes the Transnational Neighborhood: Calypso Buys a Bungalow." *Callaloo* 25.2 (2002): 620–38.

Ellis, Patricia. 1986. *Women of the Caribbean*. London and New York: Zed Books.

———. 2003. *Women, Gender, and Development in the Caribbean: Reflections and Projections*. London and New York: Zed Books.

Eriksen, Thomas Hylland. 1990. "Liming in Trinidad: The Art of Doing Nothing." *Folk* vol. 32 (1990).

Espinet, Charles, and Henry Pitts. 1944. *Land of the Calypso*. Port-of-Spain: Guardian Commercial Printery.

Figueroa, Mark. 2004. "Male Privileging and Male 'Academic Underperformance' in Jamaica." In Rhoda Reddock, ed. *Interrogating Caribbean Masculinities: Theoretical and Empirical Analyses.* University of West Indies Press.

Finden-Crofts, Justin. 1998. "Calypso's Consequences." In Daniel Miller, ed. *Material Cultures: Why Some Things Matter.* Chicago: University of Chicago Press.

Franco, Pamela R. 1998. "'Dressing Up and Looking Good': Afro-Creole Female Maskers in Trinidad Carnival." *African Arts* vol. 31, no. 2: 62–67, 91, 95, 96.

———. 2000. "The 'Unruly Woman' in Nineteenth Century Trinidad Carnival." *Small Axe* 7 (March 2000): 60–76.

———. 2001. *Shifting Ground: An Early History of Afro-Creole Women's Mas' in Trinidad Carnival.* Diss., Emory University.

———. 2004. "The Martinican: Dress and Politics in Nineteenth-century Trinidad Carnival." In Milla Cozart Riggio, ed. *Carnival: Culture in Action: The Trinidad Experience.* New York: Routledge.

———. 2007. "The Invention of Traditional Mas and the Politics of Gender." In Garth Green and Philip Scher, eds. *Trinidad Carnival: The Cultural Politics of a Transnational Festival.* Bloomington: Indiana University Press.

Freeman, Carla. 1997. "Reinventing Higglering Across Transnational Zones: Barbadian Women Juggle the Triple Shift." In Consuelo Lopez Springfield, ed. *Daughters of Caliban: Caribbean Women in the Twentieth Century.* Bloomington and Indianapolis: Indiana University Press.

Gibbons, Rawle. 1994. *No Surrender: A Biography of the Growling Tiger.* Tunapuna, Trinidad: Canboulay Productions.

———. 1999. *A Calypso Trilogy: Sing de Chorus; Ah Wanna Fall; Ten to One.* Tunapuna, Trinidad: Canboulay Productions.

Glazier, Stephen D. 1983. *Marchin' the Pilgrims Home: Leadership and Decision-Making in an Afro-Caribbean Faith.* Westport: Greenwood Press.

———. 1997. "Embedded Truths: Creativity and Context in Spiritual Baptist Music." *Latin American Music Review* vol. 18, no. 1 (Spring/Summer 1997): 44–56.

Gonzalez, Sylvia. 1978. *Steelband Saga: A Story of the Steelband—The First 25 Years.* Port-of-Spain: Ministry of Education and Culture.

Gottreich, Anna Stephanie. 1993. *Whe She Go Do: Women's Participation in Trinidad Calypso: A Socio-historical Study.* M.A. thesis, University of California, Berkeley.

Green, Garth L., and Philip W. Scher, eds. 2007. *Trinidad Carnival: The Cultural Politics of a Transnational Festival.* Bloomington: University of Indiana Press.

Grosz, Elizabeth. 1994. *Volatile Bodies: Towards a Corporeal Feminism.* Bloomington: Indiana University Press.

Guilbault, Jocelyne. 1990. "On Interpreting Popular Music: Zouk in the West Indies." In John Lent, ed. *Caribbean Popular Culture.* Bowling Green: Bowling Green State University Popular Press.

———. 1993. *Zouk: World Music in the West Indies.* Chicago: University of Chicago Press.

———. 2000. "Racial Projects and Musical Discourses in Trinidad, West Indies." In Ronal Rodano and Philip V. Bohlman, ed. *Music and the Racial Imagination.* Chicago and London: University of Chicago Press.

———. 2005. "Audible Entanglements: Nation and Diasporas in Trinidad's Calypso Music Scene." *Small Axe* 17 (March 2005): 40–63.

———. 2007. *Governing Sound: The Cultural Politics of Trinidad's Carnival Musics.* Chicago: University of Chicago Press.

———. 2014. *Roy Cape: A Life on the Calypso and Soca Bandstand.* Durham: Duke University Press.

Hall, Stuart. 1995. "Negotiating Caribbean Identity." *New Left Review* (January/February 1995).

Harewood, Susan. 2005. "Masquerade Performance and the Play of Sexual Identity in Calypso." *Cultural Studies—Critical Methodologies* vol. 5, no. 2.

Hegelberg, G. B. 1985. "Sugar in the Caribbean: Turning Sunshine into Money." In Sidney Mintz and Sally Price, eds. *Caribbean Contours.* Baltimore: Johns Hopkins University Press.

Hebdige, Dick. 1987. *Cut 'n' Mix: Culture, Identity and Caribbean Music.* London and New York: Comedia.

Herndon, Marcia. 1990. "Biology and Culture: Music, Gender, Power, and Ambiguity." In Marcia Herndon and Suzanne Ziegler, eds. *Music, Gender, and Culture.* New York: C.F. Peters.

Henry, Frances. 1998. "Race and Racism in Trinidad and Tobago: a Comment." *Caribbean Dialogue: A Journal of Contemporary Caribbean Policy Issues* vol. 3, no. 4 (October/November 1998): 45–48.

———. 2003. *Reclaiming African Religions in Trinidad: the Socio-Political Legitimation of the Orisha and Spiritual Baptist Faiths.* Barbados/Jamaica/Trinidad and Tobago: University of the West Indies Press.

Herskovits, Melville J., and Frances S. Herskovits. 1947. *Trinidad Village.* New York: Alfred A. Knopf.

Hill, Donald R. 1993. *Calypso Callaloo: Early Carnival Music in Trinidad.* Gainesville: University Press of Florida.

Hill, Errol. 1972/1997. *The Trinidad Carnival: Mandate for a National Theatre.* Austin: University of Texas Press.

———. 1986. "Calypso and War." *Seminar on the Calypso.* University of the West Indies, St. Augustine, Trinidad, Institute of Social and Economic Research.

Hodge, Merle. 1982. "Introduction." In Erna Brodber. *Perceptions of Caribbean Women: Towards a Documentation of Stereotypes.* Cave Hill, Barbados: Institute of Social and Economic Research.

———. 1996. "The People of Trinidad and Tobago." In *Insight Guides, Trinidad and Tobago.* Boston: APA Publications.

Honoré, Brian. 1998. "The Midnight Robber: Master of Metaphor, Baron of Bombast." *Drama Review* vol. 42, no. 3 (fall 1998): 124–31.

Houk, James. 1995. *Spirits, Blood, and Drums.* Philadelphia: Temple University Press.

Hughes-Tafen, Denise. 2006. "Women, Theatre, and Calypso in the English-speaking Caribbean." *Feminist Review* 84, no. 1.

James-Bryan, Meryl. 1991. "'Get Something and Wave': The Rallying Cry of a Nation on the Mend." *Caribbean Quarterly* 37, nos. 2-3 (June-September): 33–37.

Johnson, Kim Nicholas. 1988. Introduction to *Trinidad Carnival* (a republication of the Caribbean quarterly Trinidad carnival issue, volume 4, numbers 3 & 4 of 1956). Port-of-Spain, Trinidad, West Indies: Paria Publishing.
———. 1996. "History of Trinidad and Tobago." In *Insight Guides, Trinidad and Tobago*. Boston: APA Publications.
———. 1996. *Festivals in the Caribbean*. Trinidad Express Newspapers.
———. 1998. "Notes on Pans." *Drama Review* vol. 42, no. 3 (Fall 1998): 61–73.
———. 2002. "Saga of a Flagwoman." In Patricia Mohammed, ed. *Gendered Realities: Essays in Caribbean Feminist Thought*. Mona, Jamaica: Centre for Gender and Development Studies, University of the West Indies Press.
———. 2011. *The Illustrated Story of Pan*. Arima: University of Trinidad & Tobago.
Koskoff, Ellen. 1987. *Women and Music in Cross-Cultural Perspective*. Westport: Greenwood Press.
Lamming, George. 1998. "The Legacy of Eric Williams." *Callaloo* 20.4 (1997): 731–36.
Lee, Ann. 1991. "Class, Race and Colour in the Trinidad Carnival." In Selwyn Ryan, ed. *Social and Occupational Stratification in Contemporary Trinidad and Tobago*. St. Augustine: Institute of Social and Economic Research, University of West Indies. 417–33.
Leu, Lorraine. 2000. "Raise Yuh Hand, Jump up and Get on Bad!: New Developments in Soca Music in Trinidad." *Latin American Music Review* 21:1 (Spring-Summer 2001): 45–58.
Lewis, Linden. 1998. "Masculinity and the Dance of the Dragon: Reading Lovelace Discursively." *Feminist Review* 59 (Summer 1998): 164–85.
———. 2003. "Caribbean Masculinity: Unpacking the Narrative." In Linden Lewis, ed. *The Culture of Gender and Sexuality in the Caribbean*. Gainesville: University Press of Florida.
Lindsay, Keisha. 2002. "Is the Caribbean Male an Endangered Species?" In Patricia Mohammed, ed. *Gendered Realities: Essays in Caribbean Feminist Thought*. Mona, Jamaica: Centre for Gender and Development Studies, University of the West Indies Press.
Lipsitz, George. 1990. *Time Passages*. Minneapolis: University of Minnesota Press.
Liverpool, Hollis ("Mighty Chalkdust"). 1993. *Rituals of Power and Rebellion: The Carnival Tradition in Trinidad and Tobago*. Diss., University of Michigan.
———. 1998. "Origins of Rituals and Customs in the Trinidad Carnival: African or European?" *Drama Review* vol. 42, no. 3 (Fall 1998): 24–37.
Lomax, Alan, with J. D. Elder and Beth Lomax Hawes. 1997. *Brown Girl in the Ring: An Anthology of Song Games from the Eastern Caribbean*. New York: Pantheon.
Lovelace, Earl. 1979. *The Dragon Can't Dance*. Essex, UK: Addison Wesley Longman.
———. 1996. *Salt*. London: Faber and Faber.
———. 1998. "The Emancipation-Jouvay Tradition and the Almost Loss of Pan." *Drama Review* vol. 42, no. 3 (Fall 1998): 54–60.
Low Chew Tung, Michael. 2007. *Kaiso Koncepts: A Modern Approach to Playing Calypso Music*. Self-published.
McBurnie, Beryl. 1950. *Dance Trinidad Dance: Outline of the Dances of Trinidad and Tobago*. Port-of-Spain: Guardian Commercial Printery.
McCree, Roy. 1998. "Carnival Calypso and Ethnicity." *Caribbean Dialogue: A Journal of Contemporary Caribbean Policy Issues* vol. 3, no. 4 (October/November 1998): 93–102.

McLane, Daisanne. 1987. "Contemporary Music in Trinidad." *Review: Latin American Literature and Arts* 37: 48–51.

McLetchie, Alison. 2013. "Doh Interfere with Husband and Wife Business: Domestic Violence in Trinidad and Tobago." Paper presented at the University of South Carolina Women's and Gender Studies Conference, Columbia, SC. February 28–March 1, 2013.

McRobbie, Angela. 1991. *Feminism and Youth Culture: From "Jackie" to "Just Seventeen."* Boston: Unwin Hyman.

———. 1994. *Postmodernism and Popular Culture*. London and New York: Routledge.

Mahabir, Cynthia. 1996. "Wit and Popular Music: The Calypso and the Blues." *Popular Music* 15/1: 55–81.

———. 2001. "The Rise of Calypso Feminism: Gender and Musical Politics in the Calypso." *Popular Music* 20, no. 3: 409–30.

Mahabir, Joy. 2002. "Rhythm and Class Struggle: The Calypsoes of David Rudder." *Jouvert: Journal of Postcolonial Studies* 6:3 (2002). http://social.chass.ncsu.edu/jouvert/v613/con63.htm.

Maison-Bishop, Carole Nathalie. 1994. *Women in Calypso: Hearing the Voices*. Diss., Department of Education, University of Alberta.

———. 1995. *Gender and Musical Performance: The Female Calypso Singer in the Caribbean*. St. Michael, Barbados: Women and Development Unit, University of the West Indies.

Manning, Frank E. 1990a. "Calypso as a Medium of Political Communication." In Stuart Surlin and Walter Soderlund, eds. *Mass Media in the Caribbean*. New York: Gordon and Breach. 415–28.

———. 1990b. "Overseas Caribbean Carnivals: The Art and Politics of a Transnational Celebration." In John Lent, ed. *Caribbean Popular Culture*. Bowling Green: Bowling Green State University Popular Press.

Manuel, Peter. 1998. "Gender Politics in Caribbean Popular Music: Consumer Perspectives and Academic Interpretation." *Popular Music and Society* 22.2: 10–30.

———. 2006. *Caribbean Currents Revised and Expanded Edition: Caribbean Music from Rumba to Reggae*. Philadelphia: Temple University Press.

Mark, Paula. 1991. "Status Attainment and Gender in Scientific and Technological Institutions in Trinidad and Tobago: Where to Next?" In Selwyn Ryan, ed. *Social and Occupational Stratification in Contemporary Trinidad and Tobago*. St. Augustine, Trinidad: Institute for Social and Economic Research.

Mason, Peter. 1998. *Bacchanal! The Carnival Culture of Trinidad*. Philadelphia: Temple University Press.

Mendes, John. 1986. *Cote ce Cote la: Trinidad and Tobago Dictionary*. Port-of-Spain: Superior Printers.

Merriam, Alan. 1956. "Songs of a Rada Community in Trinidad." *Anthropos* 51 (1956): 157–74.

Miller, Daniel. 1991. "Absolute Freedom in Trinidad." *Man* 26: 323–41.

———. 1997. *Modernity, An Ethnographic Approach: Dualism and Mass Consumption in Trinidad*. Oxford: Berg.

———. 2011. *Tales From Facebook*. Polity Books.

Miller, Daniel, and Don Slater. 2000. *The Internet: An Ethnographic Approach*. Oxford: Berg.

Miller, Errol. 1986. *The Marginalization of the Black Male: Insights from the Development of the Teaching Profession*. Kingston, Jamaica: Institute for Social and Economic Research.

———. 1991. *Men at Risk*. Kingston, Jamaica: Jamaica Publishing House.

Minshall, Peter. 1998. "A Voice to Add to the Song of the Universe." *Drama Review* vol. 42, no. 3 (Fall 1998): 170–93.

Mintz, Sidney Wilfred, and Richard Price. 1976. *An Anthropological Approach to the Afro-American Past: A Caribbean Perspective*. Philadelphia: Institute for the Study of Human Issues.

Mintz, Sidney Wilfred, and Sally Price. 1985. *Caribbean Contours*. Baltimore: Johns Hopkins University Press.

Mohammed, Patricia. 1991. "Reflections on the Women's Movement in Trinidad: Calypsos, Changes and Sexual Violence." *Feminist Review* 38 (Summer 1991): 33–47.

———. 1997. "Midnight's Children and the Legacy of Nationalism in Trinidad." *Callaloo* 20.4 (Fall 1997): 737–52.

———. 1998. "Towards Indigenous Feminist Theorizing in the Caribbean." *Feminist Review* 59 (Summer 1998): 6–33.

———. 2000a. "The Future of Feminism in the Caribbean." *Feminist Review* 64 (Spring 2000): 116–19.

———. 2000b. "Engendering Masculinity: Cross Cultural Caribbean Research Initiatives." *Pensamiento Propio: Greater Caribbean Bilingual Journal of Social Sciences* 12 (July-December 2000): 29–52.

———. 2002. "Introduction: The Material of Gender." In Patricia Mohammed, ed. *Gendered Realities: Essays in Caribbean Feminist Thought*. Mona, Jamaica: Centre for Gender and Development Studies, University of the West Indies Press.

———. 2003. "A Blueprint for Gender in Creole Trinidad: Exploring Gender Mythology through Calypsos of the 1920s and 1930s." In Linden Lewis, ed. *The Culture of Gender and Sexuality in the Caribbean*. Gainesville: University Press of Florida.

———. 2004. "Unmasking Masculinity and Deconstructing Patriarchy: Problems and Possibilities within Feminist Epistemology." In Rhoda Reddock, ed. *Interrogating Caribbean Masculinities: Theoretical and Empirical Analyses*. University of the West Indies Press.

Myers, Helen. 1998. *Music of Hindu Trinidad: Songs from the Indian Diaspora*. Chicago: University of Chicago Press.

Neptune, Harvey R. 2007. *Caliban and the Yankees: Trinidad and the United States Occupation*. Chapel Hill: University of North Carolina Press.

Niranjana, Tejaswini. 2006. *Mobilizing India: Women, Music, and Migration Between India and Trinidad*. Durham and London: Duke University Press.

Noel, Samantha. 2009. *Carnival Is a Woman! Gender, Performance, and Visual Culture in Contemporary Trinidad Carnival*. Diss., Duke University.

Nunley, John W., and Judith Bettelheim. 1988. *Caribbean Festival Arts*. Seattle: University of Washington Press.

Oliver, M. Cynthia. 2009. *Queen of the Virgins: Pageantry and Black Womanhood in the Caribbean*. Jackson: University Press of Mississippi.

Osborne, Anne. 2000. "Steel Pan in Academia: Establishing a Programme at the University of the West Indies, Trinidad." *Caribbean Journal of Education* 22:1&2 (April/September 2000): 56–60.

Osirim, Mary Johnson. 1997. "We Toil All the Livelong Day: Women in the English-Speaking Caribbean." In Consuelo Lopez Springfield, ed. *Daughters of Caliban: Caribbean Women in the Twentieth Century*. Bloomington and Indianapolis: Indiana University Press.

Ottley, Rudolph. 1992. *Women in Calypso*. Arima, Trinidad (self-published).

Pacini, Deborah Hernandez. 1995. *Bachata: A Social History of a Dominican Popular Music*. Philadelphia: Temple University Press.

Pasley, Victoria. 2001. "The Black Power Movement in Trinidad: An Exploration of Gender and Cultural Changes and the Development of a Feminist Consciousness." *Journal of International Women's Studies* vol. 3, no. 1 (2001). www.bridgew.edu/SoAS/JIWS/fall01/index.htm.

Patton, John H. 1994. "Calypso as Rhetorical Performance: Trinidad Carnival 1993." *Latin American Music Review* vol. 15, no. 1 (Spring/Summer 1994): 55–74.

Paur, Jasbir Kaur. 2001. "Global Circuits: Transnational Sexualities and Trinidad." *Signs* vol. 26, no. 4 (Summer 2001): 1039–65.

Pearse, Andrew. 1956. "Mitto Sampson on Calypso Legends of the Nineteenth Century." *Caribbean Quarterly* iv (1956): 250–62.

Post, Jennifer. 1994. "Erasing the Boundaries between Public and Private in Women's Performance Traditions." In Susan Cook and Judy Tsou, eds. *Cecilia Reclaimed: Feminist Perspectives on Gender and Music*. Urbana and Chicago: University of Illinois Press.

Powrie, Barbara E. 1956. "The Changing Attitude of the Coloured Middle Class Towards Carnival." *Caribbean Quarterly* iv (1956): 91–107.

Quevedo, Raymond ("Atilla the Hun"). 1983. *Atilla's Kaiso: A Short History of the Trinidad Calypso*. St. Augustine: University of the West Indies School of Continuing Studies.

Ramnarine, Tina. 2001. *Creating Their Own Space: The Development of an Indian-Caribbean Musical Tradition*. Barbados, Jamaica, Trinidad: University of the West Indies Press.

Reddock, Rhoda. 1988. *Elma Francois*. London: New Beacon.

———. 1991. "Social Mobility in Trinidad and Tobago." In Selwyn Ryan, ed. *Social and Occupational Stratification in Contemporary Trinidad and Tobago*. St. Augustine, Trinidad: Institute for Social and Economic Research.

———. 1994. *Women, Labor and Politics in Trinidad and Tobago: A History*. London: Zed Books.

———. 1998a. "Women's Organizations and Movements in the Commonwealth Caribbean: The Response to the Global Economic Crisis in the 1980s." *Feminist Review* 59 (Summer): 57–73.

———. 1998b. "History of the Women's Movement in the Caribbean." Feature address to the HIVOS/UNIFEM meeting of women's organizations organized by the Caribbean Association of Feminist Research and Action (CAFRA). Grenada, December 1–2, 1998. Available at www.cafra.org/article681.html.

———. 2004. "Interrogating Caribbean Masculinities: An Introduction." In Rhoda Reddock, ed. *Interrogating Caribbean Masculinities: Theoretical and Empirical Analyses*. University of the West Indies Press.

Regis, Louis. 1998. "Calypso: Anatomy of a Controversy." *Caribbean Dialogue: A Journal of Contemporary Caribbean Policy Issues* vol. 3, no. 4 (October/December 1998).

———. 1999. *The Political Calypso: True Opposition in Trinidad and Tobago 1962-1987.* Gainesville: University of Florida Press.

Riggio, Mila Cozart. 1998. "Resistance and Identity: Carnival in Trinidad and Tobago." *Drama Review* vol. 42, no. 3 (Fall 1998): 7–23.

———. 2004. *Carnival: Culture in Action: The Trinidad Experience.* New York: Routledge.

Rodman, Hyman. 1971. *Lower-Class Families: The Culture of Poverty in Negro Trinidad.* New York: Oxford University Press.

Rohlehr, Gordon. 1990. *Calypso and Society in Pre-Independence Trinidad.* Tunapuna, Trinidad: Gordon Rohlehr, self-published.

———. 1997. "The Culture of Williams: Context, Performance, Legacy." *Callaloo* 20.4 (Fall 1997): 849–88.

———. 1998. "We Getting the Calypso We Deserve: Calypso and the World Music Market." *Drama Review* vol. 42, no. 3 (Fall 1998): 82–95.

———. 2001. "The Calypsonian as Artist: Freedom and Responsibility." *Small Axe* 9 (March 2001): 1–26.

———. 2004a. "Calypso Reinvents Itself." In Milla Cozart Riggio, ed. *Culture in Action: The Trinidad Experience.* New York: Routledge.

———. 2004b. "I Lawa: the Construction of Masculinity in Trinidad and Tobago Calypso." In Rhoda Reddock, ed. *Interrogating Caribbean Masculinities: Theoretical and Empirical Analyses.* University of the West Indies Press.

———. 2007. "Carnival Cannibalized or Cannibal Carnivalized: Contextualizing the 'Cannibal Joke' in Calypso and Literature." In Sandra Pouchet Paquet, Patricia J. Saunders, and Stephen Stuempfle, eds. *Music, Memory, Resistance: Calypso and the Caribbean Literary Imagination.* Kingston/Miami: Ian Randle Publishers.

Rommen, Timothy. 2002. "Nationalism and Soul: Gospelypso as Independence." *Black Music Research Journal* (Spring 2002): 37–63.

———. 2007. "Localize It: Rock, Cosmopolitanism, and the Nation in Trinidad." *Ethnomusicology* (Fall 2007): 371–401.

Ryan, Selwyn, ed. 1991. *Social and Occupational Stratification in Contemporary Trinidad and Tobago.* St. Augustine, Trinidad: Institute for Social and Economic Research.

Ryan, Selwyn. 1998. "Calypso and Politics in Trinidad and Tobago 1996-1998." *Caribbean Dialogue: A Journal of Contemporary Caribbean Policy Issues* vol. 3, no. 4 (October/December 1998).

Ryan, Selwyn, and Taimoon Stewart, eds. 1995. *The Black Power Revolution 1970: A Retrospective.* St. Augustine, Trinidad: Institute for Social and Economic Research.

Ryan, Selwyn, Roy McCree, and Godfrey St. Bernard, eds. 1997. *Behind the Bridge: Poverty, Politics, and Patronage in Laventille, Trinidad.* St. Augustine, Trinidad: Institute for Social and Economic Research.

Safa, Helen I. 1995. *The Myth of the Male Breadwinner: Women and Industrialization in the Caribbean.* Boulder: Westview Press.

Saft, Elizabeth, ed. 1996. *Insight Guides: Trinidad and Tobago.* Boston: Houghton Mifflin.

Sankeralli, Burton. 1998. "Indian Presence in Carnival." *Drama Review* vol. 42, no. 3 (Fall 1998): 203–12.

Saunders, Patricia J. 2003. "Is Not Everything Good to Eat, Good to Talk: Sexual Economy and Dancehall Music in the Global Marketplace." *Small Axe* 13 (March): 95–115.

Scher, Philip. 2002. "Copyright Heritage: Preservation, Carnival and the State in Trinidad." *Anthropological Quarterly* 75(3): 453–84.

———. 2007. "When 'Natives' Become Tourists of Themselves: Returning Transnationals and the Carnival in Trinidad and Tobago." In Garth Green and Philip Scher, eds. *Trinidad Carnival: The Cultural Politics of a Transnational Festival*. Bloomington: Indiana University Press.

Senior, Olive. 1991. *Working Miracles: Women's Lives in the English-speaking Caribbean*. Bloomington: Indiana University Press.

Shaw, Andrea. 2005. "'Big Fat Fish': The Hypersexualization of the Fat Female Body in Calypso and Dancehall." *Anthurium: A Caribbean Studies Journal* 3:2 (Fall 2005). http://scholar.library.miami.edu/anthurium/volume_3/issue_2/shaw-bigfatfish.htm.

Sheller, Mimi. 2003. *Consuming the Caribbean*. London: Routledge.

Shepherd, Verene, Bridget Brereton, and Barbara Bailey, eds. 1995. *Engendering History: Caribbean Women in Historical Perspective*. Kingston, Jamaica: Ian Randle Publishers.

Sherzer, Joel. 1974. "*Namakke, Sunmakke, Kormakke*: Three Types of Kuna Speech Event." In Richard Baumann and Joel Sherzer, eds. *Explorations in the Ethnography of Speaking*. New York: Cambridge University Press.

———. 1990. *Verbal Art in San Blas: Kuna Culture Through Discourse*. Albuquerque: University of New Mexico Press.

Sierra, David Lizardi. 2009. *Jean, Dinah, Dorothy, and the Rest: Representations of Women in Calypso and Literary Works of the Caribbean*. Diss., University of Puerto Rico.

Skinner, Ewart. 1990. "Mass Media in Trinidad and Tobago." In Stuart H. Surlin and Walter C. Soderlund, eds. *Mass Media in the Caribbean*. New York: Gordon and Breach.

Smith, Hope Munro. 2001. *Gender Misbehaving: Women in Trinidadian Popular Music*. Diss., University of Texas at Austin.

———. 2004. "Performing Gender in the Trinidad Calypso." *Latin American Music Review* 25/1 (Spring/Summer 2004): 32–56.

———. 2013. "Children's Musical Engagement With Trinidad's Carnival Music." In Patricia Campbell and Trevor Wiggins, eds. *The Oxford Handbook of Children's Musical Cultures*. New York: Oxford University Press. 281–97.

Solie, Ruth. 1993. *Musicology and Difference: Gender and Sexuality in Music Scholarship*. Berkeley and Los Angeles: University of California Press.

Springfield, Consuelo Lopez. 1997. *Daughters of Caliban: Caribbean Women in the Twentieth Century*. Bloomington and Indianapolis: Indiana University Press.

Stewart, John. 1986. "Patronage and Control in the Trinidad Carnival." In Victor Turner, ed. *The Anthropology of Experience*. Urbana: University of Illinois Press.

Stuempfle, Stephen. 1995. *The Steelband Movement: The Forging of a National Art in Trinidad and Tobago*. Philadelphia: University of Pennsylvania Press.

Tarradath, Selwyn. 1991. "Race, Class, Politics and Gender in the Steelband Movement." In Selwyn Ryan, ed. *Social and Occupational Stratification in Contemporary Trinidad and Tobago*. St. Augustine: Institute of Social and Economic Research, University of the West Indies Press. 377–84.

Thompson-Ahye, Hazel. 1998. "Calypso and Gender." *Caribbean Dialogue: A Journal of Contemporary Caribbean Policy Issues* vol. 3, no. 4 (October/December 1998): 55–59.

Trotman, D. V. 1991. "The Image of Indians in Calypso: Trinidad 1946-1986." In Selwyn Ryan, ed. *Social and Occupational Stratification in Contemporary Trinidad and Tobago*. St. Augustine: Institute of Social and Economic Research, University of the West Indies Press. 385–98.

Turner, Victor. 1986. *The Anthropology of Experience*. Urbana: University of Illinois Press.

———. 1988. *The Anthropology of Performance*. New York: PAJ Publications.

Walke, Olive. 1970. *Folk Songs of Trinidad and Tobago*. London: Boosey & Hawkes.

Wallis, Roger, and Krister Malm. 1984. *Big Sounds from Small Peoples: The Music Industry in Small Countries*. New York: Pendragon Press.

Warner, Keith Q. 1985/1999. *Kaiso! The Trinidad Calypso: A Study of the Calypso as Oral Literature*, Rev. 3rd ed. Pueblo, CO: Passeggiata Press.

———. 1993. "Ethnicity and the Contemporary Calypso." In Kevin Yelvington, ed. *Trinidad Ethnicity*. Knoxville: University of Tennessee Press. 275–91.

Waterman, Richard. 1943. *African Patterns in Trinidad Negro Music*. Diss., Northwestern University.

Williams, Eric. 1970. *From Columbus to Castro: The History of the Caribbean*. London: Andre Deutsch.

Wilson, Peter. 1973. *Crab Antics: The Social Anthropology of English-speaking Negro Societies of the Caribbean*. New Haven: Yale University Press.

Yelvington, Kevin, ed. 1993. *Trinidad Ethnicity*. Knoxville: University of Tennessee Press.

———. 1996. "Flirting in the Factory." *Journal of the Royal Anthropological Institute* 2:2 (June 1996): 313–33.

———. 2001. "The Anthropology of Afro-Latin America and the Caribbean: Diasporic Dimensions." *Annual Review of Anthropology* 30 (2001): 227–60.

Index

Andall, Ella, 77, 95
Arrow (Alphonsus Cassell), 124
Asche, Karene, 4, 97, 112, 121
Atilla the Hun (Raymond Quevedo), 13, 32, 42, 65, 66, 67, 69, 70, 71, 115, 186n4
Atlantik (Bakanal), 130, 136, 140, 142
Atwell, Winifred, 160

Bajan cook mas, 41–42
Barriteau, Eudine, 53
bel air, belair, belé, 28, 31
Belafonte, Harry, 186n5, 186n7
Belasco, Lionel, 40–41, 69
Ballantyne, Gregory "GB," 114
Baron (Timothy Watkins), 135
Baston, Ester, 161
Batson, Nadia, 135, 145, 146
Belfon, Denise, 55, 84, 123, 126, 127, 132, 133, 137–39, 142, 145
Best Village Competition, 47–48, 74, 107
Black Power Movement, 50, 77, 116, 160
Black Stalin (Leroy Calliste), 77, 115, 119, 126
Blackman, Abbi, 20, 53, 80, 84, 187n27, 188n2
Blue Boy. *See* Super Blue
Blue Ventures, 3, 130, 136
Bodicea, 32, 33, 36
Bolduc, Kelley, 84
Brother Resistance, 77
Bruno, Wayne, 125

CAFRA (Caribbean Association for Feminist Research and Action), 24, 53

calinda, 32, 35, 36, 62
Calypso Queen competition, 80–82
Calypso Princess (Veronica De Labastide), 74, 75, 80
Calypso Rose (McCartha Lewis), 10, 48, 74–76, 79, 80, 83, 84, 85, 94, 96, 97–106, 133, 135, 141, 145
calypsonian: emergence of female calypsonians, 44, 49, 70–76; origins, 39–40; professionalization, 39–40, 63, 69–70
Cape, Roy, 55, 125, 130, 136, 137, 140, 146
Caribbean Quarterly, 13, 47
Carnival fetes, 51, 53, 54, 57, 62, 69, 79, 82–84, 128–31
Carnival mas (masquerade), 51, 58–59, 95, 134–35, 152–53
Carr, Andrew, 44
chantwell, 28, 31, 32, 35, 39
chutney soca, 55, 57, 96, 113, 116, 118, 126, 138
competitions, calypso, 39, 50, 80–82, 96–97, 121; "dying," 55–56; gender relations, 63–68; new releases, 53–54; origins, 35–36, 61–62
de Coteau, Art, 73, 78
de Coteau, Merle Albino, 160, 161
Crosby, Nikki, 129, 136

Dempster, Sanelle, 3, 84, 112, 130, 134
Diffenthaller, Kees, 123, 133
Divas Calypso Cabaret, 84
Dr. Zhivago (Felix Scott), 107
drum dance, 28, 31, 34, 35, 57, 151

217

Eccles, Karen, 81
Esdelle, Chantal, 84, 146, 175
Explainer (Winston Henry), 77

Francis, Frankie, 73, 78
Francois, Elma, 38

Garlin, Bunji (Ian Alvarez), 84, 123, 127, 135, 139, 143, 146, 147
Garcia, Destra, 55, 84, 95, 123, 126, 132, 133, 135, 139, 140–42, 145
Garvey, Marcus, 39
George, Neil "Iwer," 84, 137, 143
Ghetto Flex (Hilton Dalzell), 127, 137
Goddard, Pelham, 79, 125, 135, 171
Grant, Christophe, 82, 83, 108–10, 117, 118, 121
groovy soca, 119, 127, 133, 139, 145
Growler (Errol Duke), 44, 66, 67
Growling Tiger (Neville Marcano), 72

Henderson, Carl "Beaver," 114
Hendrickson, Shirlane, 81, 82
Henley, Hazel, 159
Hinds, Alison, 84, 95, 124, 133, 135, 142, 145
Hindu Women's Organization, 52
Holman, Ray, 82, 158, 166, 171
Hudson, Melanie, 81, 82, 136
Huggins-Watts, Michelle, 4, 57, 162, 165, 172–73, 175, 176

Jamette, 30, 32–35, 132, 150, 170
Jeffers, Audrey, 37–38
Johnstone, Helen May, 40
Joseph, Natasha, 57, 84, 173–75

Kes the Band, 55, 123
King, Christina, 38
King Radio (Norman Span), 66, 67, 70

Lady B (Beulah Bob), 80, 111–12
Lady Baldwin (Mavis Baldwin), 71

Lady Divine, 74
Lady Excellence, 74, 75
Lady Gypsy (Lynette Steele), 53, 142
Lady Iere (Maureen St. John), 44, 71–72
Lady MacDonald (Doris MacDonald), 71
Lady Trinidad (Thelma Lane), 70–71
Lady Wonder (Dianne Hendrickson), 81
La Petite Musicale, 45–46, 73, 113, 159
Ladies Night Out, 84, 112, 118
Lee, Byron, 124, 126, 127
Lewes, Karissa, 56, 82
Lord Beginner (Egbert Moore), 44, 67
Lord Executor (Philip Garcia), 65, 115
Lord Iere (Randolph Thomas), 44, 71–72
Lord Invader (Rupert Grant), 43, 66, 69
Lord Kitchener (Alwyn Roberts), 66, 68, 73, 74, 76, 78, 79, 94, 99, 102–3, 113, 115, 125, 135, 140, 157
Lord Shorty (Ras Shorty I) (Garfield Blackman), 78–79, 135
Lucas, Colin, 124, 137
Lyons, Fay-Ann, 4, 84, 95, 105, 123, 127, 135, 139, 142–47

Marvelous Marva (Marva McKenzie), 111–12
Mataloney, Sophie/Sophia, 32–33
McBurnie, Beryl, 44–45, 155–56, 159
McIntosh, Heather, 81, 121
McIntosh, Ronnie, 111, 130, 140
McLean, Daisy James, 157–58
McShine, Umilta, 159, 160, 161
Merchant (Dennis Franklyn), 77, 82
Mighty Duke (Kelvin Pope), 77, 135
Mighty Sparrow (Slinger Francisco), 48, 49, 64, 67–68, 73, 74, 75, 76, 78, 83, 93, 94, 99, 100, 102, 103, 107, 111, 113, 133, 135, 186n8
Mighty Spoiler (Theophilus Philip), 67, 68, 74, 99
Miranda, Marcia, 119, 136
Mohammed, Patricia, 14, 25, 53, 65, 185n26

Montano, Machel, 55, 84, 105, 123, 126–27, 132, 136, 139, 140, 143
Muttoo Brothers, 72

NJAC (National Joint Action Committee), 50
NWAC (National Women's Action Committee), 50, 80
National Calypso Queen Contest, 80–82

Panorama, 149–50, 157, 158, 160, 162, 163, 164, 166–71
Paul, Leston, 125
Persad-Bissessar, Kamla, 8, 180, 183n6, 190n60, 195n4
Pierre, Jocelyne, 159–60
Plummer, Denyse, 4, 80–81, 83, 84, 85, 94, 95, 97, 112–20, 123, 126, 135, 136, 137

ragga soca, 126–27
Reddock, Rhoda, 39, 53, 185n26
Roaring Lion (Rafael De Leon), 13, 42, 66, 69, 71, 77
Roberts, Kernal, 125, 126, 140
Robertson, Raf, 197n32
Robin, Juliet, 146
rock music: Trinidad, 56
Rudder, David, 62, 77, 83, 84, 119, 140, 166
Ruiz, Kizzie, 112, 121

Shadow (Winston Bailey), 78, 118
Shanaqua (Rachel Fortune), 20, 53, 81, 82, 136
Sharpe, Len "Boogsie," 114, 115, 166, 171, 172–73, 174–75
Singing Dianne (Dianne Davenport), 49, 74, 76, 80
Singing Francine (Francine Edwards), 49, 74, 76, 82
Singing Sandra (Sandra des Vignes), 3, 48, 76, 80, 83, 84, 85, 95, 97, 106–12
Smith, Yvonne "Bubalups," 154

soca: origin, 51, 77–79; musical features 124–26; new releases 53–54
steel pan: origins, 152–54
Super Blue (Austin Lyons), 78, 114, 115, 135, 142, 145
Sylvester, Michelle, 139

tamboo bamboo, 151–52
TASPO, 156–57
Tigress (Joanne Rowley), 111–12
Tobago Crusoe (Orthniel Baccus), 107
Tudor, Ursula, 161, 169
Twiggy (Ann Marie Parks), 80, 112, 145

United Nations Decade for Women, 51
United Sisters, 111–12

Walke, Olive, 45–46, 159
Watson, Ed, 49, 78–79
Williams, Eric, 8, 45–46, 48, 98
Winchester, Shurwayne, 84, 133
wining (dance), 47, 101, 103, 130–32
Women Working for Social Progress, 52

CPSIA information can be obtained
at www.ICGtesting.com
Printed in the USA
BVHW030032220419
545974BV00008B/6/P